EXTRAORDINARY TALES

To Karl —

Stories from the Road

Wishing you extraordinary travels!

CRAIG KARGES | J. DAVID DIOSI

Copyright © 2009 by Craig Karges and J. David Diosi

River Valley Publishing
Post Office Box 369
St. Clairsville, OH 43950
740-699-1111
www.extraordinarytales.com

First Edition: November, 2009

ISBN Number: 978-1-61584-061-8

Printed in the United States of America

Dedications

Craig Karges dedicates this book to:

Judy Lawhead, my travel agent for over twenty years, I couldn't have done it without you Judy!

Joel and Cynthia, we'll always have Paris (and Coldplay!).

As always, to my extraordinary wife, Charlotte, who is often by my side and always in my heart wherever I go.

J. David Diosi dedicates this book to:

My Mother, Francie Martin, who is a remarkable woman and an inspiration to everyone who knows her.

My sons Devin and Dylan—now will you listen to Daddy? I love you both!

To Ted and Becky Showalter for introducing us to Craig and Charlotte—what *extraordinary* friends you all have been to us.

Nana—love forever!

And last but not least to the most lovely person I know—my best friend AND wife, Dana. You are my soul mate and I love you with all my heart <u>forever</u>!

Table of Contents

Acknowledgments
Author's Note

Bon Voyage

Acknowledgments

To Melinda Koslik, for doing an extraordinary job creating the cover of *Extraordinary Tales* as well as designing the entire book.

To Patricia Walther, for working her editing magic on the manuscript and making it so much better.

To my writing partner on this project, Dave Diosi, and all the fine folks at River Valley Publishing; without Dave's persistence this book would never be a reality.

Author's Note

I'm not quite certain how to label this book. I guess I'll call it creative nonfiction. The events described in this book are "realish" (to quote David Sedaris). I've embellished (and outright fabricated at times), blended multiple people into one personality, changed names to protect both the innocent and the guilty and compressed time all to make for more concise and, hopefully, enjoyable reading. The people described in the book—or people very much like them—exist or existed. The places and locations are all real and my descriptions are accurate from my point of view of actually being there. I can't vouch for the accuracy of all the stories and theories expressed in this book. Oftentimes the information was related to me, but I hope you find these stories both entertaining and thought provoking.

Throughout the book, you will find references to my work as an entertainer and a speaker. For those of you who aren't familiar with my work (and I'm hoping that's many of you because that would mean the book has found a larger audience!) I am a self-described "extraordinist"—a performer who entertains by creating the extraordinary onstage. You can think of me as a mind reader, mentalist, illusionist or magician if that helps. I entertain by combining the art of illusion with the science of psychology and the power of intuition, creating mystery while opening minds to unlimited possibilities.

And now that the stage is set, let the journey begin ....

CHAPTER ONE

The Mothman

In 1980, my heart brought me to Point Pleasant, West Virginia, where I lived for two years. During my last year of college at Marshall University, I met and fell in love with Charlotte Pearson, a fellow student and a Point Pleasant area native. After a whirlwind courtship, we married and I moved in with her and her high school aged sister, Brenda. Charlotte's father had died several years before this and her mother, Annabelle, had remarried. Annabelle was dividing her time between the family's home near Point Pleasant and her new home forty-five minutes away in Ripley, West Virginia. The idea was that with Brenda's living with Charlotte and me, Annabelle could spend more time with her second husband in Ripley, and we would make sure Brenda graduated from high school.

I'm a native West Virginian and West Virginia is definitely a rural state. However, my new home was more country than anything I had experienced before. I even woke one morning to find a herd of cows in the front yard. Apparently, the cows had organized a mass break out from a nearby farm.

Point Pleasant is a sleepy little Ohio River town. It was named by George Washington when he first set foot there and proclaimed the area a "pleasant point." What, if anything, of an extraordinary nature could happen here? I was in for a surprise!

The Mothman

When some of my college friends discovered I was moving to "Point," one or two of them jokingly warned me to, "Watch out for the Mothman!" This piqued my curiosity; so I asked Charlotte about the Mothman.

"A local legend when I was a kid… all kinds of people saw this big creature with glowing red eyes and huge wings the size of a man. Some people say it had something to do with the Silver Bridge collapse," Charlotte explained.

I knew about the Silver Bridge. Early in the evening on December 15, 1967, the 700-foot bridge which spanned the Ohio River and connected Point Pleasant to the Gallipolis, Ohio area suddenly collapsed while packed with rush hour traffic. Vehicles and the bridge went into the Ohio River and 46 people were killed. It was a real tragedy and made the national news.

"What would a Mothman have to do with a bridge falling down?" I asked.

"Oh, I don't know," Charlotte replied. "That was a terrible time for everyone. I think people just wanted something to blame. They couldn't understand this Mothman and they couldn't understand why so many good people had to die. The Mothman was always seen around power lines and the like. They say it lived in TNT."

"TNT?" I was full of questions for my new bride.

"Yeah, it's part of a wildlife preserve north of town. The military stored a lot of ammunition there in these mounds. We call them igloos. It goes on for miles, winding roads and underground tunnels. It's a creepy place. When we were in high school, we used to go up there at night on the weekends and scare parkers. Couples would be making out and we would sneak up on them and shine flashlights in their cars. It would scare them to death. Tandy (one of Charlotte's good friends) had a couple of flashlights with red bulbs. We might have been responsible for a few of the more recent Mothman sightings," she said with a laugh.

"So do you think that's all the Mothman is, practical jokes?"

"Oh, no. Mom saw it." This startled me. My mother-in-law is one of the sanest and most practical people I have ever met. If she said she saw the Mothman, she definitely saw something.

"We were out at Aunt Hilda's, way out in the country near Cornstalk Park. We had homemade ice cream. Hilda always made the best. It was getting dark; so Mom decided to head home. The road out there is terrible. Nothing more than rocks, gravel and a bunch of potholes. Anyway, we were headed back, Brenda, Rodney, me and Mom when all of a sudden, Mom floors the gas and starts driving like a maniac with all three of her kids in the car. Needless to say, this wasn't like Mom. Anyway, we were petrified and we asked her what was wrong. 'Nothing,' she says. 'Don't talk to me.' She kept racing along the country road until we reached Route 2 when she finally slowed down and drove at a normal rate of speed until we got home. When we got home, Mom was shaking. We asked her what was wrong and she said she saw it. 'Saw what?' we asked. 'The Mothman!' she yelled. She said she saw a pair of glowing, red eyes in the trees and that the eyes followed her as she raced out of the hollow. You know Mom, nothing would shake her like that unless something was really there."

This entire Mothman phenomenon intrigued me as did another Point Pleasant legend, Ben Franklin. No, not *the* Ben Franklin, the famous statesman, inventor and founding father; but a man who claimed to be a direct descendant. Point Pleasant's Ben Franklin IV was a magician and I was anxious to meet him.

Ben Franklin IV lived by himself in a large white house, not far from downtown Point Pleasant where for years he ran a local dry goods store. He was retired from both of his professions, magician and merchant, by the time I moved into town. He greeted me with a hearty handshake and a big smile. Ben was a small man with boundless energy and eyes that contained a mischievous glint. He ushered me into the parlor of his large, rambling house and we talked magic for an hour or two.

The subject of card throwing came up and Ben confessed that he was quite good at it. In fact, *Ripley's Believe It or Not* featured him once for his ability to sail a playing card through several sheets of newspaper.

"I'd love to see that," I said.

"Thought you'd never ask," Ben said as he led me down the hall and into the formal dining room. Ben had five black frames positioned along his massive dining room table. Each frame had a page from the *Point Pleasant Register* mounted in it. The old magician pulled a deck of cards from his pocket, selected a single playing card and with a flip of his small wrist sent it sailing toward the papers. *Phft, phft, phft, phft, phft,* the card passed cleanly through each piece of paper and landed on the other side of the table. He was like an ancient ninja with a deck of cards. Extraordinary!

"Here, you try," he said while handing me the deck of cards.

I pulled one out, let it fly, and then embarrassingly watched as it fluttered to the floor before hitting the first paper. He told me to try again. "It's all in the wrist," he said as he demonstrated by whipping another card through all five layers of newspaper. I tried again and failed miserably. This time, the card made it to the first paper but hit the frame and bounced down to the floor.

"Never mind. You practice, you'll get it. It took me a long time to learn to do that," Ben said as he patted me on the back and ushered me back into the parlor. "Hey, have you ever heard of the Mothman?" he asked with a gleam in his eye. This was a nice coincidence. One of Point Pleasant's most fascinating residents, Ben Franklin, discussing another of Point Pleasant's most fascinating residents, the Mothman.

"My wife, Charlotte, told me a little."

"Well, son, let me tell you a lot! You know, we magicians love a good mystery, and the Mothman is an enigma like none other.

"The hysteria started around here in November of '66. A group of gravediggers were preparing a grave in the Clendenin Cemetery when all of a sudden something that looked like a cross between a human and a bird flew out of the trees and scared them half to death.

"The sightings continued. A few days later, a carload of two married couples was driving near the old, abandoned power plant near TNT. They described seeing a large, manlike creature, six or seven feet tall with glowing, red eyes and bat-like wings. They were petrified and sped down the highway towards Point Pleasant and away from the power plant. The creature kept up with them even though they were driving in excess of 100 miles an hour. The creature didn't give up the chase until they reached the city limits, and then it just seemed to vanish.

"That same night the Mothman was sighted no less than four more times. A fella in Salem heard his dog barking and went to investigate. He shined his flashlight in the direction the dog was facing, towards his hay barn. A pair of red glowing eyes were looking back at him. It spooked him. The dog took off in the direction of the eyes and the man ran into his house to get his gun, but then he was too frightened to go back outside; so he spent a sleepless night with his gun by his side. In the morning, the dog was nowhere to be found. What was really strange was that the couples who were chased by the creature that night said that they saw a dead dog on the side of the road. When they went back later to find the dog, the body was gone. The dog matched the description of the Salem man's pet and you know Salem is about 90 miles away from here. That man's dog was never found.

"There were tons of sightings. All of them pretty much agreed that the creature was between five and seven feet tall, manlike, but wider than a normal man, and it had human legs. Didn't really have much of a head and the eyes were located near the top of the shoulders. Huge wings, maybe a 14

9

foot wing span, and they didn't flap. The Mothman just kind of glided. It could also go straight up, you know, like a helicopter. The creature's skin was described as gray or brown and they said it made a humming noise when it flew. No one ever heard it speak, but it did make a screeching noise described by some as like a woman screaming. Most people thought the creature lived in TNT. You could hide forever up there with all the woods, the trails and tunnels.

"The hullabaloo lasted for about a year 'til '67 when the bridge fell. I guess that gave us something else to talk about. In fact, just before the bridge fell, there was a rash of UFO sightings. You know, unidentified lights in the sky. People thought all this might have been connected. There was a lot of interest at the time. A bunch of Asian fellas came here looking for the Mothman. They were a little odd. Short men, all dressed in black with thick eyeglasses and a weird, almost robotic speech pattern. Personally, I never saw one but I know a lot of folks around here who did. They would interview people and ask strange, unrelated questions. They were dubbed 'The Men in Black;' so, we had the Mothman, UFOs and the 'Men in Black' harassing the local populace for an entire year.

"A man named Keel came here to study all this extraordinary phenomena. He felt that Point Pleasant was some kind of a window to another world and that the window opened for a time and then shut.

"Others felt that the Mothman was a banshee, a portent of doom. It was trying to warn us that something disastrous was going to happen. After the Silver Bridge collapse, the Mothman disappeared. If it were a banshee, I wish it would have been a little more detailed in its warning. A lot of good people could have been saved.

"Mothman-like sightings have occurred near disaster areas before. Back in the '20s, in China, one of the largest dams in the world collapsed. An estimated 40 million gallons of water flooded the farmlands below the dam, killing over 15,000 people. Almost every survivor of the disaster claimed to have seen a 'man-dragon' appearing to the townspeople and around the dam. This man-dragon seemed to look exactly like our Mothman.

"Just a couple years ago in Germany, a group of miners were barred from entering the mine by a huge manlike bird which kept hovering around the mine's entrance making terrible screeching noises. The men were driven away. An hour later, a huge underground explosion shook the earth and black smoke came billowing out of the mine's entrance. Had the men been in the mine, they would have certainly been killed. I guess that's one example of a banshee doing some good," Ben smiled grimly.

The Mothman

A half dozen years after my visit with Ben Franklin, I also learned that a huge, manlike, winged creature which appeared headless but somehow had large, glowing red eyes attached to its body often was seen in a particular area of the Soviet Union. The sightings became more and more frequent until one day in April, 1986, a reactor at the Chernobyl nuclear plant exploded and killed 30 people. Another ten died later as a result of radiation exposure. The graphite of the reactor burned for nine days. Helicopters continued to fly over the area, dropping tons of sand, clay and various chemicals to try to control the blaze, but it wasn't just helicopters flying over the site. Eyewitness reports say a manlike bird with a 20 foot wing span was seen to be soaring over the area as well.

"Do you think Mothman had anything to do with the Silver Bridge collapse?" I asked while seated on the edge of my chair.

"I don't know. But if you're of a superstitious mind, let me tell you about an even older mystery which may have had some bearing on all this, 'The Cornstalk Curse.'"

This was getting to be too much. My new hometown was populated with eccentric, card throwing ninja magicians, monsters, UFOs, 'Men in Black,' and now a curse! Perhaps it would have been better if a herd of cows in the front yard had been the most unusual thing I experienced in Point Pleasant.

Ben fixed me with his gaze and began another tale of the supernatural.

"This curse goes back two-hundred-years, to the American Revolution. Chief Cornstalk united seven Indian nations in an effort to keep the white man out of the region. His name struck both fear and awe in the minds of Indians and white men up and down the Ohio River. He was a military genius, a born leader, naturally endowed with great fighting skills, and a marvelous speaker. The earliest settlers here were attacked by Cornstalk and his 1,200 warriors during what has become known as the 1774 Battle of Point Pleasant. However, the Indians were no match for the frontiersmen with their rifles. The Indians managed to kill about 140 settlers but lost almost a fourth of their own men. Because of the attack, a fort was built here in Point Pleasant as a defense against the Indians.

"Cornstalk was tired of fighting and wanted to make peace with the colonists. He did so, but the British were constantly trying to enlist the various tribes to fight on the side of Britain against the colonists.

"The British had persuaded many of the tribes to attack the fort here in Point Pleasant. The warriors assembled along the banks of the Ohio River.

Cornstalk wanted to avert the battle and went to talk with Captain Arbuckle who commanded the garrison. Cornstalk was accompanied by his son, and Red Hawk, a Delaware chief. The three men were taken hostage in an effort to prevent the Indians from attacking. It appeared that the men willingly accepted their role as hostages to further stall the fighting.

"This seemed to work for a time, but a few days later one of the soldiers from the fort was killed while hunting deer outside the compound. His mutilated body was returned to the fort. The soldiers were furious. Against all orders they broke into the room where Cornstalk was being held. As they burst through the door, Cornstalk stood to greet them. He had such a powerful presence that it was said the men stopped cold in their tracks, but only for a moment. Red Hawk, Cornstalk's son and Chief Cornstalk himself were killed on the spot. It took eight musket shots to bring Cornstalk down. As he was dying, he uttered his famous curse." Ben reached up to a nearby bookcase and pulled down a hardbound volume of West Virginia history. He thumbed through it, found the spot he was looking for and began to read the words of Chief Cornstalk.

"I was the border man's friend. Many times I have saved him and his people from harm. I never warred with you, but only to protect our wigwams and lands. I refused to join your paleface enemies with the red coats. I came to the fort as your friend and you murdered me. You have murdered by my side, my young son. For this, may the curse of the Great Spirit rest upon this land. May it be blighted by nature. May it even be blighted in its hopes. May the strength of its peoples be paralyzed by the stain of our blood." Ben closed the book with a bang and then returned it to the bookcase.

"Many believe the 'Cornstalk Curse' had something to do with the bridge collapse. Just as they believe it had something to do with any misfortune this little town has suffered over the years," Ben said.

"They dumped the bodies of the other Indians in the river, but not Cornstalk's. No, they respected him too much. He was buried right here in Point Pleasant, overlooking the junction where the Kanawha and Ohio Rivers meet. The point that George Washington liked so much. There is no rest for the dead, though. In 1840, they moved his bones to the grounds of the Mason County Court House, and in 1899, they erected a monument to Cornstalk's memory there. In the '50s, we built a new courthouse and we had to move him again. This time his remains, just a couple of teeth and a few bones, were placed in an aluminum box and buried at Tu-Endie-Wei Park. They erected a big 12-foot monument there.

"You know what's eerie though? In addition to the Cornstalk monuments, in 1909 the town was erecting an even bigger monument, an 86-foot tall monster. The night before the dedication, on a clear evening without a cloud in sight, a lightning bolt hit the crane that was supposed to lift the monument in to place. This prevented the ceremony from taking place. They finally got the monument up and dedicated but on the Fourth of July, 1921, it was hit by lightning again and suffered considerable damage. Again, it was a perfectly clear day. Do you know what the monument commemorated?" Ben asked.

I simply shrugged my shoulders.

"The men who died in the 1774 Battle of Point Pleasant, when Cornstalk was defeated."

A little tingle ran down my spine.

"Mr. Franklin, it was a real pleasure meeting you," I said as I started to make my way to the door. I thought this was an appropriate time to take my leave as the intended brief visit had stretched into more than four hours.

"Going so soon? Did the curse scare you off?"

"No, I just feel I'm monopolizing your time."

"Poppycock. I'm enjoying this. It's rare for me to have such a good audience for my stories."

"These aren't just stories though, they really happened. That's what's fascinating and a little frightening all at the same time," I said. "I'd be curious to know what you think of all this."

"Nonsense, pure and simple. The 'Cornstalk Curse,' just an excuse people give when something doesn't go their way. There's no such thing as a curse, just misfortune. It's going to happen, there is nothing you can do about it but you can't let misfortune get the best of you.

"The Mothman? An unusually large sandhill crane combined with people's overactive imaginations and a practical joker or two. And the Silver Bridge, a barge hit it a month or so before it collapsed. It was never reported. Had they done a proper job of reporting, the structure would have been examined and a disaster might have been prevented."

I stared at him. He had a pat answer for all of Point Pleasant's supernatural occurrences. I wasn't quite buying it though. I thought there might be something more to it than that.

"Now, you want to see a card trick," Ben asked as the deck of cards materialized at his fingertips.

Over the years, I hiked through Chief Cornstalk Park as well as the TNT area. While I never saw anything I could label as supernatural, I truly enjoyed my two years in Point Pleasant and concurred with George Washington. This truly is a pleasant point and an eerie one as well!

CHAPTER TWO

Crystal Skulls and Bill Gates

By 1985, I had been a professional entertainer for five years, earning 100% of my income delivering presentations to college audiences and at corporate events. After five years of professional "trouping" and a bit of "hand-to-mouth" existence, I started making some headway. I had established a good reputation on the college market and some high level corporate engagements were coming my way. One of the most memorable of these early corporate appearances took place in San Francisco.

I was in town to present after-dinner entertainment for a Macintosh® user group composed of chief information officers (CIOs) of some very big companies. I'm not much of a computer person. In 1985, I was a complete novice when it came to technology and this was the first time I had ever heard the term CIO!

A uniformed driver greeted me at the SFO baggage claim. We gathered my bags and went to the curb. He told me to wait there while he brought the car around. Within minutes, a huge, gold, stretch limo pulled up to the curb. I stepped out of the way and scanned the road looking for "my" black Lincoln Town Car, the norm for airport pickups. At the same time, I wondered who might be getting into or out of the stretch limo. My curiosity was satisfied seconds later when "my" driver jumped out of the car, took my luggage and began placing it in the cavernous trunk.

"This is for me?" I asked, my mouth hanging open (not a very cool pose).

"Of course, make yourself at home," replied the driver as he held the door open for me and I entered the luxurious vehicle.

As I was settling in (the passenger area seemed as big as my living room at home), the driver asked, "Do you want the privacy screen up?"

"No, that's OK, we can talk. I have to admit, this is quite the ride."

It was as I looked over the various newspapers available while picking through some fresh fruit, and opening a bottle of Perrier, and beginning to feel very special and important, that the driver burst my bubble!

"Well, you know, you were scheduled for a regular sedan, but I have to do a pick up at the St. Regis and bring her back to the airport. This vehicle is really for her. You've lucked out because of your arrival time."

"Well, let me enjoy myself then," I said as I took a bite of apple and spread open that day's *USA Today* on the large, leather seat. Even at that time, the three-year-old national newspaper had already become a daily "road habit" with me.

As we pulled up to the St. Regis Hotel, I was ushered out of the car and my luggage was quickly taken by a bellman. As fast as my luggage left the trunk, piles of matching Louis Vuitton were placed into the trunk, and an elderly lady with her much younger escort entered the car. I noticed she was struggling under the weight of a highly polished mahogany case. The woman was either oblivious to, or chose to refuse, the offered help from the doorman, the bellman and her escort when it came to handling the case.

"Our apologies, but your room is not yet ready Mr. Karges," said the pretty receptionist, "Check-in isn't until four o'clock," she smiled.

I smiled back as I thought, *Great! It's always like this at these fancy hotels. At the Red Roof Inn® I can check in at eleven o'clock in the morning and park at my door. Plus, I don't have to pay to use the phone!*

"Why don't I issue your key now," queried the receptionist. "It will give you access to the lounge where you can enjoy yourself while your room is being prepared. We'll send a staff member up to inform you when your room is ready and your luggage will be waiting for you."

After a quick elevator ride, I was in a beautiful lounge which covered what seemed to be an entire floor of the hotel. A wonderful choice of food was spread all about the room. A remarkably courteous concierge tended the room and a number of servers bustled about. There were windows all around offering wonderful views of the city. I was encouraged to enjoy any of the food, as well as any of the drinks available.

16

"Can I charge something to my room," I asked.

"Oh, no sir, this is all complimentary."

Wow! Jackpot!

I pretty much had the place to myself. I did notice one middle-aged man sitting at a corner table. He was well dressed in a dark blue, three-piece, pinstripe suit, a brilliant white shirt and red power tie. He just stared into space. A glass of red wine was in front of him as well as a plate filled with assorted cheeses, but everything looked untouched. I didn't want to be rude, but I couldn't help glancing in his direction from time to time. He seemed to be mumbling something.

I thought it might be a good idea to leave my finger sandwiches and cheese and see if he was all right. As I got closer, his mumbled words became clearer, "It was right here, it was right here."

"Sir, are you OK?" I asked.

"Sorry, what did you say?" he replied as he looked up at me, a confused expression on his face.

"Are you OK sir? Do you need some water? Is there anything I can do for you?"

All at once, his eyes focused and his stare became intense. "No son, there's nothing you can do for me, but what I can do for you, oh my! Sit down here and let me tell you a story that will change you forever!"

He grabbed my forearm and pulled me onto the seat next to his.

"The Crystal Skull," he sputtered as he stared at me in wide-eyed amazement.

I wasn't certain what he was talking about and my expression surely said so.

"That Mitchell-Hedges woman… she was here, and she had it with her."

I still must have looked confused, because I was.

"In the 1920s this woman, she told me to call her Sammy, but if I remember correctly her proper name is Anna. Anyway, Sammy or Anna, was in Belize with her adoptive father, F.A. Mitchell-Hedges, she called him Mike. They were on an archeological dig at an ancient Mayan city. Her father believed the city was a link to Atlantis, the fabled lost continent. This young girl, I believe she was just a teen at the time, she's ancient now, was messing about at the dig site apparently searching an area of the excavation thought to be a temple, and she saw something shiny. She dug around and unearthed a skull made out of crystal."

"And that's what she had here?" I asked.

17

"Oh yes. The thing was beautiful but terrifying at the same time. I was attracted to it and repelled by it," he said. "It was absolutely perfect. It looked just like a human skull, perhaps slightly smaller."

"She said her father called the thing 'The Skull of Doom' and said publicly that it was the embodiment of all evil. She said he gave the skull to the local tribesmen, but when they left, the tribesmen gave the skull back to Mitchell-Hedges. He didn't want to take it, but he had to or risk insulting the locals. She didn't share the opinion that the skull was all doom and gloom. She's lived with the thing for decades. She did believe that it was older than old, three-thousand-six-hundred years old to be exact. She said many psychics had worked with it. Some claimed it came from Atlantis. Some said it came from the stars. Many feel it contains knowledge to be shared with all of mankind and that it can usher in a spiritual awakening right here, right now. Sammy wasn't sure what to believe. She did believe it was old, and she felt if it wasn't extraterrestrial then it had to come from an ancient civilization that was much more advanced than ours."

"Why?" I asked.

"There's no damn way to create the thing. In the '70s it was studied at the Hewlett-Packard Labs. They found that the skull was carved against the axis, which is impossible because it would have shattered. H-P could find no trace of tool marks. The best guess, if it were made by man, was that it was roughly traced out of the crystal with diamonds and then detailed with sand and water. People going over the details of the skull time and again, generation after generation. It could have taken 150 or even 300 years to create using this technique. One of the H-P scientists said that the skull just shouldn't be!"

"What was it used for?"

"No one knows for certain. Anna said she believed it was used in Mayan ceremonies. She said when the current shaman or high priest found his successor, he would look into the eye sockets of the skull. All of his knowledge, all of his power would leave him and enter the skull. The new shaman would then take the skull and stare into the sockets and the knowledge and the power would enter him, and the old shaman would die. She also said the skull could be used by the shaman to will the death of another."

"Do you believe all this?" I asked.

"Yes, I believe it's all possible, and you would, too, if you saw the thing, touched the thing like I did."

"You *touched* it? What happened?"

18

"I'll tell you in a moment, but first, there's something else you should know. The Mayans believe that on December 12, 2012, the earth will be destroyed. There is a legend that there are actually 13 crystal skulls. If the skulls can be found and united they would conjure up a massive power that would prevent the destruction of the earth. But, there is another theory, another legend. Some believe uniting the skulls won't save the earth, but will actually be the catalyst to destroy the earth! The gathering of the skulls will bring about Doomsday! I don't think I'll be around in 2012, but you will!" he said, punctuating his proclamation by jabbing a forefinger in my direction.

As the hairs were rising on the back of my neck, one of the hotel staff entered the room. "Mr. Karges?"

I jumped and spun around to face the man, "Yes, what is it?" I probably sounded a bit irritated to have this story of the crystal skull interrupted so suddenly.

"Mr. Thomas from your group wanted to make certain you had arrived on property. He also wanted to invite you to the ballroom to hear Mr. Gates' talk."

"Did he say if it was required?"

"No, not at all. He knew we were a bit slow getting your room ready and wanted to make certain you had something to do while you were waiting."

"Oh, I have something to do all right. Please tell Mr. Thomas I will see him at five o'clock for the sound check and thank him for me."

"Of course sir," the man said as he smartly turned and left the room.

I was anxious to find out more about this incredible artifact.

"Are you with the computer people?" My new friend asked.

"I'm hired help, just here for the evening and then on my way."

"Well, you know, they have a ballroom set up for some sort of demonstration with multiple work stations. Anna said she carried the skull by the room and all hell broke loose! Computers crashed, people were running around. She said that sort of thing happened all the time."

"What happened when you touched the skull?"

He shivered. "I asked if I could place my hand on it. She said, 'Do it son, but gently, gently.' I rested my palm on the top of the skull," he said as he mimed the action for me, his eyes distant, almost as if he were in a trance.

"I looked directly into the eye sockets. I saw twin flashes of blue light, like a pair of lightening strikes and I heard a deep moaning. 'Look deeper into the skull man, what do you see?' She prodded me on. That's when I saw myself, resting, in a casket! I was much older but it was definitely

19

me. I saw my death. I pulled my hand away from the thing like I was touching a cobra!"

"Wow," was the only response I could muster.

"Anna chuckled, placed the skull back into its case and said 'Good day' and that was it. She's gone and now I'm a mess."

"Here, have some water," I offered, "and maybe something a little stronger than that wine. There's a full bar over there," I nodded toward the corner of the room.

Just then, the St. Regis staff member reappeared and told me my room was ready. I looked toward my acquaintance and he indicated that he would be fine.

"You go on, have a nice stay. This is a wonderful place. You know it's the hotel they use for the exterior shots on that TV show, *Hotel.*"

I thought that the place looked familiar when we pulled up. *Hotel* was a mid '80s ABC television show with several independent stories happening in and around the hotel during the hour long broadcast. A landlocked *Love Boat,* which was another old TV show.

"The crystal skull would make a great story for that show," I said as I hurried off to my room.

After the performance that night, I was chatting with Mr. Thomas who had brought me to San Francisco for his group of CIOs.

"You really missed an interesting presentation. That Gates is a genius," he said.

At first, I didn't know what he was talking about. Then, I remembered the unaccepted invitation to hear someone named Gates speak that afternoon.

"Really?" I said not knowing who Bill Gates was or what he could have been talking about.

"Oh yes, he's launching something called Windows®. It's an operating system that will rival Mac's. It will be an add on to MS-DOS®. It's Microsoft's response to Macintosh's GUI."

I must have looked puzzled because he quickly clarified, "You know GUI, graphical user interface."

"Oh," I said and nodded wisely. Frankly, the whole thing sounded like Charlie Brown's teacher, "WAA WAA WA WA, etc., etc."

Of course, now I know who Bill Gates is. You have to remember, this was 1985, and I was only twenty-seven-years-old. And, while in retrospect, I probably would have been better off leaving the lounge and sitting in a room with Bill Gates and 100 CIOs, I probably wouldn't have understood half of what they were talking about. Plus, as the decades rolled by and I was forced into the "computer age" I discovered, I'm a Mac® guy!

Reflecting back on this particular tale from the road, I wanted to find out what became of the Mitchell-Hedges skull. I also reflect on the fact that if I had heard Bill Gates speak in 1985, and if I had been as moved by him as I was by my mysterious friend in the lounge, I might have bought Microsoft stock. Oh well!

The H-P story checks out. The actual discovery of the skull, not so much. While the Mitchell-Hedges family claimed the skull was discovered in 1924, there is no public mention of the artifact by Mike Mitchell-Hedges until 1943. There is a record of F.A. Mike Mitchell-Hedges purchasing a crystal skull at a London Sotheby's auction in 1943. The seller of the skull was one Sidney Burney. To cloud the issue further, Burney was apparently a friend of Mitchell-Hedges. While the Mitchell-Hedges side does not deny that the skull was purchased at auction, they clarify the provenance of the artifact by claiming that Mike Mitchell-Hedges left the skull for safe keeping with Sidney Burney. Mitchell-Hedges heard rumor that for some reason the skull was going to the auction block. He raced to London and purchased the skull for 400 British pounds when he couldn't persuade Sotheby's to pull the item from auction. Is the Mitchell-Hedges version of the auction story true? Burney claimed that he purchased the skull in 1934, but there is no record of the purchase and Burney never identified from whom he purchased it. However, he denied that Mitchell-Hedges found the skull or was the owner of the skull prior to 1943. Is the Burney version of the story true?

There are several other famous crystal skulls. None matches the notoriety or quality of the Mitchell-Hedges skull, but two of the most famous are The Paris Skull (property of the Quai Branley Museum) and The British Museum Skull. In 2008, electron microscopic examinations of these skulls (along with a third skull at the Smithsonian Institution in Washington, D.C.) revealed tool marks of the industrial age meaning they were created in recent times, not by ancient Mayans.

The British Museum Skull and the Paris Skull can be traced to a French antiques dealer, Eugene Boban. Boban had a shop in Mexico City with a collection of over 2,000 pre-Columbian artifacts. The collection included several crystal skulls. In 1887 he sold at auction what has become known as The British Museum Skull to Tiffany & Co. in New York. In 1889, Tiffany's sold the skull to a wealthy California businessman who went bankrupt years later and tried to get Tiffany's to buy the skull back. Tiffany's vice president, George Kunz, persuaded The British Museum to buy the skull in 1897, and it has resided there ever since.

Boban claimed that his skulls were Aztec, Mayan and/or Mexican. Many experts believe that all of these skulls were created in the mid 1800s, most probably, in Germany, and are fakes.

It is important to note that the Mitchell-Hedges skull, the subject of this story, has never been traced to Boban, and despite numerous scientific examinations, has never been explained. As the Hewlett-Packard researcher said, "The damned thing simply shouldn't be."

Anna "Sammy" Mitchell-Hedges died in 2007 at the ripe old age of one-hundred. Upon her death there were some legal arguments among her family as to who owned the skull. It is now in the possession of Bill Homann who took care of Anna for the last eight years of her life.

I truly believe that the man I spoke with at the St. Regis had a profound experience with the crystal skull. I believe that he believed he saw a vision of himself within the eye sockets. But that doesn't mean that I think the skull is some supernatural instrument from another world, although it could be! He could have had one too many Bloody Marys that morning. Or, more than likely, his imagination kicked into high gear and suggestion took over. Suggestion is a very powerful force. It can make you see, feel and hear things that aren't really there.

I remember when I was a young boy, my older, neighborhood friends told me there was no Santa Claus. I came to believe that the jolly old man didn't exist, and I told my younger brother, Brian. We then told our parents. They were a bit upset. I think they wanted Brian, who is three years younger than me, to believe for another year or two. That Christmas Eve, as we were lying in bed, both of us distinctly heard reindeer hooves on the roof of our house! Our faith in Santa was restored. Of course, I know there were no reindeer on the roof that night, and I suspected my father of concocting some sort of scheme to create a noise on the roof we might believe to be Santa and his reindeer. I asked him about it years later. He said he remembered that Christmas, but he didn't do a thing to sway our belief in Santa. So what did we hear? I think we wanted Santa to be real. As we were lying in bed trying to fall asleep and thinking of all the toys we would find under the tree in the morning, we imagined the noise. Or, a squirrel ran across the roof and we amplified the noise to suit our idea of what reindeer hooves on the roof would sound like. We both experienced it, and at the time, it was magical. This type of suggestive hallucination may well have been what the man in the lounge experienced when he came face-to-face with the crystal skull.

Crystal Skulls and Bill Gates

I know crystal skulls do have some power. The legend of the crystal skulls was powerful enough to lure Harrison Ford back into his fedora and the role of Indiana Jones in the 2008 film *Indiana Jones and the Kingdom of the Crystal Skull*!

The Mitchell-Hedges skull still tours the world, causing awe and wonderment. I've yet to see it. I hope one day to meet it face-to-face, perhaps rest my hand upon it, and stare into the eye sockets.

CHAPTER THREE

Ripping Good Times in London

In celebration of our 15th wedding anniversary, Charlotte and I decided to take our first "real" vacation. I knew it was our first real vacation because of my friend Jeff. Jeff insists that you're not on vacation unless you're gone for two weeks. This was news to me! So despite the many trips Charlotte and I had been on for rest and relaxation, it wasn't until 1995 that we took on the task of going on vacation!

At the start of our marriage, we had no money—and I mean NO money—so we couldn't afford leisure travel. Then, as my career began to grow, my travel schedule exploded! In the 1990s I averaged 175 performances a year. It was an intense and exhausting schedule. I know what you're thinking—*You only worked one-hundred-seventy-five days a year and you're complaining?* No, that's just the number of shows I averaged a year. You have to add on travel days and days spent at conferences and trade shows to get the complete picture. When you do that, the number of nights I spent away from my home would top two-hundred annually. Fortunately, Charlotte would be with me about half the time. I'm not certain our marriage would have survived otherwise. And just so you know, those two-hundred days on the road are just part of my job. There's the office time too, with marketing, promoting, writing, developing new performance material and all the rest of the duties an entrepreneur running a small business has. Believe me, it's more than a full-time job.

When you spend that much time on the road, you don't really want to travel much for fun. All you really want to do is be home. There are several songs that have popped up over the years that perfectly describe what I'm trying to express. To quote rocker Chris Daughtry from his song, *Home:*

> *So I'm going home, back to the place where I belong*
> *And where your love has always been enough for me*
> *I'm not running from, no, I think you got me all wrong*
> *I don't regret this life I chose for me,*
> *But these places and these faces are getting old*
> *So I'm going home, well I'm going home.*
>
> *Be careful what you wish for,*
> *'Cause you just might get it all.*
> *You just might get it all,*
> *And then some you don't want.*
> *Be careful what you wish for,*
> *'Cause you just might get it all.*
> *You just might get it all, yeah.*

The first song that really resonated with me along these lines was the work of one of my favorite artists, Dan Fogelberg, in *False Faces* he sings:

> *False faces and*
> *Meaningless chases*
> *I travel alone*
> *First places and*
> *Calendar races*
> *I need a home*

And you might be familiar with Michael Buble's *Home*:

> *Another summer day*
> *Has come and gone away*
> *In Paris and Rome*
> *But I wanna go home*

May be surrounded by
A million people I
Still feel all alone
I just wanna go home
Oh, I miss you, you know

Another aeroplane
Another sunny place
I'm lucky, I know
But I wanna go home

Let me go home
I've had my run
Baby, I'm done
I gotta go home

These artists express my feelings much better than I could. I'm hoping you understand what a touring performer goes through, torn between doing what he/she loves to do and being applauded for it yet yearning to return to a place he/she can truly call home.

As things got better for us financially in the late '80s and early '90s we did start to take quick trips (I used to call them vacations until Jeff corrected me) for three or four days to some tropical location like the Virgin Islands, the Bahamas or Bermuda. But these getaways were always short and not very challenging. We would pick a nice hotel, lie in the sun, and enjoy tropical drinks and nice dinners. It was a way to unwind after all those road miles.

In 1995, our vacationless lives changed. Both of us had always wanted to go to England, so a Great Britain, two-week vacation was planned. Come to think of it, it's the only "Jeff vacation" we've ever taken since it's the only time we've traveled for pleasure for two weeks or more.

I cashed in some of the hundreds of thousands of frequent flyer miles I had accumulated for two round trip tickets to London. As you can probably tell, I fly a lot! My record for elite frequent flyer status was in 2005 (based on 2004 mileage). I was a top tier elite frequent flyer on both Delta and US Airways; a second tier elite frequent flyer on both Northwest and United; and a third tier elite frequent flyer on American. Basically, that translates into over 275,000 actual miles flown in 2004, and that's a lot of time in the air.

Ripping Good Times in London

I used to wear my elite frequent flyer "badges" with honor like any road warrior. By the way, you can always tell us at the airport. Before the plane starts boarding, we all puff up and jockey to be first in line. Look at me! I'm in the air all the time! Then, I realized, who wants to fly that much? I still fly a lot. I'm always a top tier or second tier elite frequent flyer on Delta and US Airways. I've flown over a million miles on each carrier. Now I do 100,000 to 175,000 miles a year.

When I travel for fun, I usually go first class on free tickets using my mileage. I "cash in" miles for a certain type of award ticket which has no blackout dates, and as long as there is a first class seat available, you can get it. It "costs" about twice as many miles as a regular first class award ticket, but I prefer it. I choose my flights on my days. I remember cashing in miles for a pair of first class tickets to France on Delta. The reservation agent asked, "That's 400,000 miles, are you sure you want to burn that many miles on one trip?" After cashing them in, I still had 200,000 miles in the account, and by the same time the following year I was back up to 400,000 miles thanks to bonus miles and an airline credit card.

After cashing in mileage for our tickets, the next thing we did to plan our Great Britain romp was to pick up a guidebook. We chose one by Rick Steves. He gets to the hot spots as well as the less known wonders of a place. He writes with wit and good humor and in a very conversational tone. He's always on the lookout for good value and tries to get you to experience a country like a native. I highly recommend any of his travel guides.

As we put together our itinerary (with Steves' help) it began to look a little intimidating. We would fly direct from Pittsburgh, to London Gatwick (the less crowded of London's airports). I was going to rent a car (automatic please, driving on the left hand side of the road and from the right hand side of the car was going to be difficult enough). After our overnight flight, we would head to the town of Bath, for two nights. Then, it would be up to the beautiful Lake District for another couple of nights before crossing into Scotland. In Scotland, we would stop over in Oban, and ferry out to an island and then move on to Edinburgh, for three nights. From Edinburgh, it was back to merry olde England with an overnight in York, before ending up in London for three days.

When I turned our desired itinerary over to our travel agent and she passed it on to an affiliate in the U.K. they said we were out of our minds. They insisted that we would be spending all our time in the car and not get to see anything. We were confident we could pull this off — one of the benefits of living out of a suitcase for fifteen years. So we leafed through a big book of Great Britain hotels, picked our spots and looked forward to our adventure.

Upon arrival in Gatwick, we headed to the rental car counter. I was supposed to get a Volvo or "other similar vehicle." A large Ford station wagon, larger than anything I remember seeing in the United States pulled up and we were told to hop in and get going!

"But, I thought I had a Volvo," I complained.

"Sorry lad, this is the only automatic we have in that class of vehicle. Now move along."

Driving wasn't horrible, but it did take some getting used to. I had to constantly remember to stay on the left hand side of the road. Then there were the roundabouts, continuous circles that you could find yourself trapped in for days! While heading towards Edinburgh, we exited a roundabout at the wrong spot and drove 15 miles in the wrong direction before realizing our mistake.

We stopped at Stonehenge, on the way to Bath. In 1995, you would be driving along and Stonehenge would just appear on the side of the road. I understand that they rerouted the roadway or something so you don't just pop up on it as we did, but it was quite a site. The prehistoric megalithic ruin marks a burial mound with remains dating back to 3000 B.C. No one quite knows who built Stonehenge or why. Best guesses include that it was used as an ancient observatory or for religious rituals. It has become a pilgrimage site for British Druids.

After marveling at Stonehenge, we got back into the huge Ford wagon and headed off. We were lost for a while. At first, it was frustrating, but then we just started to laugh. We were on a country road that could barely accommodate our car, trying to find another stone circle. When another car came along one of us had to back up to a point where you could pull over and let the other vehicle pass. And remember, I'm driving for the first time on the "wrong" side of the road after an overnight plane trip and in a gigantic station wagon.

We made it to the town of Avebury, a beautiful little village that is completely surrounded by a stone circle. The circle of stone around Avebury is actually 16 times the size of Stonehenge and consists of more than 100 huge stones.

We were getting a little hungry, so we stopped for a bite to eat. I had heard bad things about English food. From our pub lunch in Avebury, my worst fears were realized. It was inedible. Two weeks of this? We went to a pastry shop and ordered some sweetness. Everything looked so good but tasted like sawdust! Charlotte and I were beginning to worry that we would be malnourished by the end of the two weeks.

Driving into Bath, the traffic was extremely heavy and we were later told that we were in the midst of a "Bank Holiday" or three-day weekend, and that Bath was a very popular destination for British holidaymakers. It was a tight squeeze, but I got the giant Ford into a car park and said goodbye to the behemoth of a rental vehicle for a day as we checked into our hotel. We found a Pizza Hut™ for dinner that night.

The next day we toured Bath. It is quite a beautiful city. One hundred-sixteen degree natural hot springs give Bath its name. The Romans enjoyed the water and there are beautiful excavated Roman baths you can tour. It's said that in 1687, Queen Mary, in an effort to cure possible infertility bathed in the warm water. Within ten months she gave birth to a son and Bath became even more popular. This was a wonderful day for us. We felt like a couple of British bankers on holiday. We toured the abbey, the Royal Crescent and the Circus (home to stunning Georgian architecture), and we had high tea at the Pump Room. Then, it was time for dinner. We decided to give English food one more try and we're glad we did. We had a wonderful meal and didn't have another bad meal the entire time we were in the U.K.

From the resort town of Bath, we traveled north to the Lake District, possibly my favorite part of the trip. We stayed at a lovely country house with a gorgeous garden and hiked around Derwentwater, one of the area's most beautiful lakes. A ferry dropped us off at one point and we were supposed to catch up with it at different stops around the lake, but we just kept missing it. What was to have been a four-mile hike ended up being seven miles, but we didn't mind. It was so peaceful and lovely. Every time I hear Sting sing *Fields of Gold,* I think of this day in the Lake District of England. I believe we only ran into one other group of people, a husband, wife and daughter with three dogs. One of the pups only had three legs. We helped them organize the pack as we all crossed a stone wall together.

In the town of Keswick, Charlotte went in and out of the various shops while I had a serendipitous moment. I went into a car museum and what a treasure trove it turned out to be. I have to confess to you that I'm a "spy geek," and inside the facility was the greatest collection of "spy cars" ever assembled in one place, or at least I like to think so. James Bond's tricked out Aston Martin DB5 was parked next to a rocket-launching BSA Lightning motorcycle used by femme fatale Fiona Volpe in one of my favorite 007 films, *Thunderball.* There was *The Equalizer's* dark green Jaguar XJ6 sedan. My favorite television show of all time is *The Avengers* starring Diana Rigg as Emma Peel and Patrick Macnee as John Steed. In this smallish building tucked away in a quiet Lake District town was Mrs. Peel's powder blue Lotus Elan and Steed's 1920s era green Bentley. The late '60s cult TV show, *The Prisoner,* was another of my boyhood TV watching habits. In fact, my only regret on this U.K. pleasure tour was that we couldn't squeeze time in to travel to Portmeirion, a quaintly unique collection of buildings, statues and gardens on a rocky peninsula on the coast of North Wales' Cardigan Bay, as it was the site of The Village in *The Prisoner* TV show. In the opening scene of each episode, Patrick McGoohan's character was seen driving a Lotus Seven Series II, a topless, two-seater roadster. It was here too. Roger Moore starred as Simon Templar in *The Saint,* another of my favorite '60s television shows. He raced around in a white Volvo P1800. I used to own one of the little Corgi metal models of the vehicle with a Saint logo on the hood, er, bonnet. The Volvo had a home in this museum along with all the other cool spy cars. In fact, when I received word from the rental car company that I would be motoring around Britain in a Volvo, I had images of me as Simon Templar. Instead it was turning out to be more like me as Chevy Chase in *National Lampoon's Vacation* driving the "family truckster!" If any of these spies is familiar to you and you're a certified spy geek, you'll know I was having the time of my life. It's the one time I was still gawking and Charlotte was waiting on me instead of the other way around.

As much as we loved the Lake District, it was time to travel farther north to Scotland. As we crossed the border it began to snow! This was late May and I started to worry that we might not have properly prepared for a Scottish spring. Our fears were short lived. As we drove along Loch Lomond, the snow drifted away.

Our destination was the town of Oban, but we were sidetracked when a beautiful, fairy tale castle appeared before us. It was like something from a dream. It turned out to be Inveraray Castle in Argyll. The Duke of the clan Campbell makes his home here and it was beautifully restored. Our first castle! We loved it and stayed for hours.

With our detour at an end, we pushed on to Oban. In Oban, we ferried out to the Isle of Mull, toured another castle and admired the "Hairy Coos," the Scottish hairy cows or Highland Cows that come in a variety of colors and have long horns and a very shaggy coat. With hair hanging down into their eyes, they are quite a sight. Back on the mainland, we toured two castle ruins on our way to Edinburgh. These ruins are National Trust sites; yet, there are no guides there and you are free to roam about them as you please.

There is no graffiti and no lawsuits against the National Trust for Scotland charity or the government because someone fell from the top of a castle tower. Personal responsibility is a wonderful thing.

We were two full days in Edinburgh, and enjoyed every minute of it. We toured the Royal Mile starting at the end, the Palace of Holyroodhouse, where the Queen still spends a week each summer. We ended at the beginning, thirteen-hundred-year-old Edinburgh Castle. There were many stops in between including an antique store where Charlotte picked up one of her favorite treasures, a large kilt pin made of beautifully etched sterling silver with blue-gray agate stones and dating from the 1860s.

One night, we took a ghost walk that consisted of a bit of an historic tour with costumed characters known as "jumper ooters" surprising you at every turn. There was a serious side to this walk, as the history of the witches of Edinburgh was revealed. Edinburgh was once considered the capital of witch burning in Europe. It is a matter of record that over 300 women were accused of witchcraft and burned at the stake on Castlehill. In all of Scotland, it is estimated that as many as 2,500 women were put to death. If you were a convicted witch in England, you would be hanged by the neck until dead. In Scotland, it was a different story. Mary Queen of Scots came back from a trip to France and brought with her the Witchcraft Act. This equated witchcraft to heresy, and the punishment was to be burned alive at the stake. The convicted witches were cruelly tortured before their final, painful demise. The last person to be executed as a witch in Scotland was Janet Horne in 1722. The law was abolished in 1736. A special plaque and cast iron wall fountain serve as a memorial to the hundreds of women who were killed as witches in Edinburgh.

We had dinner that night at a restaurant on Castlehill called the Witchery, and a coven of witches joined us. Actually, I think it was some university students and their professor out for a good time, but it added to the atmosphere.

We left Edinburgh, toured a ruined abbey at the Scottish-English border and before we knew it, we were back in England. The plan was to stay in York, a walled medieval city, and try to catch up with our English friend, Peter, who lived not far away in Chesterfield. Our time in York was short but we did get to tour York Minster, considered England's finest gothic church and The Shambles, the town's extremely well preserved medieval section.

Peter Zenner is a British hypnotist and mentalist and has been a friend of mine for twenty years or more. We primarily communicated via audio cassette tapes for years and first met face-to-face when he traveled to the United States to attend an International Brotherhood of Magicians gathering (no, I'm not making that up). The following year, he made another trip to the U.S. and stayed with us for two weeks. We traveled together to Washington, D.C. for the International Psychic Entertainers Association convention (no, I'm not making that up, either).

Peter, his new wife Jules, and his stepson, Sammy, were gracious hosts. We had a grand evening and we parted agreeing to meet in four days time in London, for a double-decker bus tour of the city (Jules had never been) along with a "Ripper Walk" Peter had been dying to go on. As we said goodbye to the Zenners, I started thinking about London and Jack the Ripper.

London was everything we expected it to be, and we did everything we wanted to do: a cruise on the Thames, the Changing of the Guard at Buckingham Palace, Westminster Abbey, the Houses of Parliament, Big Ben, St. Paul's Cathedral, strolls through St. James's and Hyde Parks, a shopping trip to Harrods and my personal favorite, the Tower of London. This castle, palace and prison is overflowing with history. From the crown jewels to the armory, to the giant ravens guarding the grounds and the entertaining Yeoman Warders or Beefeaters who take you on lively tours, I was constantly drawn to this place. And it was there, at the Tower of London, where we met our guide and began to retrace the steps of Jack the Ripper.

The group gathered at twilight. There were eleven of us. There would be far less than that at the conclusion of the tour. The group consisted of an older couple, two men and a younger couple with a baby in a stroller, plus Peter, Jules, Charlotte and me. Our guide was an academic, a college professor. He was dressed in blue jeans, black boots and a black leather jacket. He wore his salt and pepper hair long. As we began our walk, our guide clued us in on the background of Jack the Ripper.

"The serial killer known as Jack the Ripper committed a series of murders in the Whitechapel area between August and November of 1888 in what became known as the 'Autumn of Terror.'

"While there has been much fiction based on the character of Jack the Ripper, rest assured the killer was quite real. The brutality of the murders, the sensational nature of the press at the time, and the inability of the police to solve the murders are all partially responsible for the legend of Jack the Ripper. The killer was never caught. His identity remains unknown, and tonight we shall trace his very steps," our guide stated.

As we walked behind our guide like schoolchildren on a field trip, Charlotte and I glanced at each other, reading each other's thoughts — *Is this the way we want to spend our last night in London?*

As we crossed through the financial district, "The Professor" stopped us.

"Do any of you have a tourist map of London?" he asked.

One of the group produced a rather detailed map.

"From here on, none of the areas we shall visit can be found on any tourist map. The tourist industry does not want you wandering about here. It is dangerous." As the professor said this, he demonstrated with the map and indeed, it seemed as if we were stepping off the edge of the map and into the unknown, at least as far as the tourism industry was concerned.

Twilight had turned to dusk as we walked through the site of a demolished building. It was rough going for the baby stroller; so that was folded up and carried by the father as the mother took the babe into her arms.

"Jack the Ripper is credited with as many as 11 murders, one as early as April 1888, and one as late as February 1891, but we shall focus on what most experts, myself included, consider the most likely victims of Jack. Those five women, all prostitutes, were murdered between August and November 1888. They are collectively known as the canonical five," proclaimed our resident "Ripperologist."

"Friday, August 31, 1888, the body of Mary 'Polly' Ann Nichols was discovered at 3:40 a.m. in front of a gated stable entrance which was located just about here," the Professor gestured with a wide arc of his arms.

"Her throat was cut deeply — twice. The lower part of her stomach was cut open — a large, jagged wound. There were other incisions across her abdomen and on her right side," the Professor glanced around at the group, settling his gaze on Charlotte.

"Let us move on and meet Dark Annie," the Professor said as he turned to walk away.

"Excuse me sir," the father with the stroller interjected.

"Yes, what is it?" the Ripperologist asked.

"Will this walking get any easier?" the man said as he looked about the gravel we were standing in.

"No sir," replied the Professor, "if anything it will get worse."

The young couple quickly conferred in private and then the man spoke, "I'm taking the baby and going back, but she wants to stay. She loves this stuff. Can you make sure she gets back to the Tower?"

"I will try my best," the Ripperologist said.

"Can I get a refund?" the young father asked.

"Afraid not. You are quite welcome to continue the walk and I've not charged you for the little one," the Professor said as he nodded toward the baby.

The couple briefly kissed goodbye. The husband hurried off with the baby tucked in one arm and the stroller in the other as the rest of us continued our walk through Whitechapel.

"Now where was I?" the Professor continued, obviously a bit irritated.

"Oh yes, Dark Annie or Annie Chapman. She was killed Saturday, September 8, 1888. Her body was discovered here," he pointed to a spot on the ground.

"Her neck was cut deeply, twice, as was Polly Nichols' you will recall. Her abdomen was entirely ripped open, and her uterus was removed," our guide informed us.

"Jack the Ripper came about his name on September 27, 1888, when the Central News Agency received a letter which contained the salutation, 'Dear Boss.' In this letter, the writer stated that he was 'down on whores and I shan't quit ripping them until I do get buckled. Grand work the last job was. I gave the lady no time to squeal. My knife's so nice and sharp I want to get to work right away if I get the chance.' This communication was signed 'Yours truly, Jack the Ripper.' Hundreds of letters were received claiming to be from the murderer. I believe only three have any real merit. This 'Dear Boss' letter primarily because it gave the Ripper his name. We shall discuss two more supposed communications from the killer before our walk is finished," the Professor lectured.

We continued to move on through the Whitechapel night, and suddenly the Professor stopped and turned to face us.

"We are now just over three weeks following the murder of Dark Annie. It is September 30, 1888, and the body of Elizabeth 'Long Liz' Stride was found at 1:00 a.m. She bled to death from one deep cut on the left side of her neck. There were additional cuts on the right side of her neck. However, her abdomen was intact. The body was not mutilated. Because of this, some believe Jack was not the murderer. Others believe he was interrupted during the attack."

"What do you believe?" Peter asked our guide.

"I believe it was Jack because September 30th is known as the 'Night of the Double Event.' Catherine Eddowes' body was found, her throat deeply cut in two places, her abdomen ripped open. Her uterus was removed along with her left kidney, and her face was horribly mutilated. You see, Jack was interrupted before he finished with Long Liz and he had to satisfy his cravings. He had to kill once more," the Professor said with a far off look in his eyes.

"Oh my!" the female half of the older couple spoke up.

"Sir, we're getting pretty far away from the Tower of London. You are going to lead us back there, aren't you?" the woman's companion asked.

"No sir. You will be on your own at the end of the evening, and unfortunately we will be even farther away from the Tower of London by then," the Professor explained.

The couple looked at each other.

"I saw an Underground station a while back. I believe we will be on our way. Goodbye!" the male half of the couple stated and off they went.

"Be careful," our guide called after them.

"This may well be a good time to tell you about the second Ripper letter which I believe to have some importance. It was a post card, actually. The card was received on October 1st, one day after the double murder. It was short, but not very sweet. In the note, the writer refers to a double event this time. He also wrote that the first victim squealed a bit and he couldn't finish her as he would have liked. In the 'Dear Boss' letter, the writer said he would send an ear to the police cut from his next victim. Long Liz did have a cut to her ear and some believe that the killer may have tried to take it. In the post card, the writer mentions that he did not have the time to get ears for the police this time. The post card is known as the 'Saucy Jacky' letter as the writer states, 'you'll hear about Saucy Jacky's work tomorrow.' The handwriting was similar to the 'Dear Boss' letter as was the language of the missive, and it was signed Jack the Ripper. Some believe this to be a genuine communication from the killer. Others believe it to be yet another hoax, one of the hundreds the police and press received during the 'Autumn of Terror,'" the professor concluded.

"What do you believe?" asked Peter.

The Professor rubbed his chin and then turned to face Peter as he said, "A probable hoax, perpetrated by a journalist close to the investigation who had inside knowledge of the crime."

Peter nodded his head in agreement.

"However, there is one other letter that I truly believe may have come from our boy, Jack," our guide went on.

"The 'From Hell' letter?" Peter asked.

"Spot on. On October 16th, George Lusk, President of the Whitechapel Vigilance Committee, received the letter. The Whitechapel

Vigilance Committee was a citizens' brigade established to investigate the Ripper murders due to the inability of the police to make any progress with regard to solving the crimes.

"Not only did Lusk receive the letter, he also received a box containing one half of a human kidney. The writer claimed to have fried and ate the other half. You will recall that Catherine Eddowes' left kidney was missing. I am not alone in the opinion that this letter may well have been from the true killer. Noted FBI criminal profiler John Douglas agrees with me," the Ripperologist said with a smug smile.

"This letter is referred to as the 'From Hell' letter because that is precisely how the return address read—'From Hell.' It wasn't as well written as the previous communications we discussed, and it wasn't signed Jack the Ripper. Instead, it was signed 'Catch me when you can Mishter Lusk,'" our guide concluded.

"If you have been keeping count, we have covered four murders. There is just one to go, " the Professor stated.

We were standing at the entrance to an alleyway that stank of urine. I looked down and saw that I was standing on a condom — a used condom.

"Mary Jane Kelly was apparently murdered in her own bed. The body was found at 10:45 a.m. on Friday, November 9th. This was Jack's most vicious attack. Her neck was severed to the spine, her abdomen was ripped open and all the organs were removed and left in the room. Her heart was cut out and missing from the crime scene," our Ripper historian informed us.

"Why don't you join me for a pint, there is a pub just through the alley and we will discuss who the killer may have been," the Professor invited us.

Our guide slipped into the alley and the seven remaining members of the group reluctantly followed him down the alley and into a Victorian era pub named The Ten Bells.

"So tell us, who do you believe the Ripper to be?" Peter prodded our guide on.

"Not so fast. Buy me a pint and get one for yourselves and I will give you my thoughts on the matter, and then you will be free to go," our guide said.

A pint was set in front of the Ripperologist and he began to pontificate.

"You realize we are sitting in a pub which dates back to the time of the murders?" the Professor asked as he glanced around the establishment.

"Yes indeed, Long Liz, Dark Annie and all the rest used to frequent The Ten Bells. Perhaps they even met Jack here," the Professor said.

"There are literally hundreds of Jack the Ripper suspects. There is also the strong likelihood that the real Ripper's name does not appear on any subject list. He could have appeared to be an unremarkable man who lived and worked in Whitechapel, a man who appeared quite normal. He had to have an intimate knowledge of the area as he stalked these women, viciously murdered them and then disappeared without a trace.

"However, if I were a betting man, I would put my money on one of two known suspects. The first was a Pole, Seweryn Antonowicz Klosowski. He came to this country in 1887 or 1888. He lived in Whitechapel during the time of the murders, working as a barber. He was a rogue, a scoundrel and a murderer—of that it is certain. He poisoned three of his wives. He was hanged for those known murders in 1903. Inspector Frederick Abberline, one of the chief investigators on the Ripper case, favored Klosowski as a prime suspect.

"My best guess though is one David Cohen, a Polish Jew who may have been a bootmaker in Whitechapel. He was very poor and very troubled as were many residents of the East End. He was incarcerated in an asylum for the criminally insane. His incarceration coincided with the end of the murders. While in the Colney Hatch Asylum, he constantly had to be restrained due to his violent behavior. He died in the asylum in October 1889. John Douglas, the FBI profiler I mentioned when discussing the 'From Hell' letter, also favors the Cohen theory," our guide concluded.

The Professor drained his beer and looked around his semi-circle of students.

"So that's it then?" a small man who had been with us the entire tour but was mute throughout, spoke up.

"Yes sir, that is the story of Jack the Ripper as well as I could tell it and as well as we could trace his steps in modern day London," the Ripperologist replied.

"Well, we're off then," the little man said pulling his much larger male companion by the arm and toward the door.

"Um, Professor," the young mother spoke up, "can you help me get back to the Tower of London?"

"After my next pint," the Ripper historian replied.

The two men heading toward the door overheard this and offered to escort her back, an offer she quickly accepted. That left Peter, Jules, Charlotte and me. Three of us were ready to leave, but not Peter.

"What about the royal-Masonic connection to the murders?" Peter asked.

"Oh, not that rubbish," the Professor responded.

"It's hardly rubbish," Peter said, obviously offended by the Ripper historian's tone.

"Haven't you read Stephen Knight's *Jack the Ripper: The Final Solution*?" Peter asked.

"It is a sensational work of fiction, nothing more," our guide answered.

"What are you talking about Peter?" I asked my English friend.

"Just this—the Ripper murders were connected to the Crown. There are two primary theories. They both revolve around Prince Albert Victor, grandson of Queen Victoria and second in line of succession to the throne," Peter said, warming to the topic.

"The first theory says that Prince Albert Victor, or Eddy as he was known to his family, fathered an illegitimate child and the Ripper murders were part of a royal conspiracy to hide the birth," Peter went on as the professor rolled his eyes and took a sip from his second beer.

"The other theory suggests that Prince Eddy was, in fact, Jack the Ripper," Peter stated.

"Bollocks!" the Professor exclaimed before draining his second pint.

"Queen Victoria, Eddy's father, the Prince of Wales who later became King Edward VII, Prime Minister Lord Salisbury and his Freemason friends plus the London police conspired to murder anyone who could trace either the child or the murders back to the Crown. It was a vast conspiracy," Peter went on, oblivious to the Professor's outburst.

"Ahem," the Professor cleared his throat, "Prince Albert Victor had alibis."

"I'm not saying it was Eddy alone, I'm just trying to point out the royal connection. I believe the Ripper was probably Sir William Withey Gull, Queen Victoria's physician. He was a Freemason and the murders were similar to a ritual killing known in Freemasonry—death by a slashed throat followed by disembowelment. That is how the famous Mason, Hiram Abiff, was executed. And, the crimes were obviously committed by someone who had anatomical knowledge, like a surgeon or physician," Peter was talking nonstop.

"No, they weren't," the Professor stated matter-of-factly, "Dr. Thomas Bond examined the bodies and clearly stated that the killer's work did not display the skill of a surgeon or even a butcher, just a savage madman and the Masonic theory is just preposterous."

Peter was not deterred, "There are many connections between the Prince and possible Ripper suspects. James Kenneth Stephen was the Prince's tutor and possible lover. His handwriting was found to be similar to the 'From Hell' letter that you yourself believe may have come from the killer. Stephen starved himself to death after Prince Eddy's death which, by the way, was carried out by an overdose of morphine ordered by the Prime Minister himself," Peter went on.

"Prince Albert Victor died in January of 1892, a victim of an influenza pandemic," the Professor bluntly stated as he motioned to the barman for another pint.

"That's exactly what *they* would want you to think! And then there's Walter Richard Sickert. He was an artist, a close associate to Prince Eddy and a likely suspect in the case," Peter went on.

"He was in France at the time of some of the murders," the Professor rebutted.

"Some, but not all. Prince Albert Victor, Sir William Withey Gull, James Kenneth Stephen and Richard Sickert may have committed some of the murders or all of the murders. It could easily have been more than one killer. That's why he was never caught. Think of it, all these men working together in a murderous conspiracy with the powers of the Queen, the Prime Minister and the police department to cover up their wicked deeds," Peter said loudly as he looked to Jules, Charlotte and me.

"Oh, that's bloody brilliant! You're grasping at straws, man," the Professor said.

I could see where this was going. When Peter visited for two weeks, I learned one thing—he will not lose an argument. He's like a dog with a bone, and our Ripperologist seemed to be cut from the same cloth.

"I'm hungry," Charlotte spoke up. Indeed, we hadn't eaten since lunch and it was getting very late.

"Come on dear," Jules said as she took Peter by the arm and the four of us waved goodbye to our host as we watched him finish off his third beer as neatly as Jack the Ripper finished off Dark Annie.

As we exited The Ten Bells, you couldn't help but notice that a cold fog had rolled in. We looked around at our surroundings and I noticed a look of panic on Peter's face.

"This isn't good, not good at all," Peter said to no one in particular.

"What is it?" Charlotte asked.

"It's not good, that's what it is. We're in a dreadful neighborhood. We need to get out of here quickly," he said as he tried to hail a cab. At that moment, it dawned on me that Peter was the only one of us who had any idea where we were and since he was worried, we should all probably be worried.

A man came shuffling toward us just as a cab pulled to the curb.

"Quickly, everyone in," Peter said.

"Not so fast, where to?" the cabbie asked.

"Anywhere but here!" cried Peter.

"Not good enough guv, I need a destination before I can allow you in," the cabbie replied.

The shuffling figure kept coming closer.

"Chinatown?" Peter said it as more of a question than a statement. "Yes, yes, Chinatown, now drive man, drive!" Peter implored as we all piled into the cab. The cabbie sped away from the curb leaving the approaching stranger far behind.

We had a very late night Chinese dinner but none of us had much of an appetite after "meeting" Jack the Ripper. The four of us parted ways and the next day we were on a plane flying over the Pond and leaving London and Jack the Ripper behind. I certainly can't say The Ripper Walk was my favorite part of our Great Britain getaway. I can't even say it was a highlight. But, I can tell you one thing—I will never forget it!

CHAPTER FOUR

The Raven

I'm certain you've heard of the theory of "Six Degrees of Separation." It's the idea that everyone on the planet is only six people away from being connected to every single person on the planet. For example, you are one step or person away from everyone you know, which means you are two steps away from every person who is known to everyone you know, three steps away from everyone they know and so on and so on. The Six Degrees concept states that, on average, you are only six steps away from any person on the face of the earth. The game, "Six Degrees of Kevin Bacon" exploited the concept. The goal of this game was to link any actor to Kevin Bacon in six "moves" or less. A connection was made if two actors appeared in a film together. For example, to connect Kevin Bacon to Val Kilmer, you could say Val Kilmer was in *Top Gun* with Tom Cruise, Tom Cruise was in *A Few Good Men* with Kevin Bacon. You've made the connection in only two moves. You get the idea. This small world phenomenon was never more apparent to me than in Alaska. I think in Alaska, there are only about two degrees of separation.

I've been to Alaska many times. The trips are usually short (not the flight but the actual time I spend in the state) and *cold*. However, one August I had a wonderful opportunity to spend some quality time in the 49th state. I was hired to do two performances for a group of insurance agents. This was an incentive event for the company's very top producers. There were two groups of award winners. The first group of agents specialized in selling life insurance and the second group sold everything else. The company had rented a cruise ship, and the plan was to fly all the life award winners to Anchorage. They would board the ship and sail to Vancouver, British Columbia, Canada. The boat would dock there, and the life insurance agents would disembark and fly home. The other agents would meet the ship in Vancouver and sail it back to Alaska.

The company wanted to do something special for the *best of the best*, the top dozen or so agents in each group. They flew these agents and their guests into Alaska and Vancouver two days early. In Alaska, they had a tour of Anchorage and then two days at a Japanese owned mountain resort, Alyeska, before heading south to Seward, Alaska, to join their peers and board the ship to Vancouver. It was a similar situation in Vancouver. The top dozen producers and their guests came in two days early and had a wonderful time touring Vancouver. It was my job to provide special entertainment for these VIPs. I performed after-dinner entertainment at the Alyeska for the group's final night in Alaska, and I entertained the other top performers in Vancouver, during a dinner cruise on a private yacht cruising Vancouver Harbour.

Charlotte traveled with me on this trip. We opted to stay in Alaska while the ship cruised to Vancouver and then to spend some more time in Vancouver after the show there. It turned out to be a wonderful work-vacation. We absolutely loved Vancouver. We hiked and biked throughout Stanley Park and had our first taste of "ice wine" at the Teahouse overlooking English Bay before joining a few hundred thousand other people on the beach for the most incredible fireworks display I had ever seen. Well, it was the most incredible fireworks display I had ever seen at that point in time. In 2006, Charlotte and I had the pleasure of attending the Bastille Day celebrations at the Eiffel Tower in Paris, but that's another story! This Canadian display was the Benson and Hedges *Symphony of Fire,* a friendly international competition with fireworks companies from around the world, and it was spectacular. We took time to leave the city of Vancouver and travel aboard a B.C. Ferry to Vancouver Island for an overnight stay and high tea at the majestic and very British Empress Hotel in Victoria. We also toured the breathtakingly beautiful Butchart Gardens while on the island.

We had a wonderful time in Alaska, too. We had an incredible helicopter tour over the harsh and rugged landscape. The helicopter was actually able to land on a glacier where we got out and had a picnic lunch complete with champagne. We traveled to Seward for a day cruise in the Kenai Fjords. We watched as whales danced, bald eagles soared and porpoises chased our boat. We were also treated to the sight of 20,000 puffins, black and white seabirds with large, brightly colored beaks, living on the islands dotting the Kenai Fjords. During the cruise, we were fortunate enough to see an iceberg created as a large chunk of ice fell from a glacier and landed in the sea with a gigantic splash.

All this Alaskan sightseeing came after the show. The performance was very intimate with about 30 people in attendance. There was a disc jockey playing some light dinner music at the Alyeska prior to my presentation. He was an Anchorage resident, and I asked him if he would give me driving directions from Seward to the Captain Cook Hotel where we planned to stay for a couple nights after our scheduled day cruise. He was very familiar with the hotel and mentioned he was going to play a wedding there that weekend, which coincided with our stay. He suggested we look him up and perhaps get a drink together. Needless to say, he gave us excellent directions to the hotel.

The day after the show, we headed down to Seward for our day cruise. On the way, we saw moose along the side of the road, wild sheep situated on mountainsides that looked impossible to scale and even spotted a bear digging through a dumpster. Alaska is a wild place! We made a quick stop at a glacier on the Kenai Peninsula. While we were there, a cute little boy with a mop of dark, curly hair and wearing a makeshift cape made from a towel was running around bedeviling his family with a toy sword. After touring the glacier, we finished the drive to Seward and boarded the boat for the day. Who should appear on the boat but the boy from the glacier and his family. We started talking and discovered that the boy's name was Edward, and his father was a photographer. They had come to Alaska to photograph the wedding of a friend of the family.

While in Alaska, we wanted to connect with a friend of our own, Mimi. Mimi had worked the college circuit, traveling around the country setting up games and inflatables on college campuses for Homecoming and Spring Fling Weeks, what's known in the "business" as "novelty attractions." She had grown tired of life on the road and tired of her personal relationships; so she made the rather sudden decision to pack her belongings, load her car, drive across the country and then ferry her way to a new life in Alaska and, hopefully, a new man. We received photos and post cards from Mimi during her cross-country journey, as well as a Christmas card during her first winter holiday season in Alaska; however, after some time, we stopped exchanging cards and letters and, as so often happens, we lost touch.

After our cruise, we drove to Anchorage and checked into the Captain Cook. We discussed trying to find Mimi.

"Just look her up in the phone book," Charlotte suggested.

"Well, that's an obvious place to start," I said, "but she's been here a few years. I know she wanted to find someone and settle down. My guess would be that she was successful and is now married; so we couldn't find her by her maiden name in the phone book. The other possibility is she didn't find a man, gave up and moved back to the lower 48. You know, we haven't heard from her in over three years."

As I was completing my analysis of the situation, Charlotte shoved the local phone directory under my nose and pointed to a listing for Mimi.

"Well, there you go, we'll call her in the morning, it's too late tonight," I said after being confronted with the obvious.

The next morning I phoned Mimi.

"Is Mimi there?" I asked.

"No, she's not. Who's this?" responded the male voice on the other end of the line.

"My name's Craig Karges. I'm an old friend, my wife and I are in town, and we'd love to see her. Now, who are *you*?" I questioned him with what I hoped was a smile in my voice.

"Craig and Charlotte? Mimi talks about you all the time. She wanted to invite you to the wedding."

"What wedding?"

"My wedding, her wedding, I mean our wedding. I'm Bob and we're getting married tomorrow."

"Getting married? We've never met you. I sure hope you meet *our* approval," I joked.

"This is just great! You two are going to be my surprise for Mimi. Do you know where the Captain Cook Hotel is?"

"Know it. We're staying in it."

"You're kidding! Aw, this is great. The reception starts at three o'clock. We'll work you into the reception line and you can surprise Mimi."

Charlotte had picked up on what was going on, even though she only heard half the conversation and was looking at me in amazement.

"We've got a date with Mimi and her new husband tomorrow at the wedding reception," I said as I hung up the phone. "He sounds like a great guy and someone who is really in love."

The Raven

The next day we found ourselves in the reception line. When Mimi came to us, she stopped, stared, did a literal double take and then started crying. It was a priceless moment. We had a great time meeting her family members, both old and new, as well as her friends. And, as you've probably figured out, Edward was there since his father was the wedding photographer, and the disc jockey from the corporate show was in charge of the tunes. See, there are no more than two degrees of separation in Alaska.

While you might call the Mimi wedding an extraordinary coincidence, it's not the story I set out to tell in this chapter. However, it does show how we are all connected. The story I want to tell takes place in Alaska, but not in Anchorage, and happened a few years after Mimi's wedding. I was doing a quick college tour with return visits to the University of Alaska campuses at Anchorage and Fairbanks. The shows were back-to-back as they had been in the past, one of those quick and cold trips. However, this time a new stop was added, the University of Alaska branch campus in Bethel.

When we booked the mini-tour, I asked my student activities contact in Anchorage how long it would take to drive to Bethel.

"Oh, you can't drive there, you have to fly," the university official responded.

I enjoy driving even over long distances so I pushed on, "What if I really wanted to drive it?"

"When I said you can't drive, you have to fly, I meant it. There are no roads to Bethel!"

The plane landed at 10:00 a.m. and it was still dark outside. Welcome to Bethel, Alaska, in early February. As I disembarked and walked into the terminal, I looked around for my contact person. It was just starting to brighten up a bit outside, and I began to notice the birds. What really stood out were the crows. They were *huge*, the size of cats!

Bethel is a small community inhabited primarily by Yup'ik Eskimos. It is built on the frozen tundra of western Alaska. The ground is permafrost; so the houses can't have foundations and they are all built on stilts. There are cars and roads in the town, but the cars are brought in by boat or airplane. Bush pilots fly supplies and people from town to town over the tundra. A group of native Alaskans met me and took me on a quick tour of town. While they all spoke English, their first language was Yup'ik, a guttural speech pattern that I couldn't begin to understand, and they would talk to each other in Yup'ik as well as English. Most homes had a fish house where they smoked fish. We stopped inside one as part of the tour, and one of my guides pulled a piece of fish from where it hung and took a bite out of it. She offered

45

it to me and I took a nibble. Actually, it was pretty good. I knew I was still technically in the United States, but I have to say that Bethel seemed as foreign to me as any place I had ever been, and no matter where we went, there were crows.

Unfortunately, like many of the unique and extraordinary places I visit, I had very little time to spend in Bethel, less than twenty-four hours. After a tour of the town, I did a mini-show in the student center to help promote the major event that evening. It must have worked, because the show that night in the school's gymnasium was packed. I spent an hour or two after the show talking with various audience members. They didn't seem to want to leave the gym and had all sorts of questions about what I did and how I did it.

Early the next morning, I boarded my Alaska Airlines flight back to Anchorage to catch a connecting flight to Salt Lake City where I would pick up the rest of my western college tour after this detour to Alaska.

I squeezed into the small commuter plane's seat and was hoping that the seat next to me would remain unoccupied. However, that was not to be. I saw an elderly woman shuffling down the aisle, a backpack slung over her shoulder. She smiled as she squeezed in next to me.

"Good morning. Where are you headed?" she greeted me.

"Anchorage and then on to Salt Lake City," I replied as I stared out the plane's window looking at the stars that still shone brightly in the Alaskan morning sky.

"The sky is beautiful, yes?" my seat companion asked.

"Oh, very much so, the stars are so bright that I can't get over the fact that it's morning," I replied.

"Perhaps they are not stars in the sky but rather openings where our loved ones shine down to let us know they are happy," the old woman said.

"What a beautiful thought."

"Were you in Bethel long?"

"Oh, about twenty hours."

"My, that is a short trip. I hope you enjoyed yourself."

"Oh, I did. I usually do and if I don't, I don't have to worry because I'll be moving on to a new location soon."

"What is your best memory of Bethel?"

I wanted to say the show because it truly was a unique situation. The majority of the audience was Yup'ik and I had the feeling that they rarely had a chance to see live entertainment and probably never had seen a show like mine before. I also had had some interesting questions after the show connecting my work with that of the native shamans. While it was all quite memorable and very deep on some levels, the following words came out of my mouth instead, "The crows."

"The crows?" she repeated.

"Yes, those big, black crows, they're everywhere. They seemed to follow me," I explained.

"Oh, you mean the trickster," she said.

"Trickster?" I asked.

"Raven is the greatest trickster of all. Raven is a shapeshifter and a creator."

"What do you mean shapeshifter?"

"According to legend, Raven can change into any animal, person or thing. This is one of the reasons he is such a great trickster!"

"That's some powerful magic," I commented.

"Raven is filled with magic. He was born to a princess in the Land of the Supernatural Beings. But because of his pranks, he angered a great chief who sent floods to destroy him. In order to escape death by drowning, Raven created the earth," she explained.

"Raven has great power," I said, as I thought this story would be great if we were seated around a campfire; but it sounded a bit weird at 30,000 feet up in an airplane. Her voice grabbed me and brought me back into the story.

"Powerful yes, but not so smart. When Raven created the earth, he forgot to include light; so he lived in a world of darkness. However, there was a remedy for this situation. He simply had to steal the sun from The Sky Chief. The Sky Chief kept the sun in a locked box in his house. His house was an impenetrable fortress, but that didn't stop Raven from trying.

"He flew to the Sky World, but despite his powers he could not gain access to the house much less the box containing the sun. So, he hatched an elaborate plot.

"The Sky Chief had a daughter. Raven changed into a hemlock needle—shapeshifting can be very handy at times—and put himself in her drinking water. She drank Raven and became pregnant, giving birth to a boy, the grandson of The Sky Chief, who in reality was Raven. Do you follow the tale?"

"I think so." I responded trying to keep all the "facts" straight.

"The Sky Chief dearly loved his grandson and, like most grandfathers, only wanted to make his grandson happy. Raven, in the form of the grandson, pleaded to play with one of the boxes that hung from the ceiling

47

of the Sky Chief's house. The Sky Chief let him have one of the boxes, but it wasn't what Raven was looking for. It wasn't the sun. It was the stars. The stars did not provide enough light for Raven's purposes; so he played with them for a time and then released the stars through the smoke hole of the Sky Chief's house and into the sky where they remain today.

"Raven pleaded for another box. This time his grandfather gave him the box containing the moon. Raven was frustrated and he flung the moon through the smoke hole and into the sky.

"Only one box remained. It must contain the sun. Raven pleaded again and again with his grandfather. The Sky Chief gave Raven the last box. The instant Raven took the box he changed back into his original shape and flew off with the sun. As he flew through the smoke hole, he changed from his original color of white to the black color that we know Raven to be today.

"When Raven arrived back on earth, he took the shape of a man and began to head north. He came to a river that he could not cross on his own. There were others on the opposite side of the river and Raven tried to get them to help him cross. They would not help him. He told them he had a box that would light up their dark world; yet they still refused to help. Raven opened the box then and there releasing light into the world.

"Upon releasing the bright blinding light the people of earth became frightened. Those that were dressed in the skins of animals plunged into the forests and they became the animals of the forests today. Those dressed in the hides of sea creatures dove into the sea to become sea creatures. Those dressed in bird feathers took flight and became birds. Thus, Raven's antics created The Forest People, The Sea People and The People of the Sky. These people still exist and take their natural forms when no one is watching," she said with a wink.

"So that's what you meant when you said Raven was a creator," I said.

"Yes, but you see, he created out of his own selfish ways. That is how the trickster is. He changed the world, though."

"What happened to Raven?"

"Oh Raven is still around, there are many stories."

"I'd like to hear another."

"I would like to tell you another, but it appears we are beginning to land, and I don't think we will have time for one more," she said.

I don't usually make conversation on an airplane, especially early in the morning, but the old woman had me captivated, and I wanted to know a little more about her. "Are you Yup'ik?" I asked.

"No, I am of the Tlingit tribe."

"Are you from Alaska?"

"But of course, native Alaskan. My tribe has occupied Southeast Alaska since time immemorial. There are many peoples who make up Alaska: Yup'iks, Ingalik, Ahtena, Haida, Tlingit. We are all native Alaskans, and we are all different. And we were all here a long time before the white man came," she said with pride.

"Were you visiting family in Bethel?" I asked.

"No, I am working my route. I am an artist. I create dolls and travel about Alaska selling my creations," she answered as she reached under her seat and pulled a fur covered figure from her backpack. It was an Eskimo doll with a carved face. She handed it to me and I petted the fur and traced my fingers over the details of the face.

"So you have a bit of Raven in you. You are a creator too," I said.

"Well, yes. And this doll is one of my better creations. It has the fur of a wolf, a mink and a beaver. It is a caribou face. The face is carved from the horn of a caribou. Would you like it?" she asked.

"Oh yes, it's beautiful."

"How about fifty dollars?"

At this point I thought I might actually be sitting next to Raven, he is a shapeshifter after all, and the old woman had just shown me that she was both a creator and a trickster!

"Sure," I said as I got my wallet out and handed over a fifty-dollar bill.

Her timing was perfect. Not long after she closed the sale we began our descent into Anchorage. The Tlingit artisan and I parted ways at the Anchorage airport.

To this day, "Caribou Face" has a place of honor in my library, sitting between a mask created by the artist Robert Shields and a crystal ball once owned by my late, great-uncle and mentor, Alain "Doc" DeLyle. Every time I look at it I smile and think of Raven, the trickster.

CHAPTER FIVE

.

Hawaii Five-O

Hawaii, the 50th state of the union and the 50th state I performed in. I had played Alaska and the rest of the 49, been to Mexico, toured Canada, the Caribbean and even the U.K. but didn't make it to Hawaii until the late '90s. It's not that I didn't have offers. It's just that it takes so long to get to "Paradise" that you typically must have two or three open days to fill just one engagement. From the East Coast, you can actually be in Europe in less time than it takes to get to Hawaii.

My first Hawaiian booking was on the island of Hawai'i (that's how the natives spell it) also known as "The Big Island." After hours of flight time, we were finally approaching Hawaii. I imagined tropical palm trees and lush green acreage all around. Imagine my surprise when I looked down and saw desolate, black and rocky sloped terrain. *This is paradise?* I thought to myself.

Yes, I found out, the Big Island is Paradise.

The Big Island may well be my favorite Hawaiian island because it offers such variety. It is bigger than all the other Hawaiian islands combined, and 11 of the world's 13 different climate zones can be found on the island, resulting in everything from lush rain forests to dry deserts and from black sand beaches to snow-capped mountaintops. The Big Island is home to

Mauna Kea, the world's tallest mountain (measured from the ocean floor) and Hawaii is still growing due to the active volcano, Kilauea.

This first Hawaiian trip was to be followed by another Aloha State booking about two months later. Charlotte was going to go with me on that one; so I was going to do a bit of reconnaissance work in order to plan our vacation. I was also fortunate enough to get another booking on Maui, during the time I would be on The Big Island. So, I went from zero Hawaiian bookings to three in just a two-month period.

I was appearing at the Kona Surf Resort, and in the lobby a video played continuously of divers interacting with giant manta rays. I asked the concierge about it, and she said she could easily arrange for me to go on a night dive.

"I'm not a certified diver. Could I snorkel?" I asked.

"I don't see why not. Let me call the dive operator and find out," she said.

I warmed up for my nighttime snorkel adventure with a little snorkeling at Kahaluu Beach just down from my hotel. This cove is known as sea turtle paradise. There were a dozen sea turtles (or *honu* as the Hawaiians call them) in the water munching on seaweed and sunning themselves on the warm lava rocks. I almost tripped over one while entering the water as his shell blended in so well with the color of the large lava rock he was resting on. I love watching the honus! I followed one out to sea, just the two of us swimming parallel to each other. When I finally pulled my head from the water in order to get my bearings, I saw that I had left the cove of Kahaluu Beach far behind and I was very far away from shore; so I bid farewell to the honu and swam back in. I'm certain the giant turtle was luring me out to sea to get even with me for disturbing his afternoon!

With my performances on both the Big Island and Maui out of the way, I headed down the road to begin my encounter with the giant manta rays of the Kona Coast. I boarded a small boat with six other people, all certified divers and we headed out to sea. The Kona Surf Resort had a series of underwater lights that attracted these monsters of the deep at night. The mantas feed off plankton and other miniscule organisms that are attracted to the glow of the lights. The presence of divers in the water (including a videographer) adds to the light source, which means there is even more plankton for the rays to feed on and more rays in the water. We were a fair distance from shore when we dropped anchor near the underwater lights.

"You can go ahead and get in," the divemaster said to me since I had no equipment to prepare, just my snorkel, mask and fins.

"OK," I said, looking around at the night sky and the black sea.

A short time later I was still in the boat and the divemaster turned and said to me, "Are you still here? Go on in. You've done this before haven't you?"

"Yeah, I snorkel all the time, just not at night, alone in the water with giant manta rays!"

He laughed, "You'll love it, jump in!"

I went over the side of the boat and started swimming around in the dark water. I immediately spotted the underwater lights; so I swam over to them. There were already four divers sitting on the bottom surrounding the lights. *Well, at least there are other people here,* I thought as I relaxed a little bit. Soon, the divers from my boat joined the others and there was a circle of ten divers on the bottom, and me, floating on top of the water. Eleven people, no mantas. Our divemaster/videographer joined us next. The light on his camera illuminated the scene even more.

Suddenly, off in the distance, you could see a ghostly, otherworldly figure floating toward the lights: a giant manta ray! It was so impressive just gliding effortlessly through the water, and it was huge. Its wingspan must have been 14 feet across. Soon there were more, a half dozen in total, all of them gliding and turning somersaults in a beautiful underwater ballet. Their wide, cavernous mouths were open as they feasted on their favorite food. The mantas soared over the divers below, and I envied them. While I had a good view, I wasn't as close as the others to these gentle monsters of the deep. The videographer must have read my mind because he swam up to me and the mantas followed his bright camera light. A manta would head right toward me (actually toward the area illuminated by the camera light). I could see right down its throat! It looked as if it would run right in to me but at the last moment it would veer off, missing me by inches. This was a night I would never forget.

A couple of months later, I found myself back on the Big Island for another performance and this time a bit of a vacation as well. Charlotte and I rented a convertible at the Kona airport and headed to the Hapuna Beach Prince Hotel. I'm all business until after the performance is over; so I was focused on the show for my first twenty-six hours back in Hawaii. However, the morning after the show, Charlotte and I were in our convertible driving around the Big Island and experiencing the amazing change in topography. We left the lava desert of the Kohala Coast and headed into the mountains. We went from beaches, palm trees and black lava slopes, to pine forests in no time. We drove by the Parker Ranch, one of the country's largest cattle ranches where the paniolos, or Hawaiian cowboys, have been working the land on the 135,000-acre ranch since 1832. We drove out of the mountains and into a lush, tropical rain forest and then found ourselves in rainy Hilo before reaching our final destination, Volcanoes National Park.

We spent the night at Chateau Kilauea, a very unique and casually elegant boutique hotel one mile from the National Park. The next day we explored Kilauea. Kilauea is the home of Pele, the volcano goddess, and ancient Hawaiians visited the crater to offer gifts to the goddess. In 1790, a group of Hawaiians bearing gifts was caught in an eruption, and many were killed. Some escaped, and you can still see their footprints in the lava to this day. We hiked through the Thurston lava tube and the rain forest, descending about 400 feet to the crater floor. We hiked across the crater. The smell of sulfur was in the air as we passed steam vents and cinder cones, and we came upon the occasional flower or plant growing in this harsh environment. Then, we returned to the crater's rim.

Leaving Volcanoes National Park behind, we returned to the Kohala Coast and checked-in to the Hilton Waikoloa Village which would be "home base" for the rest of our vacation. This is a big property of 62 oceanfront acres and 1,240 guest rooms. There are boats traveling a canal system to take you from your room to the various restaurants and pools that are located throughout the property. During our stay, I was fortunate enough to get to swim with the dolphins as part of an organized interactive program the resort offers on property. Swimming with dolphins, manta rays and giant sea turtles, no wonder I like the Big Island so much!

We played the role of Hawaiian tourists to the hilt over the next few days including spending a day in the luxurious spa at the resort and attending the Island Breeze Luau under the stars on the historic grounds of King Kamehameha's former estate. We also took a horseback ride into the beautiful Waipio Valley. The steep, mile long road into the valley drops 1,000 feet. Waterfalls surround the valley, including the breathtaking 1,400 foot Hi'ilawe Falls, the highest waterfall in Hawaii. The valley is sparsely populated, mostly with farmers working their taro fields, and there is no running water, electricity or phone service. But there is beauty everywhere; in the form of exotic flowers, ferns and fruit trees, their branches weighed down heavily with over ripened fruit. There is also a black sand beach, and wild horses roam the basin. It is a special place, to be sure. We revisited Kilauea, this time aboard a Blue Hawaiian helicopter. The chopper took us over the most active areas of Kilauea where we were able to witness lava flows from above. From the volcano, we headed back to the valleys of the Kohala

Mountains and the Hamakua Coast, our eyes bugging out of our heads as we tried to take in all the beauty of the towering sea cliffs, beautiful waterfalls and lush rainforests we were flying over. The helicopter would drop into a valley and we would find ourselves face-to-face with a waterfall. The pilot would then climb straight up, the water rushing down in the opposite direction right in front of us. We ended our Hawaiian Big Island vacation with a champagne toast at Buddha Point on the Hilton's property as we watched an extraordinary Hawaiian sunset.

I've been back to the Big Island many times since, and there is always something new to discover. At the Hilton, I met a special individual, Sammy Kaoo. Sammy works at the spa but also created an online business called Big Island Sam's. He specializes in sending Hawaiian themed gift baskets around the world.

During one visit to the Big Island, Sammy provided Charlotte and me with a magical moment I will never forget. We hiked into the mountains past an abandoned sugar cane plantation as we followed the big Hawaiian with the easy smile and laid back attitude. After an hour of uphill hiking, we were on a small trail looking down upon the clouds, or at least that's how it seemed. What we were actually looking at was a fog-filled valley. Sammy asked us to just look at the fog and wait a moment. An ocean breeze blew through, and the fog vanished leaving us with a stunning view of a lush green valley complete with waterfalls. We also noticed we were right on the edge of the trail, a sheer 1,000 foot drop-off just past our toes! After a bit of time, the fog returned and the valley disappeared. It was more magical than any magician's trick.

The Hawaiian Island chain is actually hundreds of islands spread over 1,500 miles. The eight main islands are: Niihau, Kauai, Oahu, Molokai, Lanai, Kahoolawe, Maui, and Hawaii, the Big Island.

In addition to the Big Island, I've also spent time on Kauai, the Garden Island. It looks like what I used to think of when I heard "Hawaii," it's very lush, very green and not very populated. Chickens still run across the road and you can't help but slow down and relax when you're on this island. I'd like to spend more time there.

Oahu is the home of Honolulu, Pearl Harbor, Diamond Head and 70% of Hawaii's population. I've spent time at the airport, but I've not really experienced the island. I have become fairly familiar with a small hotel within the airport when my best laid travel plans of getting to Paradise are waylaid by the "travel gods."

Hawaii Five-O

I've probably spent more time on Maui than any other island. It's more of a tourist spot than the Big Island and Kauai, but it is a wonderful place to visit. The Four Seasons has some of the best service I've ever experienced. Charlotte and I would be sunning by the pool, and every forty-five minutes or so a pool attendant would stop by and ask, "Spritz Mr. and Mrs. Karges?" "Cold towel Mr. and Mrs. Karges?" "Frozen pineapple Mr. and Mrs. Karges?" "Popsicle Mr. and Mrs. Karges?"

Getting to Paradise is not always easy. In June of 2001, I was appearing at the Boca Raton Resort and Club in South Florida for the parent company of the travel agency I work with locally. This was an international meeting, and I was presenting the opening general session. It was a special day as Sally and Bill, the owners of Uniglobe Ohio Valley Travel, *my* agency, plus *my* travel agent, Judy, were in the audience. I spoke to the fact that I considered the travel agency and Judy a part of my team, and I really meant it. I have monthly in person meetings with Judy over coffee in her office as we lay out the following month's tour schedule, and we have been doing this for over twenty years. The Ohio Valley Travel team has saved me many times. In fact, they saved me on this very day!

The plan was to fly from South Florida to the Big Island for another presentation the following morning. As I was leaving the stage and meeting my driver in the foyer of the convention center, I heard a window-rattling "BOOM!" One of those famous South Florida thunderstorms was just beginning. The West Palm Beach airport was a mess with delayed and canceled flights. I was going to fly from West Palm, to L.A., to Honolulu and then finally, Kona. It was going to be a long day even if everything worked perfectly. My flight to L.A. was delayed by hours; so I called Jeanne at Ohio Valley Travel (since Judy was away from her desk in Boca Raton), and she gave me some options. If I could catch a commuter flight to Orlando which was at least showing a departure time, I could connect to an American flight to Dallas that would get me to Hawaii, or if I missed that one, a United flight from Orlando to L.A. that would allow me to catch up with my original Delta flight to Honolulu. Jeanne had me booked on both the American and the United flights. My little commuter flight was delayed further, and when we touched down in Orlando, I called Jeanne from the tarmac.

"American's gone. You're protected on United; so hurry to that gate, and I'll see that Delta doesn't give away your L.A. to Honolulu portion," Jeanne informed me.

I made it to L.A. but the Honolulu flight was delayed; so I missed my connection from Honolulu to Kona. It was one of the nights I spent in the tiny

Honolulu airport hotel-sleeping-showering room. Jeanne had me on the first flight to Kona from Honolulu the next morning. It would get me there just in time to travel to the Mauna Kea Resort for my after-breakfast presentation.

I phoned my contact's office and cell numbers, but the voice mailboxes were full. People, even meeting planners, tend to really relax after a few days in Hawaii. I left a message for him through the Mauna Kea's hotel operator and hoped that he got the word that I would be there in the morning.

When I landed on the Big Island, there was no one there to meet me and no taxis in sight. I walked over to the Hertz rental car counter (which was just opening for the day) and asked if they had anything I could rent.

"All we have is that little Mazda Miata convertible," he said.

"Cool car, but I don't know if I can fit all my luggage in it," I responded.

The Hertz representative helped me pack it all in, and I headed up the Kohala Coast to the Mauna Kea Resort, strolling in just as breakfast was starting. The presentation was a major success, and I was able to secure another booking with the company before leaving Hawaii.

After a nap on the beach, I "relaxed" by taking the Miata through the mountains at high speed and getting a speeding ticket before the day was over. Lesson learned.

Had this travel scenario unfolded three months later, I probably wouldn't have made it to Hawaii. This happened in the days just before 9/11 when you could still travel like a cowboy, carry on all your needed bags, switch flights on a whim and not be required to fly with your luggage. Travel has certainly changed.

In February of 2006, I had a booking at the Grand Wailea Resort on Maui. I then had to travel to Salt Lake City for a show, Boston for another, and then, guess what? Return to Maui! As I said, it takes a long time to get to Hawaii, and two trips to the Aloha State in a five day period was a bit intimidating; so Charlotte decided to go with me on the second trip, and we planned an extended stay.

As it turned out, we would be leaving Maui and going to Boston to attend a college entertainment trade show for a week. I booked Charlotte's round trip flight, Pittsburgh – Boston – Pittsburgh, on US Airways. She would meet me in Boston, attend that show, and together we would fly round trip on Delta, Boston – Maui – Boston, a perfect plan! Beware the "travel gods!"

The second Maui booking was at the Hyatt Regency. While I was on the island, I decided to drop off some of my props and equipment at the Hyatt before my night flight to Salt Lake City. These were items I would need for my presentation when I returned but didn't need for the Salt Lake City and Boston engagements. On the roadway from Wailea to the Hyatt in Kaanapali a brush fire had broken out, and traffic was traveling at a snail's pace as smoke choked the road. I was beginning to worry that I wouldn't make it to the Hyatt and then to the airport in time for my flight. I finally made it through the jammed traffic and reached the Hyatt where I made arrangements to store my equipment for a few days. I didn't want to drive back through the brush fire; so I consulted my rental car map. I noticed a road that wrapped around the northwest of the island and would lead me right back to the airport; so I made the decision to reroute on route 340.

It was dusk when I left the Hyatt and headed toward the airport. After leaving the resorts of Kaanapali and Kapalua behind, I found myself on route 340, a narrow, serpentine road. What a spectacular seacoast highway with jaw-dropping views! At one point, I screeched to a halt in front of a huge boulder that had fallen across my lane of traffic on a hairpin turn. It was nerve wracking negotiating the turn and hoping I wouldn't meet a Maui version of my Big Island self on a speedy joyride in a Miata convertible! As it began to get dark, I realized that the rental car company sent me out with a near empty gas tank. While most rental car companies send you on your way with a full tank and you are required to return the car with a full tank, a few will just mark the level of gas in the vehicle and you have to return it with the same amount of gas that was in it when you started the rental. I was running out of gas! There were no gas stations anywhere in sight. In fact there was not much of anything in sight, no people, no cars just breathtaking scenery, and now that it was dark, I couldn't enjoy that. My low fuel light was on, and my tank was showing empty. Finally, I made it around the northwest coast and found a gas station, making it to the airport in time for my flight.

The Salt Lake City engagement went off without a hitch and then it was on to Boston. As I arrived in Boston, news of the season's biggest snowstorm (a Nor'easter dumping two feet of snow up and down the East Coast and closing all airports in its path) reached me, courtesy of Charlotte, who was stuck in Pittsburgh. They canceled her Boston flight and rerouted her to Philadelphia and then to Boston. The storm was rapidly making its way up the coast but had yet to reach Boston. In fact, it was in Philadelphia. In fairness to the US Airways people, they thought Charlotte's destination was Boston, not realizing she was headed to Hawaii. We talked them into sending her to Atlanta where she spent the night. We were hoping I would make it in from Boston the following day, and we could travel to Maui together. The only problem was, all our vacation luggage was checked to Boston on US Airways and we wanted it on Delta to Hawaii!

The storm just reached Boston as I was performing. By the time my show was over, Boston's Logan International Airport was closed. I called my trusty travel agents and they re-scheduled me on a flight out of nearby Manchester, New Hampshire, to Atlanta where I would meet up with Charlotte. I was the only one on the road that morning, driving in the aftermath of the blizzard. Manchester is more inland than Boston and wasn't hit as heavily by the storm. The Delta flight was the first (and possibly only) flight out that morning, but I made it and Charlotte and I reunited in Atlanta. Our vacation bags arrived twenty-four hours later which I didn't think was too bad considering they had to be moved from one airline to another and changed from Boston to Maui all in the middle of a monster snowstorm!

After my presentation, Charlotte and I had a grand time for four days, shopping and dining in Lahaina, enjoying the spa at the Hyatt and just hanging out by the pool and walking the beach. February is the very best time to be in Hawaii. The whales were "in town," and I went on a snorkel cruise where we spotted whale flukes and saw the massive mammals breaching and slapping their tales on the surface of the water. Snorkeling underwater, I could hear the whales' song as they communicated back and forth.

Back at the Hyatt, I was studying a mixed media art piece in a gallery. I've always been attracted to Hawaiian petroglyphs and this modern piece was a representation of those figures along with a few scattered shells. It was the work of Michael Stark who was inspired by this ancient rock art to create newer pieces. You can find petroglyphs carved on boulders, in lava fields and on cliffs throughout Hawaii. The primitive looking figures depict people, animals and mysterious symbols.

"You know, nowhere in Polynesia are petroglyphs more common than in Hawaii," a voice behind me said as I turned to face a smiling, pleasant faced man.

"These rock carvings were created by ancient artists to record history. They cover one-thousand-two-hundred years of history on these islands and they are most commonly found on the Big Island. I also think they were a weapon of survival in a world that was hard to understand. The predominate theme of the rock art was procreation and power over man and nature," he continued as he studied the artwork before us.

"The art's demise coincided with the arrival of missionaries around 1860. Ironically, some of the last petroglyphs depict churches and European sailing ships," he concluded.

"Now this piece," he said as he touched the wooden frame, "is done on coconut palm fabric and is called Ho'omaikai Nui."

"I'm sorry, but what does that mean?" I asked.

"It's the marriage blessing. The two people there are man and wife," he said as he pointed to a couple (one complete with stylized breasts) joined together.

"Below the couple is the Kahuna Nui or high priest," he said as he pointed to another figure with a turtle-like body holding a staff.

The man continued, "To the right of the high priest are the mirrored human figures. The top one is the ancestral guardian spirit looking over the living descendant below him. Above them is the shark tooth motif, offering protection. To the far left, is the eyes symbol which means wisdom.

"There are the aumakua or animal symbols too. They are guardian spirits — you recognize the bird and the honu?"

I nodded my head "yes" as I studied the piece.

"That spiral represents the spiral of life. On either side of it are the symbols of Lono, god of peace and of plenty. Upper left and right ...."

"Sun and moon?" I offered.

"Exactly," he said with a smile.

"How do you know so much about this?" I asked.

"I'm Michael Stark, the artist."

Michael is a fascinating person, and we talked for an hour before I purchased the piece that now hangs in my office as an artful and constant reminder of all my trips to Hawaii. Our trip coincided with Valentine's Day, and Charlotte felt this was a great Valentine's Day gift for me while she found one of her own in Lahaina — a golden south sea pearl necklace.

We didn't want to leave Hawaii, but Boston beckoned. We capped off our trip with a drive on route 340 back to the airport, this time with a full tank of gas!

As I've said, I've been to Hawaii many times, and there is always something new to discover. One of my most extraordinary discoveries was atop the Maui volcano, Haleakala, courtesy of "The Wise Old Man."

Most tourists will take a bus around 4:00 a.m. to the top of the Haleakala volcano and ride their bicycles down the mountain to witness a beautiful sunrise. That sounded cool to me, but I couldn't resist the offer when a very nice and interesting person I started talking with after one of my shows offered to "hook me up" with a personal tour of the volcano with a native Hawaiian known as "The Wise Old Man" (we'll call him Wom, short for Wise Old Man). It sounded like something right up my alley.

Fortunately, I didn't have to wake up in the middle of the night to meet with Wom. He was rumored to prefer giving his special tours a little after lunchtime. I arrived at our pre-determined meeting spot, and his appearance did not disappoint (nor surprise) me. I knew that he had the "Old" and "Man" parts of his name covered; I guess I would just have to wait and learn if he was truly "Wise." My companion for the next few hours stood about 5'5" tall, wore an authentic Hawaiian style shirt and shorts. I was a little concerned to see him wearing a pair of sandals considering the "hiking" I expected us to do all afternoon. He had a very long, pure white beard that flowed nearly to the middle of his chest. He also had long, white hair that was neatly pulled back into a ponytail. Wom's face looked nearly ninety years old. I could tell he had ventured miles upon miles on this mountain. He was probably in better physical shape than me. He had a friendly way about him right off the bat, and we shook hands as he told me the game plan. We would actually explore inside the crater as well as the surrounding park. The tour began with Wom wasting no time by freefalling into the history of this mountain with scientific and folklore explanations. He told me that the volcano is considered "active," but it has not erupted since 1790. Much to my delight, he seemed to have a passion for the ancient and mystical stories. Wom claimed that Haleakala was the home to the grandmother of the demigod Maui. She used to help him capture the sun and force it to move more slowly across the sky so the days would be longer. He also told me about the actual "birth" of the Hawaiian Islands. With seriousness in his eyes and a passion from his soul, he told me the story of Pele and how she created Hawai'i.

Pele followed a very bright star from the Northeast for days and finally caught up to it one morning. She could see and smell the smoke from a very large mountain in the distance and knew this would be her new home. She called her new discovery Hawai'i. Pele was very pleased with her new home, but there was another inhabitant named "The Forest Eater" who did not like her living there. They both wanted Hawai'i for their own and began to throw fireballs at each other. "The Forest Eater," in defeat, moved under the earth and he is the sole reason many of Hawai'i's volcanoes have erupted and continue to erupt.

Pele also had an egg that her mother had given her. This egg hatched one day, and her sister Hi'Aika was born. One night Pele had a dream of a man named Lohi'au. She immediately fell in love with him and sent her sister out to find him and bring him back to her. Pele was concerned that if her sister found Lohi'au that she might fall in love with him and not return. So,

Pele gave Hi'Aika forty days to find and bring back her man, or she would turn her sister's best friend into stone. In the meantime, when Hi'Aika finally found Lohi'au, he was dead. She used her magical powers along with herbs and spices to bring him back to life.

Unfortunately, when Pele's sister returned with her dream man, Hi'Aika discovered that since it had taken her longer than forty days to come back home, Pele had turned her best friend into stone. Hi'Aika was furious at Pele and acted like she was in love with Lohi'au to get back at her. Pele engulfed Lohi'au with flames and lava and he died.

Both sisters were angry, but later became very remorseful that they had lost two companions for no real reason. This led to Pele's decision to bring Lohi'au back to life and let him choose (she was confident it would be her, of course) between the two sisters. Lohi'au selected Hi'Aika instead of Pele. They moved away from Pele, and in loneliness and despair, Pele retreated back to her home in Kilauea on the island of Hawai'i where she still rules as the "Fire Goddess of Volcanoes."

"Do you smell that sulfur in the air, my friend?" Wom asked me.

"Yeah, I guess so, a little bit," I answered.

He looked me straight in the eyes and said with total conviction: "Well that is Pele reminding us that she is still in her home."

"I thought Pele lived in Kilauea?" I asked.

"Pele is the Goddess of all volcanoes, she is everywhere," Wom explained with a smile.

Wow. Pretty interesting. I was enjoying the tour of the crater and leaned down to pick up a small lava rock. "No!" screamed Wom. "That will upset Pele and the Menehunes, too," he said.

"The Mini whats?" I asked.

"Pele and the Menehunes," he repeated.

Sounds like a new rock band.

"Pele gets very angry and will curse those who disturb the building blocks of her home. Many have suffered great despair if they chose to remove a precious lava rock from where she lives," he explained.

"I wasn't going to take it home with me," I told him. He ignored me and started to explain that in combination with Pele's wrath and these "Mini Wheat things" that countless people have experienced the worst repercussions and horrible luck because they took a rock from a volcano.

The Menehunes. Well, when Wom settled down a little (and I gently placed the lava rock back to its original spot) he continued walking (at a brisk pace, mind you!) and told me about these tiny mythical creatures that also protect beautiful Hawai'i.

"Even before Pele arrived, the Menehunes occupied the islands of Hawai'i. Every single plant and tree was planted by the Menehunes," he explained

"Who are the Menehunes and where do they live?" I asked.

"They are tiny, magical creatures that cannot be seen," he said with a look of total seriousness plastered across his face.

Yeah, right. And they're going to gang up on me for taking a lava rock.

"You do not believe, my son?" Wom questioned me.

"Tell me more about this magical race," I responded.

"The Menehunes are very kind. They always want to help. When my ancestors came to Hawai'i from Tahiti, the Menehunes actually took care of and fed my great-grandfather when he was very young. They are very shy and do many of their good deeds at night. Many of the Menehunes will fly on the backs of seagulls and search the islands to see if they can help in any way," he said.

"How can they help out if they are invisible and so tiny?" I played along.

"They are not invisible. They just choose not to be seen because they are very shy. They may be tiny, but there are so many and they work together so well that they can assist anyone because of the vast number of these creatures. They all wear tiny horns around their necks and they will use them to call the seagulls and other Menehunes when they see trouble.

"You will know they are around sometimes if you see the feathers on the back of a seagull's neck ruffled. The only way you can see a Menehune is if they decide to give you a special potion, *or,* if you have some of their blood in you. Although most people cannot see them, there are many who claim to hear the humming of their voices at times," he said. "I have," he added.

"Really?" I asked interestedly.

"Yes. I remember when my two older brothers and I were in a small outrigger canoe near Molokini and ventured out too far in the sea. We should have been more careful, but we were only ten, twelve and thirteen years old at that time. Before we knew it, we could barely see land and a storm was forming. My oldest brother took control and told us to remain calm and listen to him, that everything would be OK. We knew we could beat the storm and get back to Molokini to find shelter; but what we didn't count on were the sharks circling us and our canoe. I will say that in all my years I have never been more afraid in my entire life and will never forget that image as long as I live. We were doomed. My older brother remained positive, but only for us. Me and my other brother could see the fear in his eyes, too. The situation was very grim, and even if we could beat the storm, there were too many sharks to fight off; and the group was growing, too," he explained.

"Then, for no apparent reason, the sharks started falling out of their attack mode and started heading out to sea. They seemed almost agitated, like someone or something gave them a command to leave us alone and swim away. Not only did they head out to sea, but they did so in a single file line. One by one, we could see the dorsal fins do a direct turn away from the three of us. It was a miracle! But what I remembered after all this happened tied it all together. It made sense to me.

"When we were trying to outrun the storm to get back to Molokini, I thought about how lucky we were, but I also remembered that there was something odd about the whole incident. I recalled that there were hundreds of seagulls flying above us when the sharks were circling us. Yes, my friend, I believe that our little friends, the Menehunes, saved our lives. The legend says that these mystical creatures patrol the islands on the seagulls and protect us—the natives, especially—from shark attacks. If they see trouble, they blow the little horns hanging from their necks and the Menehunes will all arrive on their tiny canoes to help. The folklore says that they use their oars to beat the sharks and scare them away. The powers of these magical Menehunes are remarkable. They are all dedicated to doing 'good deeds' for the land that they love.

"Back to the seagulls," Wom continued. "There were so many of them and I do recall (even with all of the commotion with the sharks and such), that there were splashes all around us like it was raining, but I felt nothing on my bare shoulders. Heavy raindrops falling around us making ripples, but no precipitation whatsoever. Once again, I did not really think much about this at the time. I was more concerned about being eaten by sharks! But I remembered this after we escaped and am positive that those were the Menehunes dropping from their seagulls with their canoes to help us.

"The most convincing part is that—and I said this earlier—I heard them. I actually heard a peaceful humming while staring death in the face at only ten years old. Not a church hymn, the sound was like something you would almost expect these mystical beings to make from a Walt Disney movie or something. It was definitely not spooky or weird. It had a peaceful and calming effect on all of us brothers. Yes, we all heard it, and we all believe that the Menehunes rescued us. Our parents agreed and believed us too," he concluded.

"Wow, what an amazing story. Have you had other encounters since you were a little boy?" I asked Wom.

"No, but many of my friends and relatives have had encounters—not as intense as me and my two brothers but little things like all of the weeds were pulled from the garden or their rooms were cleaned and beds were made. I know of one friend who has *seen* a Menehune. He claims that he was in his woodshop one day and saw a little creature with a tiny broom sweeping up sawdust for him. I believe him. He is the nicest and most sincere person I know. Maybe he has a little Menehune blood in him as well.

"Do not forget what I said to you about the lava rock," he reminded me. "Although Menehunes take pride in helping all of us here on the islands and have good intentions in their hearts, they will take revenge on anyone who will desecrate their home. They love Hawai'i and just want others to respect their sanctuary.

"I recall that someone once picked a bunch of Silverswords, a rare plant indigenous to Haleakala. These flowers are sacred to some on the islands. Not only did Pele take her revenge on this person, but the Menehunes taught this man a lesson as well. He was a tourist and meant no harm, but the streak of bad luck that he experienced over the week he was on vacation was horrible. I hope he enjoyed the flower arrangement of Silverswords, because the rest of the week was not pleasant. He lost his wallet; wrecked his rental car but was not injured; got food poisoning after eating mahi-mahi; accidentally erased all of the photos he took on his digital camera; and lost his swimming trunks as he was exiting from the water in front of all the sunbathers at the resort where he was staying. Not a coincidence. Respect the legends, my friend," he advised.

When our tour was finished, I thanked Wom for his insightful stories and knowledge about the volcano as well as Hawaiian folklore. "I truly enjoyed our time together. You are a very kind, curious and *wise* person," I said to him. As I was driving back to my hotel, the thoughts of Pele, Hi'Aika, Lohi'au and the Menehunes lingered in my mind. What extraordinary tales! Could they really be true? Was I really given a "house tour" at one of Pele's residences today, or was it just a volcano crater? Was I the only one in the car or were a few Menehunes hitching a free ride back to town? I had a funny vision of tiny, mystical and magical creatures sitting in the passenger seat next to me.

When I returned home, I shared my experience with Charlotte and told her what a fascinating tour I had had with "The Wise Old Man." After listening to me rehash the stories, she asked me one question: "Why didn't you bring a few Menehunes home with you to help clean up around the house?" Not a bad idea.

Just a few weeks after returning from Hawaii, I read something fascinating in a sports magazine concerning a coach in the National Football League. Supposedly, this man was hiking in Hawaii near Diamond Head, and he picked up a small lava rock (no kidding) and brought it back home with him. A few years after that, he was watching a PBS documentary about Hawaiian traditions and legends and learned that these rocks are considered sacred and those who remove them may experience a long period of bad luck. He still blames himself for taking that rock. Indeed, the worst luck came his way while coaching the Buffalo Bills during the 1990s. In Super Bowl XXV, a placekicker named Scott Norwood missed a 47-yard field goal to win the game as the final seconds ticked away. The Bills were defeated 20-19. These same Buffalo Bills also lost four times in as many trips to the "Big Game" from 1991 to 1994. That's right. They went to the Super Bowl *four years in a row* and never won! The coach blamed himself for a very long time, and the memories of these losses haunted him. There was only one thing to do, return the lava rock! He did just that after Super Bowl XXV, but obviously the dark cloud did not disappear. Years later, while the coach was in Hawaii for the Pro Bowl, he confessed his wrong doings to a Hawaiian friend and former NFL player. This player was familiar with the legend and sacredness of the lava rock; so he took the coach to see the authority on the matter, his grandmother! She listened to the coach's story and simply answered: "It will pass. It will pass." He is still waiting for that elusive Super Bowl victory. Don't mess with lava rocks, and don't anger Pele or Menehunes!

I will never forget the stories told to me by "The Wise Old Man" and the enjoyment I received from listening to his tales of Hawaiian legends. I have been very fortunate to run into interesting, strange, peculiar, weird and even crazy people during my time on the road. Coincidence? I think not.

CHAPTER SIX

Beneath Arabian Sands

"So, how would you like to go to Saudi Arabia?" my manager asked over the phone.

"Saudi Arabia? Gee, I don't know. What's in Saudi Arabia?" I replied.

"The world's largest oil company and you if you say yes to their offer."

It was a very nice offer, and in November of 1995, I found myself headed to the Kingdom of Saudi Arabia to work for Saudi Aramco.

Saudi Aramco is indeed the world's largest oil company with the world's largest proven crude oil reserves. It is also considered to be the world's most profitable company. Commonly known as Aramco (which was an acronym for Arabian American Oil Company), the state-owned national oil company changed its name to Saudi Aramco in 1988.

In 1933, Standard Oil of California began exploring Saudi Arabia for oil under an agreement with the Saudi Arabian government. It took years, but in 1938 oil was discovered. Originally known as the California-Arabian Standard Oil Company the name was changed to Aramco in 1944.

Twelve years after the initial discovery of oil, in 1950, King Abdul Aziz Ibn Saud threatened to nationalize Saudi Arabia's oil industry. The threat resulted in Aramco agreeing to share profits with the government in an even 50/50 split.

In 1973, the Saudi Arabian government acquired a 25% share of Aramco. By 1974, the government owned 60% of the company. It had full control of Aramco by 1980; thus, the name change in 1988 to Saudi Aramco to reflect that this was indeed a Saudi Arabian owned enterprise.

While the Saudis owned the company, there were still many Americans working in Saudi Arabia along with expats from dozens of countries from around the world. This was the audience I was being sent to entertain. There were five Saudi Aramco communities in the Eastern Province of the country. These were gated, guarded communities that resembled suburban U.S. housing developments from the 1960s except for the gates and the guards.

In 1995, you couldn't choose to visit Saudi Arabia. You had to be invited, and it took some time and some paperwork. I remember they asked my manager if he wanted to travel with me. He declined. When I finally got to Saudi Arabia, I mentioned that my wife had thought about coming in place of my manager. "Oh no," I was told by a Saudi Aramco employee, "your wife would not be invited. Your manager, yes, he's a man. Your wife, no, she's a woman!"

I remember signing one particular document as I was acquiring my business visa that stated that I understood drugs were illegal in Saudi Arabia and if I was caught carrying drugs, it was a crime punishable by death. I remember death being in bold, capital letters and accompanied by a skull and crossbones. I was also told to apply for a month long visa even though I would be in the country for less than ten days.

Saudi Arabia has some pretty strict laws. The Koran is the constitution of the country and Saudi Arabia is governed under Islamic law. Criminal cases are tried in Sharia courts, and all foreigners in the country are tried in these religious courts. The Saudi legal system believes in capital and corporal punishment. Execution, as well as amputation of hands or feet, are punishments for things like murder, robbery, rape, drug possession, homosexual activity and adultery. The courts can also order punishments like flogging for less serious crimes such as public intoxication. During my visit, I was asked if I wanted to visit "Chop Chop Square" where the amputations and beheadings are carried out in public one day a week. I declined. However, I was constantly reminded by residents during my stay in the kingdom that there is very little crime in Saudi Arabia as the extreme punishments act as a pretty powerful deterrent.

Saudi Arabia is the largest country on the Arabian Peninsula, and is literally surrounded by the smaller countries of Jordan, Iraq, Kuwait, Qatar, Bahrain, the United Arab Emirates, Oman and Yemen. The kingdom is home to the two holiest places in Islam, the holy mosques at Mecca and Medina. The Prophet's Mosque in Medina is built on the site of a mosque the Prophet Muhammad built next to his house. The Prophet's Mosque contains Muhammad's tomb. The Holy Mosque in Mecca is the primary site of the Hajj pilgrimage. It is considered the holiest mosque in the world as it is built around the Kaaba, a black stone building allegedly built by the prophet Ibrahim (Abraham) and his son, Ismail, (Ishmael). It was built to be a house of worship on earth to resemble a house in heaven. The building contains Islamic holy relics including the mysterious Black Stone. The stone is believed to have been found by Abraham and Ishmael as they were gathering stones to build the Kaaba. Father and son were attracted to this unusual black stone and decided to make it part of the building. There are two lines of thought about the Black Stone in the Muslim belief system. One states that it is just a stone and is useful as a marker as the pilgrims make their way around the Kaaba. The other theory states that the stone itself has supernatural powers, and that it can cleanse worshippers of their sins by absorbing those sins. It is believed by some who subscribe to the supernatural theory that the stone was once a bright white and turned black over time due to the amount of sins it absorbed. When Muslims pray, they face Mecca, the Holy Mosque and the Kaaba. During the Hajj more than 800,000 Muslims can gather around the mosque and pray.

I wouldn't be visiting Mecca or Medina. I would be based in Dhahran, the location of Saudi Aramco's corporate headquarters. I flew through London on British Airways and directly to Dhahran. During the flight, they announced that we would be entering Saudi Arabian airspace in thirty minutes. That meant it was the last opportunity to order alcohol as no liquor would be served once we were in Saudi airspace. Upon landing in Dhahran, I entered the worst airport I've ever been in! Customs took forever as we followed a planeload of Pakistanis whom the customs officials seemed especially hard on. My bags sat unattended in baggage claim for over an hour, and I was worried that someone might have put something in them that would result in my being flogged, or worse! After clearing passport control, I collected my luggage and went through the second phase of customs where my bags were searched. The customs agent began ripping out the foam-lined bottom of one of my cases thinking it might be a false bottom and yelling at me in Arabic every time I made an attempt to explain it was just padding. I finally made it through baggage claim, and a big, friendly American dressed in jeans and wearing a baseball cap greeted me on the other side. I was never so glad to see a friendly face.

"Hey Craig, I'm Richard, I'll be taking you to your hotel," my new friend said.

"Great, can't wait," I replied with a tired smile. I had been traveling for over twenty hours.

"You'll be in the Aramco community, nice little hotel. There's a grocery store, restaurant and everything else you'll need, plus everyone speaks English," Richard explained.

"That's nice to know."

"I know a first time arrival can be a bit disconcerting. It's an unusual country. At least you're here in the winter. In the summer months you can be stuck in customs for hours and the heat can be brutal, 110, 115 degrees," Richard said.

"You're kidding."

"No, I'm not. Saudi is one of the few places in the world where temperatures above 122 degrees have been recorded. The record was set right here in Dhahran in 1956, 124 degrees!"

"Don't ever invite me back in the summer!"

"You also had the bad luck of coming in behind that Pakistani plane," Richard stated.

"I thought they were being pretty hard on them in customs," I said.

"Yes, it's drugs. A lot of these Pakistanis are coming in to work the oil fields, and a lot of them try to smuggle drugs into the country. Just last week they caught an entire family carrying drugs."

"What happened to them?"

"They're all in jail now. The father will be executed, and the rest of the family will be sent back to Pakistan."

"Wow, they're serious about drugs, aren't they?"

"They're serious about a lot of stuff: drugs, alcohol, religion. You know you can't bring a Bible, rosary, crucifix or Star of David into Saudi?"

"I remember reading that when I was applying for my visa."

"You also can't wear shorts, and your arms should be covered. Women have it even worse. That's why Aramco originally built these compounds. It's a little more relaxed in the Aramco communities, but you still have to live by the rules."

On our car ride to the Saudi Aramco community in Dhahran, Richard gave me a little history of the Kingdom.

"You have to understand, you're in a monarchy ruled by Muslim law. The descendants of Abdul Aziz Ibn Saud rule the Kingdom. The Saud dynasty goes back to 1744. Muhammad Ibn Saud ruled a town near the current capital city of Riyadh. He joined forces with a Muslim cleric, and they created a political party. The Saud family had varying degrees of success and failure. It was Abdul Aziz who really solidified the family's holdings and created the realm we now know as the Kingdom of Saudi Arabia through a series of military conquests and political maneuverings that began in 1902 when Abdul Aziz was only twenty-two years old and ended in 1932 when the Kingdom of Saudi Arabia was officially established," Richard explained.

"The current king is Fahd bin Abdul Aziz Al Saud, or King Fahd. He is one of 36 sons fathered by Abdul Aziz Ibn Saud," Richard went on.

"Thirty-six sons? How many wives did Abdul Aziz have?" I asked.

"Many! The Koran limits the number of legitimate wives to four, but then there are the concubines," Richard said.

"King Fahd is actually sick, just hope he doesn't die while you're here," Richard went on.

"Why's that?"

"You won't be able to leave the kingdom for at least a month. The whole country will shut down in mourning," Richard said.

Oh great, I thought as I looked out the window at the bleak desert landscape.

After clearing security, we entered the gated Saudi Aramco community. I turned over my passport and checked into the hotel where I fell deep asleep, dreaming of deserts and Arabian sultans.

The following day, I was given a quick tour of the Saudi Aramco community. It did seem like I was in an American suburb in 1960. There was a running track and a pool and a gym with separate hours for men and women. The most interesting thing was the golf course. It was all sand. If you were playing a round of sand golf, you carried a mat of artificial turf with you and you would hit from the mat. There was a bit of a controversy going on concerning round and square mats. In tournament play, round mats were required because it was felt that with the square mat you could line your shot up with the green. The greens were compacted sand and a green attendant would squirt oil on them to keep the surface just right. It was bizarre.

In the grocery store, Richard handed me a copy of *Time* magazine and asked me to look through it. As I did, I noticed some pages were torn out. There was also an advertisement for panty hose with the model kicking high in the air. The model's legs were covered over with the scribbling of a black marking pen.

"Ministry of Censorship," Richard explained. "They have an entire room filled with women, and someone directs them to each page in every foreign magazine coming into the country. If there is an objectionable image, like that model, the objectionable part is covered up and if there's too much to cover, the page is simply ripped out."

"Amazing," was all I could think to say as I imagined a room filled with burkha-clad women turning magazines page by page, day after day.

I was scheduled for five performances. The first was a dinner theater show in Dhahran. From Dhahran, I would travel to Udhailiyah, the smallest of the Saudi Aramco communities. It was originally set up as a bachelor camp for drilling crews but was converted to accommodate a family lifestyle for American and other expat workers. The Udhailiyah compound is surrounded by rocky hills called jebels and the show was in the Wahat Al-Ghawar, a large, air-conditioned tent. After Udhailiyah, it was on to Abqaiq which I was told meant "father of the sand flies," and then Ras Tanura on the Persian Gulf coast where the world's largest offshore oil-loading facility is located. The final performance was a theater show back in Dhahran. Actually, I never stayed overnight anywhere but Dhahran as all the compounds were within driving distance of the primary Saudi Aramco community.

My driver, an Englishman named Trevor, was ex-military. He was a solidly built redhead, and we had a good time driving through the desert. I filled the theater in Dhahran on the last night of the tour, and the following day the Saudi Aramco employees hosted a going away party for me. I have to say, I was treated very well, and the shows were extremely interesting to do because of the variety of nationalities making up my audiences. A Saudi would be sitting next to some guy from Norway who was best friends with an Aussie. The people I met were all interesting, and each possessed an adventuresome spirit that brought them to this desert kingdom in the first place. While I felt a bit constrained in Saudi Arabia, I nevertheless found the entire experience incredibly interesting. In early 1997, I found myself headed back to Saudi Arabia for one last tour of the kingdom.

As we taxied in to the Dhahran airport terminal, we passed a beautiful building. *Thank God, they built a new terminal,* I thought. But no, we pulled up to the same old, dilapidated structure. I was in the passport control line with a man who was coming to Saudi Arabia to work for one of the major soft drink manufacturers. He had a pair of brightly colored sweatpants on and looked nervous.

"First time here?" he asked.

"No, I'm a repeater. I was here a little over a year ago. I'm doing some work for Saudi Aramco."

"Is it as strict as they say?" he asked.

"Pretty much. I always stay in the Saudi Aramco communities; so it's a little more relaxed there," I answered.

"Well, I had a buddy who was coming over to work, and he swiped a couple of the little liquor bottles from the plane. They caught him at customs and arrested him. Put him in jail for a few days and then deported him, and he was not allowed back in the country. Man, was corporate pissed!"

"Yeah, I wouldn't mess around here," I advised as I told him the story of the Pakistani drug smuggling family from my first trip.

Trevor greeted me after I cleared customs with a big grin and a slap on the back. "Welcome back to Saudi," he said.

"Hey Trevor, we passed this beautiful airport terminal on the way in. I thought they rebuilt the old terminal."

"No, that's the Royal Family's private terminal," Trevor informed me.

"Trevor, how's King Fahd's health?"

"He's still sick. He had a stroke when you were here last. His half-brother, Abdullah, is really running the country now. But King Fahd is still king," Trevor clued me in.

As I checked in with security on the Dhahran compound and surrendered my passport, a look of concern spread over the Saudi Aramco employee's face.

"You were supposed to get a month long visa," she said. "This is only for two weeks."

"I know, but I'm only going to be here for seven days. That's twice the amount of time I need," I said, knowing that I had gone against instructions partly because I wanted to make certain I could get out of the country in case anything happened to King Fahd. I mean if my visa expired, I had to be deported, right?

"You don't understand. I'm going to have to send this off to the government, and we're going to have to get an extension. I only hope we get your passport back in time for you to leave."

Oh boy! I thought. *What have I gotten myself into?* I still don't understand why I had to have a thirty day visa, but I've learned one thing from this experience. When traveling in a foreign country and you have been instructed how to act, follow those instructions. You don't have to understand them. You don't have to agree with them. But you're better off doing what those in the know say to do.

The 1997 schedule was exactly the same as the 1995 tour. However, this time I was a little more relaxed and a bit better prepared for the experience. I wanted to make the best of any free time I had. I brought some workout clothes in an attempt to start to get in shape and "get me training in," as Trevor was fond of saying. The Brit promised to take me to Khobar for some shopping and sightseeing. Unfortunately, one of the sights was Khobar Towers. On June 25, 1996, a terrorist group exploded a fuel truck in an eight-story building in the Khobar Towers complex which housed United States Air Force personnel. Nineteen U.S. servicemen and one Saudi were killed, and 372 others from a variety of nations were wounded. We stood and stared at the rubble.

"It was terrible," Trevor said. "You know, the acts of terrorism in this country are growing, acts against the U.S. military and against any strong foreign presence, including Aramco. That's why the compounds are so heavily guarded," Trevor's statement served as a reminder of exactly where I was and that I should remain on guard.

"In fact, that's part of the reason you're here," Trevor added.

"What do you mean?" I asked.

"The Saudi government is putting pressure on us to turn over the jobs that many foreigners have to the Saudis or at least to people from Muslim nations. They feel the foreign presence, especially you Yanks and us Brits is detrimental, and we'll probably all be gone before long. We wanted to have you back for one more go round before we were all kicked out," Trevor informed me.

"Now, let's think happier thoughts, what would you like to shop for?" Trevor asked.

"You know, I always wanted one of those Arab knives, the kind that curl up at the end," I said.

"I know just the place. There's an antiquities dealer I'm friendly with who has quality merchandise and will give you a fair price. Let's go see him."

I followed the big, redheaded Brit into a mall and then into a second floor antique shop.

"Greetings Trevor," a small Arab man approached us as we entered the shop.

73

"And who is this?" he added nodding his head in my direction.

"This is Craig Karges, he's an entertainer we've hired to work the Aramco compounds. He does some amazing stuff. And Craig, this is Khalid, the shop's proprietor," Trevor explained.

"It's a pleasure sir," I acknowledged the shopkeeper.

"He's after a Bedouin knife for a souvenir of his trip," Trevor said.

"You have come to the right place," the proprietor responded as he led me to a glass display case.

He removed a knife from the case as he explained, "This is a classic example of the Bedouin knife or Gudamiya in Arabic. As you no doubt know, the Bedouin are a nomadic people, a series of tribes really, who make their home in the desert. A craftsman named Dagget Mizale made this particular blade. He was from Al-Jouf in northern Saudi Arabia. It is about one-hundred-twenty years old, crafted in silver with handmade work. It was used by Bedouins on ceremonial occasions."

It was a thing of beauty. We quickly negotiated what Trevor indicated was a fair price.

As we were closing the deal, the Adhan or the Muslim call to prayer began. Loudspeakers at mosques broadcast the announcement to "hasten to prayer." This is based on the tradition of the muezzin, a man who would climb the minaret of a mosque and call all believers to pray. The call to pray is heard five times a day: at dawn, midday, in the middle of the afternoon, just after sunset, and at nightfall, or about two hours after sunset. When it is time to pray, everything stops. The shops close down. A traveling Muslim will have his prayer rug with him. As Trevor and I would leave Dhahran for the other compounds our travel would often coincide with the Adhan. Many a devout Muslim could be seen on the roadside, out of his car, prayer mat spread by the side of the road as he faced Mecca and prayed. For some reason, the car was usually a big, Chevy Impala, a very popular vehicle when I was in Saudi Arabia.

"We better be going," I said.

"No, please stay here," the shopkeeper, said as he shuttered the shop's windows.

"Not all Muslims are so devout," he said as he packaged up the knife.

"Are you a religious man, Mr. Karges?" Khalid asked.

"I'm a Catholic," I replied.

"On a scale of one through ten, how devout would you say you are?"

"Maybe a five," I said somewhat ashamed.

"That would be me as well with my religion," Khalid said.

"There are many truly devout Muslims in Saudi Arabia. Then there are the fanatics, the ones who pervert our religion, the ones who bombed Khobar Towers in the name of Allah. What blasphemy!" Khalid's voice had risen and he was visibly upset.

"And then there are the rest of us," Khalid suddenly calmed down. "Some of us like to sneak away to Bahrain where we may even partake in— how would you say it — earthly pleasures?"

I could feel my eyebrow involuntarily cock as Trevor nodded his head in agreement, "Yeah, I've spent some wild nights in Bahrain!"

"Yes, Bahrain can provide a momentary escape from the very strict religious laws of Saudi Arabia," Khalid concurred.

"When do you leave?" Khalid asked me.

"In a couple days."

"What airline are you flying?"

"British Airways to London."

"First class, business class or coach?"

"Why do you ask?" I had to admit I was getting a little suspicious as I looked at my packaged antique knife, wondering what else may have been slipped into the packaging and thought about Khobar Towers.

"I have a little observational exercise for you to attempt. You will enjoy it, I promise," Khalid explained.

"OK, I'm in business class."

"Good, not as good as first, but it is still good. Watch to see how many women in burkhas join you in your business class compartment. Count them. Then count the number of women wearing burkhas when you land in London. Some will have mysteriously disappeared."

"Ah, the burkha babes," Trevor chimed in.

Khalid shot a disapproving glance Trevor's way and Trevor lowered his eyes, but I noticed a slight smile on his lips.

"These women wear the burkha when in Saudi Arabia. However, as soon as the plane leaves Saudi Arabian airspace they will discreetly head toward the restroom and remove the burkha. Underneath they will be wearing brightly colored clothing," Khalid went on.

"Of course, all women do not do this. However, the laws in my country can be very stifling and there is need for an escape from time to time," Khalid concluded.

"Here is your knife, a treasure worthy of Ali Baba himself," the shopkeeper said as he handed over my recent purchase.

"Well, I hope the 40 thieves stay away from my knife," I said with a smile.

"Open Sesame!" cried Trevor.

"You two are familiar with the tales of the Arabian Nights?" Khalid asked as he pointed back and forth between Trevor and me.

"Certainly," Trevor said. "Every schoolboy knows of the tales of the *One Thousand and One Arabian Nights.*"

"Yes, told by Sultan Shahryar's bride Scheherazade. The sultan discovered that his former wife was unfaithful, and he had her executed. He then declares that all women are unfaithful, and he asks his official minister to find virgins for him to marry. He marries the virgins and then executes them the following morning. Finally, the official can find no more virgins in the kingdom. The minister's daughter, Sheherazade, offers to be the king's next bride. This Sheherazade was a very clever lady. Each night, she began to spin a magical tale, stories that totally entranced the sultan. Just before the end of the night, she would stop telling her story, and the king could not have her executed because he needed to hear the end of the tale. The following evening she would conclude the story but start another. She did this for one thousand and one nights. At the end of the one thousand and one nights, the sultan pardoned Sheherazade and all ends happily," Khalid explained.

"*Ali Baba and the Forty Thieves* was just one of those entrancing tales," Khalid went on. "Ali Baba overhears a group of 40 thieves hiding their treasure in a cave. The cave is a magical place, the secret words to enter the cave are 'Open Sesame' and the cave would seal itself closed when one of the thieves uttered the words 'Close Sesame.'

"After the band of thieves departs, Ali Baba enters the cave by saying the magic words, takes some treasure and leaves the same way, sealing the cave by saying the magic words. He takes his stolen goods to his brother's house and weighs them. Ali Baba's brother, Cassim, discovers what Ali is up to and makes a trip to the cave himself. Once inside, he forgets the magic words to get out of the cave. The thieves return and find Cassim with their treasure. They cut him into tiny pieces and leave him at the mouth of the cave as a warning to others.

"Ali Baba finds his brother's body and brings it home. One of Cassim's slave girls, Morgiana, helps Ali Baba find a tailor who is led to Cassim's body. The tailor stitches Cassim up and makes him whole again so that he can be given a proper burial without arousing suspicion.

"The thieves return to the cave to find Cassim's body has vanished and they realize someone else knows where their treasure is hidden. They discover the tailor who stitched Cassim's body together, and he leads them to Ali Baba's home. One of the thieves marks a symbol on Ali Baba's door. The 40 thieves intend to return in the dead of night and murder everyone in the house. The slave girl, Morgiana, overhears this plot and puts a similar symbol on every house in the vicinity of Ali Baba's home. When the thieves return that evening, they cannot locate the proper home. The leader of the thieves is filled with anger and kills the thief whose idea it was to place a symbol on the door.

"They try again the following day. This time one of the thieves decides he will chip a chunk of stone from the front steps of Ali Baba's home. Morgiana catches them in the act, realizes what is going on and chips similar chunks of stone from all the neighbors' steps. That night the 39 thieves are foiled again, and one more thief falls to the hand of the chief thief as he is murdered for his stupidity.

"The chief thief then decides to take matters into his own hands and finally locates Ali Baba's home. He memorizes every detail of the house so he cannot mistake it for another. He disguises himself as an oil merchant and brings Ali Baba 38 jars supposedly containing oil. In reality, only one jar contains oil, while the other 37 contain the remaining thieves. The plan is for the thieves to leave their hiding places once everyone in the house is asleep and murder them. However, Morgiana, the wise and clever slave girl, is on to them, and she pours boiling oil into each jar, killing the 37 thieves. When the chief thief returns to get his men, he finds them all dead—boiled alive in oil!"

"What happens next?" Trevor asked, we were both as transfixed as the schoolboys the Brit mentioned earlier.

"Some time passes and then the chief thief returns for revenge. He enters into business with Ali Baba's son who now runs Cassim's business. Eventually, the chief thief is invited to Ali Baba's home. As part of the entertainment, Morgiana performs a traditional dance with a dagger not unlike your newly acquired dagger, Mr. Karges," Khalid said nodding his head toward the package in my hands.

"As she danced, she came to recognize the thief. She danced closer and closer to him. As the thief became entranced with the lovely slave girl, Morgiana plunged the dagger into the thief's heart!

"Ali Baba was in shock until Morgiana explained who the dead man was. He was then overjoyed that the slave girl had saved his life and undoubtedly the life of his son. Ali Baba gave Morgiana her freedom and she married his son," Khalid concluded.

"Thanks for the story Khalid, we should be going," Trevor said.

"I don't think it is wise for me to permit you to leave until after prayers," Khalid said.

"OK, tell us another story. This time, tell a true one, about real treasure," I challenged the friendly shopkeeper.

"Would you like to know the location of King Solomon's Mines?" Khalid asked.

"The biblical Solomon?" I asked.

"Yes, King Solomon is in the Koran as well," Khalid informed me.

"He was the King of Israel, son of David, and he was Israel's last ruler before it split into the northern Kingdom of Israel and the southern Kingdom of Judah. Solomon built Jerusalem's First Temple, and he was great in power, wealth and wisdom," Khalid stated.

"I remember the biblical story about the two women claiming the same child to be theirs," I offered.

"Ah, yes. Solomon said he would slice the baby in two with a sword so the women could share the child, at which time the true mother showed herself by allowing the second woman to take the child to avoid killing the baby. Solomon awarded the child to the true mother," Khalid finished the story.

"The source of Solomon's great wealth (King Solomon's Mines) is right here in Saudi Arabia," Khalid stated matter-of-factly.

"Really? Where?" Trevor said interested.

"Solomon is said to have brought his treasure in from the country of Ophir," Khalid said.

"Ophir, never heard of it," Trevor replied.

"There are very few hints as to the location of Ophir. Archeologists and treasure hunters have searched the wide world from Africa to Peru looking for Ophir and the source of Solomon's wealth, but it is here in Saudi Arabia," Khalid said.

"Come on Khalid, out with it, where is this treasure," Trevor prodded the shopkeeper.

"In 1932 an American mining engineer named Karl Twitchwell found evidence of olden mines in Saudi Arabia. The richest of these mines was Mahd adh Dhahab or the *Cradle of Gold.* It is located halfway between Mecca and Medina, our holiest cities. The mine was ancient and the evidence was plentiful that it had been heavily mined, but it still contained more gold and silver than any other location in Saudi Arabia. The mine was immediately reopened and was operated successfully for another twenty years. Many archeologists, scholars, historians and, of course, Twitchwell himself believe that the Mahd adh Dhahab and the surrounding mines were, in fact, King Solomon's Mines. It made perfect sense," Khalid recounted.

"Just across the eastern sands in Oman lies another treasure," Khalid continued, "the lost city of Ubar. The Koran describes it as 'the many-columned city whose like has not been built in the whole land.' It was a city of riches to be certain, with streets paved with gold. It became wealthy due to trade between the coastal regions and the population centers of the Middle East and Europe. Caravans would carry frankincense far and wide. However, the city's riches became its downfall. The land became corrupt and Ubar was swallowed by the sands of the desert," Khalid continued.

"Kind of like Atlantis meets Sodom and Gomorrah," I observed.

"You certainly could say that. Some refer to Ubar as the 'Atlantis of the Sands.' Now, do you two believe Ubar to be mythical or real?" Khalid asked as he looked back and forth from Trevor to me.

"I'm guessing it's a fairy tale," Trevor said.

"Well, I'm betting it's real," I said with a smile.

"You are quite correct Mr. Karges," Khalid said as I smiled at Trevor.

"Just a few years ago a group of adventurers and amateur archeologists tried to find Ubar by using modern technology. They utilized NASA remote sensing satellites, ground penetrating radar and even images taken by the space shuttle in an attempt to locate the ancient camel caravan routes that they believed could lead them to Ubar. They were successful and found an area in Oman that was a likely location for the lost city. They found evidence of an impressive ancient fortress built atop a massive limestone cavern. The cavern was filled with water, and this provided a convenient water source for the fortress. As you know, water in the desert is a treasure in and of itself. At the dig site, they unearthed artifacts from far and wide, some dating back two thousand years, further proof that this was an ancient trading location. The team theorized that as the water in the cavern was depleted, the walls of the cavern dried out, and without the support of the water, the cavern collapsed. As the cavern collapsed, it took the city with it. The desert swallowed Ubar in accordance with legend. The team verified that the collapse occurred around 100 A.D. just as the legend says—an ancient mystery solved from outer space. You see, yesterday's fable, Ubar, is today's fact. Who can say how many more mysteries and treasures are buried beneath the Arabian sands," Khalid concluded.

"Ah, prayers are at an end," Khalid said as he went to the shop windows and opened the shutters.

"Enjoy your remaining time in the desert, Mr. Karges and enjoy your knife," Khalid added as we said goodbye and exchanged the traditional Muslim greeting *as-Salamu alaikum* (peace be unto you) and the response *wa alaikum assalam* (and on you be peace).

I did enjoy my remaining time in Saudi Arabia. I got my passport back in time to catch my flight home, and King Fahd was still alive when I left. He was a tough man. Despite suffering a massive stroke in November of 1995, he lived almost ten more years, passing away in August of 2005. At that time, King Abdullah officially succeeded him and remains the ruling monarch of the Kingdom of Saudi Arabia today. I have subsequently learned that the old Dhahran airport has been converted into an air base for the Royal Saudi Air Force, and a brand new facility, King Fahd International, was opened in 1999. On my return flight, I tried to spot the disappearing burkha trick. I caught three of Trevor's "burkha babes" in the act. A burkha–clad woman would shuffle up the aisle and enter the lavatory. You would never see her again. Instead, out of the lavatory would appear a woman with long, flowing dark hair, extreme eye makeup and dangling golden jewelry, dressed in a colorful, trendy outfit!

On a more somber note, in February of 2006, members of the al-Qaeda terrorist group attacked the Abqaiq facility. Terrorists in multiple vehicles laced with explosives tried to enter the facility but were halted by the security force. The vehicles exploded and a gunfight erupted resulting in the death of four terrorists and two security guards. This was the first direct attack by al-Qaeda on a Saudi oil installation. Osama bin Laden called for attacks against the oil industry in Saudi Arabia in 2004, and his deputy, Ayman al-Zawahiri, repeated that message in 2005. A subsequent website message by al-Qaeda claimed responsibility for the attack saying it was part of al-Qaeda's "war against the Christians and Jews to stop their pillage of Muslim riches and part of the campaign to chase them out of the Arabian Peninsula."

CHAPTER SEVEN

Walk Like an Egyptian

Communication has changed so dramatically in the past decade. In 1998, most business was conducted over the telephone, the office telephone. Cell phones were generally reserved for emergencies (the per minute rates were so high) and while I had a website and an e-mail account, the amount of business e-mail we received was minimal.

Of course today, as soon as my plane lands, my iPhone is out and I'm checking e-mail, voicemail and surfing the Internet before I'm even at the gate! But this was 1998, and I had been on the road for about a week. Charlotte was out of town as well, attending a business conference; so e-mail had not been checked for a few days. I had a long layover at Chicago O'Hare; so I was checking voicemail from a payphone (remember those?) and I was surprised to hear an Arabic accented voice on one of the messages.

"This is Dr. Kalib. I sent you an e-mail days ago requesting your presence in Cairo, Egypt, for the Worldwide Lessons in Leadership conference. Please get in touch with me as soon as possible if you choose to take part. Here is my number (he rattled off a long string of digits). Thank you, goodbye."

I immediately phoned my manager and gave him the details of the call before boarding my next flight. Within thirty-six hours, I had a confirmed booking in Cairo that would take place two months later.

The 1998 Worldwide Lessons in Leadership Series featured top management speakers like Ken Blanchard, Stephen Covey and Tom Peters as well as CEO's Jack Welch of General Electric and Herb Kelleher of Southwest Airlines. Dr. Kalib had purchased the Middle Eastern rights to the satellite broadcast of this event. He would be hosting management types from the gulf region at the El Gezirah Sheraton hotel, located on the tip of an island in the middle of the Nile. I was to entertain the delegates and then conduct an intuitive management session of "Ignite Your Intuition."

Originally, I was going to perform at the Cairo Opera House for the conference attendees as well as anyone in Cairo who wished to purchase a ticket. However, my visit coincided with the first anniversary of what became known as "The Luxor Massacre." On November 17, 1997, terrorists ambushed, shot and killed 63 tourists at Luxor. In the mid-morning hours, a group of six terrorists disguised as part of the tourism security force and armed with automatic weapons and knives trapped a group of tourists inside Hatshepsut's Temple near Luxor. Over a forty-five minute period, they systematically murdered their victims. The dead included a five-year-old British child and four Japanese couples on their honeymoons as well as tourists from France, Germany, Switzerland, Columbia and Egypt. After committing mass murder, the terrorists hijacked a bus but were stopped by the Egyptian military. A gun battle ensued. One of the terrorists was wounded and taken prisoner while the rest escaped into the hills. Their dead bodies were found in a cave, victims of a mass suicide.

Apparently, there were some credible threats of terrorism targeting foreign tourists in Egypt to mark the first anniversary of the "Luxor Massacre." All foreigners were instructed to keep a low profile; so the Opera House performance was changed to a private, after-dinner cabaret show with a question and answer session for the conference attendees at the El Gezirah.

Checking into the hotel, I passed armed guards. It was exactly like going through airport security with my bags being x-rayed as I took a stroll through a metal detector. I guess the terrorist threats were pretty specific, because I was checked into the hotel under an assumed name. Dr. Kalib accompanied me to my room where he paid me in American cash and invited me to have dinner with his family.

Before heading down to dinner, I walked out to my balcony and looked at the stunning view I had of Cairo. It would have been even more stunning if the air hadn't been filled with smog. Cairo has a bit of a pollution problem. Still, I couldn't believe it. *I was in Egypt!*

Walk Like an Egyptian

We had a wonderful meal that night at the hotel's restaurant that was literally in the river Nile. As the waters of the Nile lapped up against the patio where we dined, I kept pinching myself.

The following morning, I was on my balcony sipping a strong cup of coffee, and I saw three distinct shapes in the distance. I rubbed my eyes and looked again. The Pyramids of Giza! I hadn't been able to see them the day before because of the smog.

Dr. Kalib had kindly arranged for a tour of the pyramids. He and his son, Ahmed, along with a driver would accompany me. Ahmed had returned to Egypt from his studies in England to help his father with the conference. He was also put in charge of babysitting me.

The Pyramids of Giza are an iconic image. The Great Pyramid or the Pyramid of Cheops is the oldest and largest of the three pyramids making up this city of the dead. This massive structure was built during the Egyptian Fourth Dynasty (between 2613 and 2494 B.C.). It is believed that Cheops, or Khufu, his Egyptian name, ordered the structure created to house his tomb and serve as a monument to his rule. But if it is a tomb, why was a body never found, and why were there no symbols or possessions of royalty in the pyramid?

The Great Pyramid is massive, covering a ground area of 13.1 acres and composed of 2.3 million limestone blocks averaging two-and-a-half tons each. There is enough stone in the Great Pyramid to build a wall of four foot square cubes two-thirds of the way around the earth, or covering 16,600 miles. The key question that is asked about the pyramids is how they could have been built and are *still* standing strong when the Egyptians lacked the technology and skills necessary during that age. The answer that some archeological experts offer is that thousands upon thousands of slaves, and years of hard labor constructed these magnificent structures. Others have an "alternative" theory. Because of the vastness and complexity of these monstrous structures, many suspect (brace yourself here) that E. T. may have had his hand in helping out the Egyptians. That's right, aliens from outer space were the project managers for the construction of the pyramids. Yes, I'm being a little sarcastic, but let me share some of these strange facts that correspond with various events in history, mathematical equations and even secret codes.

Let's take a look at the precise arrangements of the pyramids in Giza. These enormous and precise structures are in the exact order of the corresponding stars in the Orion constellation. I know, weird. Hold on to your hats, there's more. Here's an equation for you: If you take the circumference of the pyramid and divide by two times its height, the result is 3.14159, the first six digits of pi. The mathematical capabilities of these primitive people were limited during this time in Egypt. Many believe the Egyptians would not have been able to compute or design these structures without the involvement of a higher intelligence.

How about this one: The passageways and chambers in the Great Pyramid are of various lengths and dimensions. When the dimensions are converted into years, some claim they coincide with the dates of important historical events such as the Jewish exodus from Egypt, the birth and death of Jesus Christ, the French Revolution and World War II. Obviously, only individuals with a clear vision of the future could predict these happenings.

OK, not enough for you? Here are just a few more oddities about the ancient Egyptians. In King Tutankhamen's tomb (which is not part of the Giza complex but was located at the Valley of the Kings), there was a specific mold found within that burial chamber that does not exist anywhere else in the entire world. Also, the strangest thing I learned about the pyramids has to do with record keeping and documentation. There aren't any records. This is one of the most intriguing facts to me. Why would the Egyptians, with their hieroglyphics and organizational skills simply neglect to write down the plans or leave a clue or two behind as to how they built these pyramids? This culture was very consistent with keeping a good, clean journal of their activities and history. An extensive list of who their rulers were, various structures they built, the many wars they fought were all extensively documented; however, not one single passage about the pyramids exists.

Then, there is the whole subject of "Pyramid Power." In the 1920s the remains of several feral cats were found in the Great Pyramid. They were naturally mummified. This led to the question of whether or not the pyramid shape had powers all its own. Does the pyramid shape create physical effects on living things and inanimate objects? Many believe that it does, citing experiments where dull razor blades were sharpened, plants had accelerated growth and food was kept fresh, all when placed under a pyramid shaped structure.

The Great Pyramid of Giza is an enigma of the first order and the only "wonder" still in existence from the original Seven Wonders of the Ancient World. Is it a tomb? Does it possess some type of power we can't currently understand? Does it embody a universal system of measurement? Is it a gigantic sundial and astronomical observatory? Was it a temple used by the Egyptians to worship the sun or a temple where a secret ritual was enacted which would allow the participant to achieve immortality? Is it a repository of ancient knowledge, or was it simply a repository for grain? All of these hypotheses have been put forth to help explain why the Great Pyramid of Giza exists. And here I was, arriving at the Giza plateau.

As soon as the Mercedes sedan pulled up, a throng of children approached the car asking for money. I wasn't even out of the car before I had dozens of hands in front of me.

Dr. Kalib barked at them and the crowd disbursed. We were out of the car and headed toward the pyramids when a cute little girl rushed up to me and tried to hand me a beaded bracelet.

"No, no thank you," I said trying to brush her away.

"No. It is a gift. It is for you. It is for free," she said as she slipped the bracelet on my wrist.

"Thank you but…"

She cut me off with, "I give you something, now you give me something."

I had to smile at her negotiating skills; so I handed over some money. The sight of the money being exchanged brought another army of children and they surrounded us. Dr. Kalib yelled something in Arabic and off they went.

"Sorry, Craig, it is the *Egyptian way*. Enjoy yourself here. We will stay parked down the road and when you are finished come back to the car and we will visit the Sphinx," Dr. Kalib said.

I was spinning around in circles trying to take everything in. I started taking some photographs of the pyramids, and I noticed a Bedouin on a camel watching me. I deliberately didn't point my camera in his direction because I didn't want to offend him by taking his photo.

He called over to me in accented English, "Sir, would you like a picture of me?"

"If that is acceptable, certainly," I replied.

He posed on his camel and I captured some images. The camel lowered itself to the ground and the Egyptian dismounted.

"Now I take a picture of you," he said.

"No, that's OK."

"No, no, come here by my camel."

It was an offer I couldn't refuse; I mean you just don't hear that every day. I stood by the camel as my new Egyptian friend took some photos. Then, before I knew it, I wasn't standing by the camel, I was *on* the camel and we were heading out to the desert!

"Really sir, I need to get back," I said as we went further into the Libyan Desert.

"You do not like your camel ride?"

"No, it's fine, really, but I have to get back."

The Bedouin slowed the camel to a stop and then he looked up at me and said, "Fine. You can pay me now."

"Pay you? I didn't ask for a camel ride."

"You must pay," he insisted.

"I only have U.S. currency."

"That is acceptable, now pay."

I handed him a twenty-dollar bill.

"That is not enough. More please."

"Look, I have to get back." I was getting nervous. We were in the desert a fair distance from the pyramids and Dr. Kalib was nowhere in sight.

I handed him another twenty and said, "That is it. Final. The end. Now take me back to the pyramids."

"Gladly, sir," he said with a smile as he led the camel back toward the Great Pyramid.

I reunited with Dr. Kalib and Ahmed at the car and the three of us headed over to the Sphinx. The Sphinx, I couldn't believe it.

"What do you think, Craig?" Dr. Kalib asked.

"It is so impressive, I just can't believe I'm here," I replied.

"The Sphinx stands 66 feet tall, and it was built from the discarded stone used to build the pyramids. It is sculpted in the likeness of Pharaoh Chephern," Dr. Kalib explained.

"Due to the many sandstorms in the desert, the Sphinx tended to get buried in the sand over time," Ahmed said.

"Yes, quite right, son. In 1400 B.C. the Sphinx was buried up to its neck. A young prince came by. Exhausted from a hunting trip, he lay down to rest in the shadow of the Sphinx. He claimed the Sphinx spoke to him as he slept. The Sphinx said the prince would be the next ruler of Egypt, ahead of his older brothers, if he would only clear away the sand covering the statue. The prince cleared the sand away and shortly after ascended to the throne becoming Pharaoh Thutmose IV," Dr. Kalib informed us.

After marveling at the Sphinx and taking in the view of the pyramids, I pivoted around and saw a Pizza Hut™! I know it's hard to believe, but when viewing the sights on the Giza plateau from one direction you only see desert in the background; however, Cairo is encroaching on the site and "civilization" is just a stone's throw away. As I thought about this and thought about my kidnapping-by-camel, I looked down and four more Egyptian children were surrounding me, hands out. I felt so sorry for them but they were everywhere and you couldn't give money to all of them. Dr. Kalib yelled once more and they vanished.

I am not a fan of organized tour groups. However, my advice to you is that if you plan on touring Egypt, go with an organized group. There is safety in numbers!

"Now, come, I have a special treat for you," Dr. Kalib said as he headed toward the car and motioned Ahmed and me to follow.

A short time later, we arrived at Saqqara, a necropolis for Memphis, the capital of Ancient Egypt. It was here that we explored Pharaoh Djoser's Step Pyramid, the world's oldest standing step pyramid. The pyramid was created to hold the mummified body of Djoser, the third king of Egypt's Third Dynasty. It was originally a traditional, flat roof mastaba, a large slab constructed of mud-bricks or stone with outward sloping sides that marked a burial site. However, by the end of Djoser's reign, it had risen to six, stepped layers and stood 204 feet high. It was the largest building of its time (2630 B.C.). The Pharaoh was buried deep beneath the ground with the pyramid erected over the burial chamber. The burial chamber is just one of many underground tunnels, shafts, galleries and rooms covering three-and-a-half subterranean miles—a maze created to thwart grave robbers.

The original complex at Saqqara was the size of a large town in the third millennium B.C. and covered 40 acres. It consisted of courtyards, tombs, temples and chapels. The south tomb chapel has large, carved cobra heads protecting the facility. The cobras still stand guard!

It is widely believed that Pharaoh Djoser's Step Pyramid was the very first pyramid structure used to mark a tomb. Imhotep, Ancient Egypt's greatest architect, created the pyramid. Imhotep was also a physician and a priest. He founded a cult of healing and was deified one-thousand-four-hundred years after his death.

Dr. Kalib had arranged for a special tour of Saqqara, and I enjoyed it immensely. It was just the good doctor, Ahmed, a private tour guide and me wandering throughout the ancient complex. Our tour at an end, we began to exit the complex through a colonnaded hallway. Ahmed and the tour guide began a heated argument in Arabic. I tried not to pay attention and gazed out at the complex's courtyard. All of a sudden, Dr. Kalib materialized from the shadow of one of the columns and asked what the problem was (at least that's what I assume he asked because I don't speak Arabic). The tour guide spoke in rapid fashion to Dr. Kalib who then turned to face Ahmed and berated him in Arabic. Ahmed hung his head low and walked away. Dr. Kalib and the guide continued to converse, and then Dr. Kalib exploded again. This time his anger was directed toward the tour guide! The guide's gaze drifted downward, some money was exchanged and Dr. Kalib walked away with me trailing behind.

I was a little uncomfortable getting into the car with father and son after that argument, but all seemed fine between the two so I asked, "I'm sorry, but what was all that yelling about?"

"Oh, it was nothing. Just the *Egyptian way*," Ahmed answered.

"My son offered the guide less money than he deserved. The guide was very upset. I scolded my son for insulting the guide with such a low offer. I then asked the guide what he would like to be paid. He answered with an unjustly high fee. I then scolded him for being unfair, and a compromise was reached. A fair price was paid. It was a simple negotiation. In Egypt, there is always a negotiation," Dr. Kalib explained.

The following day while Dr. Kalib was busy attending to the last minute details of the conference, Ahmed took me to the Cairo Museum.

I have to tell you that Ahmed had not been in Egypt in almost two years. He was enrolled in university in England. He spoke perfect English with a British accent. While his hair was dark and curly, his skin was not as dark as the rest of his family due to the amount of time he had spent in the sun-deprived U.K. As we walked up the steps to the museum, I noticed a sign listing the entrance fees. There was a price for Egyptian citizens and a slightly higher price for foreigners. Ahmed approached the window and said in English, "One Egyptian and one non-Egyptian."

The man in the booth looked back and forth between Ahmed and me and said, "Which one is the Egyptian?"

"I am, of course!" Ahmed replied.

With our tickets in hand, we entered the museum and Ahmed confessed to me that he felt a bit out of place in his native land. He was experiencing a little "culture shock" after spending so much time in Britain.

"That negotiation back at Saqqara for example, it just felt so strange and uncomfortable," he explained, "and now I have a museum ticket seller questioning my heritage."

"I think he was just trying to be funny," I offered.

"No, it has been happening ever since I returned."

We engaged a private tour guide and embarked on an experience I will never forget. The Cairo Museum is a treasure trove of Egyptology. There are obelisks, statues, mummies and sarcophagi strewn throughout the complex any one of which would probably qualify as the prized exhibit in a North American museum. As you walked down a hallway, you would literally run into a sarcophagus in the middle of the walkway, and not under glass, not in a formal display, just there, right in front of you. You could easily trip over a millennia old artifact.

Our tour guide took us through the over three-thousand-year history of Ancient Egypt. It covered the Late Pre-dynastic Period (3100-2950 B.C.) during which the earliest hieroglyphic writing was recorded, to the Early Dynastic Period (2950-2575 B.C.) when Memphis was established as the capital and Imhotep built Djoser's pyramid, the Old Kingdom (2575-2150 B.C.) when the pyramids at Giza were created; and the First Intermediate Period (2125-1975 B.C.) when Egypt actually split into two smaller states with Memphis, the capital of the north and Thebes, the capital of the south. Egypt was reunited under Pharaoh Mentuhotep during the Middle Kingdom (1975-1640 B.C.) and then split again during the Second Intermediate Period (1630-1520 B.C.). The New Kingdom (1539-1075 B.C.) was the time of the brief reign of Tutankhamen, the long, sixty-seven year reign of Ramesses II and the creation of the elaborate tombs at the Valley of the Kings. In the Third Intermediate Period (1075-715 B.C.), the Nubians conquered Egypt. This was followed by the Late Period (715-332 B.C.) when the Nubian-conquered Egypt was conquered in turn by the Assyrians and the Persians before becoming independent again in 404 B.C. Last was the Greco-Roman Period (332 B.C. to 395 A.D.), the time of Alexander the Great's conquest of Egypt. Alexander made his general, Ptolemy, king. Ptolemy went on to create a dynasty. Cleopatra VII also reigned during the Greco-Roman Period until Egypt became a province of the Roman Empire in 30 B.C. I apologize for the history lesson, but just consider for a moment the millennia of recorded ancient Egyptian history. It is staggering, and I felt like I was standing in the middle of it all at the Cairo Museum.

As we left the museum, our tour guide suggested a detour before returning to the hotel. He knew a papyrus dealer just across the street. The three of us entered a small shop and were introduced to the owner, Islam Samaha. Our museum tour guide left, leaving Ahmed, Islam and me in the shop. Islam began to pluck various papyrus paintings from their cubicles and unfold them on a table in the middle of the room.

Papyrus is really the world's first paper, made from the stem of the Cyperus papyrus plant that grows in the damp regions of Egypt's Nile Delta. It was the main writing surface used by the ancient Egyptians. Islam's papyrus paintings were not ancient, but newer, and were adorned with hand painted artwork, each more beautiful than the next. I purchased an astronomical ceiling papyrus as a gift for Charlotte's mother and stepfather. It depicted Nut, the goddess of the sky, as she supports the sky with her back, swallowing the sun at night only to give birth to it the next day. I was told the painting was based on images found in the tombs of the Valley of the Kings.

As we were leaving the shop, an older, more faded papyrus painting caught my attention. It wasn't rolled up and shoved in a pigeonhole as most of the others were, but it wasn't really on display either. It was in a corner of the shop atop a small, glass topped table. The weight of the glass pressed the painting flat against the table top. It depicted a large scarab beetle, an army of smaller scarabs, a pyramid surrounded in light and a man.

"What about this one? What story does it tell?" I asked.

"That one tells my story," Islam said as he went on to recount a childhood memory.

When he was just a schoolboy, Islam and one of his friends visited the pyramids of Giza—no, not the regular tour, one of Islam's uncles had special clearance to get "behind the scenes" and take the real tour of the pyramids into strange corridors and passageways that no tourist had ever seen.

Islam and his friend got the tour of their lives. The extensive history and the folklore as told by his uncle, and the pyramids themselves were astonishing. After his uncle finished giving the two youngsters their private tour, Islam remembered that he had left his backpack near one of the secret doors near a passageway. Fearing that he would be running late and that Islam's mother would be angry, his uncle allowed Islam to go back inside the pyramid and retrieve the item. Although Islam told his uncle he could find his way back in and back out without a problem, it was a little more confusing inside than he had anticipated. After making a few wrong turns and running into a few dead ends, Islam finally got his bearings and found his backpack.

He was about ready to hustle back out to meet his friend, but curiosity got the best of him. A small scorpion skittered across Islam's path and then suddenly disappeared under an obscure and extremely small opening in the floor. Surely nobody would care if he sneaked a peek! Islam carefully peered down this opening and saw another secret room, but this room wasn't like the others. First of all, it was beneath the ground floor, and secondly, it was built like a pyramid shape within the pyramid. That's not all he saw. Islam was staring in a trancelike state at the most beautifully crafted statue he had ever seen. He just had to explore this close up! He grabbed a flashlight from his backpack and approached the opening. Although the opening was small, Islam knew he could squeeze through it. He obviously shouldn't have been in that room, but if it was totally off limits, then why was there a "humongous" one-by-one foot opening in the first place, right? When he squeezed through the small opening, he fell a lot further down than he had expected. It might be tough climbing back *up* to that opening. His uncle would be furious if he couldn't get out of this secret room! Oh well, he'd worry about that later....

Since he was already in the pyramid *within* the pyramid room, he just had to see that statue! He approached the sculpture and shined the flashlight toward the face. He didn't know for sure, but he guessed that this effigy (possibly made of solid gold) was forged in the image of Khepri, the scarab-beetle god. This god was usually identified with Ra, the sun god and both were creator-gods. Why would this beautiful statue be left unattended, and why would Khepri, a lesser-known figure in Egyptian mythology, be deserving of such a large and costly representation? Well, he was in an area where most people would not have had access; and he had barely squeezed through a small vent to gain access to this secluded area. The statue was definitely in a secluded spot; however, why wasn't it on display in a museum somewhere? Instead, it was stored in a cobweb-infested dungeon underneath the pyramids. Islam was definitely more excited than afraid.

He approached the statue and guessed that it most likely weighed 500 kilograms (or just over a half ton) and was approximately 12 feet tall. As he neared the icon, he felt a tingling sensation first in his fingers and toes, but then it engulfed his entire body. Islam described it as if your foot "went to sleep" and you had that "pins and needles" feeling. Although the tingling was strange, he was not in any pain or even discomfort. He actually felt more invigorated than he had ever felt in his life. Islam described his physical and psychological condition as: "An overwhelming absence of fear, an aire of confidence and a clear mind."

Should he touch the scarab statue? He was not afraid at all. He almost felt that he was destined to be in this position. Islam reached out his hand and cautiously approached the massive artifact. He touched the statue! Islam immediately felt an electrical pulse throughout his entire body. This was definitely more intense than the numbing sensation. He was not in any discomfort, nor was he concerned that he might have made a mistake.

Out of respect for his uncle and his waiting friend, Islam decided it was time to start back. This definitely had been an experience of a lifetime, but he had to get moving. He must have been gone for at least half-an-hour. Islam was concerned about getting back up through the tiny opening. *I dropped nearly three meters or so* he thought. Islam didn't think of it at the time (mainly because he was concerned about the time and his wonderful experience seeing the statue), but he recalled later that one of the most fascinating things that had happened to him that day had been the strength and agility he had demonstrated when jumping up to get back through the opening. Islam was not an exceptional athlete; however, that day he felt he could have tried out for the Egyptian Olympic basketball team and possibly have made the cut with his vertical jump and newfound coordination. If only he had had an outside jump shot, too!

When he crawled out of the vent, Islam brushed himself off and continued down the passageway to meet his friend. He hoped he was not upset. Islam decided to keep his little adventure to himself; he did not want his uncle to get into any trouble.

When Islam retreated from the pyramid, he did not see any trace of his uncle but profusely apologized to his patient friend for having taken so long. "What do you mean? You were only gone for five minutes or so," his friend said.

This could not be possible, thought Islam. He thought his friend was joking. "I had to have been in there for at least forty minutes or so," Islam said to his friend.

"No. Six minutes at most," said his friend.

Islam couldn't believe it, but he didn't press the issue. If his friend truly thought that he had been gone for only a few minutes, then his "secret" would be even safer than he had imagined, because there was nothing to explain about the "time lapse."

The next few days were particularly strange for Islam. He had a clearer mind than he had ever had during his entire life. He could see things clearly, *very clearly.* Schoolwork was easier. He found himself questioning the "hows and whys" of everything but then answering the questions himself! Islam felt that he was possibly smarter than usual and obviously attributed this to the peculiar encounter with the Khepri statue. It just had to be. He could do math equations that would normally have troubled him in a snap! His reading speed *and* comprehension were also noticeably improved. He tore through ten books (all on mathematical theories) over a three day span. He just knew that everything that was happening to him had to do with the statue. He was very focused and felt that he could achieve just about anything... until the dream.

Islam was very excited about his new energy and increased intelligence. He was especially pleased to find such an amazing passion for math, one of his favorite subjects but not necessarily his strongest. He was getting ready for bed the fourth night after having discovered the statue and was amazed at all that he had accomplished during the past three days. He really didn't sleep much over that period of time. Maybe it was just the adrenaline and unbelievable happenings. Islam was exhausted on the fourth night, though. He crawled into bed and was asleep within minutes. He started dreaming immediately.

He found himself on the very top of the pyramid where he had found the statue and saw a single small scarab crawling up the front side of the massive structure. He was not concerned. He looked to the east and saw that there were literally thousands of the same sized scarabs climbing toward him while he was still standing on the top of the pyramid. He looked behind him and saw one enormous scarab making the ascent toward him. It may have been nearly half the size of the pyramid. This scarab was clawing its way up the side of the pyramid with great speed and the vast structure was suffering severe damage from the insect's force. He had to do something. He looked in front and saw the single, small, non-threatening scarab approaching him at a fast pace. The thousands of small scarabs to Islam's right were nearly at the top now. The enormous scarab was on a mission to reach the top of the pyramid, and Islam did not want to meet this creature face-to-face.

Only one option, he thought. Islam took the plunge and slid all the way down to the bottom of the pyramid on the west side. He made it safely to the ground unharmed! He backed away and looked up to the top of the structure and saw that the gigantic scarab had positioned itself directly on top of the pyramid. It stabilized itself with its legs while thousands of small scarabs climbed on the large beetle's back. They unfurled and evenly covered the enormous scarab's back as if someone had dumped an entire truck of jellybeans on the back of the monster beetle. All the insects were facing in Islam's direction. It was eerily quiet when the final small scarab approached the front of the thousands of others and positioned itself near the forehead of the giant bug. The small scarab turned a bright green color, and then a major energy surge pulsated up the north, south and east sides of the pyramid, creating a bright light that swirled around all the scarabs positioned atop the pyramid.

The light was spinning at a fast pace and was gaining speed. Spinning, spinning. Faster and faster. The bugs were now taking a different form, a discus shape. They were still spinning and getting louder. All of a sudden, a loud "BANG" and the pyramid disappeared. It just vanished. There was no destruction, it was just invisible. The discus was taking form. It looked just like all the alien spaceships Islam had seen in comic books and movies. The sound was intense and reached a decibel level that was deafening. Islam could see a single green light. He couldn't make out the details of the light, but he assumed it was the small scarab and it seemed to take control of this spaceship. Then, in an instant, the alien craft that was hovering over what was once a pyramid only a short time ago took off toward Islam and disappeared in the starry Egyptian sky.

Throbbing pain. That is what Islam felt in his head when he awoke. "People talk about migraines. Although I have never had one, I would not wish the torture I experienced that day upon my very worst enemy," Islam said. He suffered the entire day with this incredible "headache" until late that evening. Then the pain stopped. Nothing. He felt perfectly normal. He felt as normal as he had prior to touching the statue. He was relieved. He also realized that those three days of gaining an outstanding level of intelligence, physical strength and stamina, and a passion for learning was a gift, a short-lived gift. The experience has affected him from his early childhood to the present day.

As Islam finished his tale, I looked toward Ahmed as if to say, "Do you believe this?"

Ahmed shook Islam's hand and they exchanged some words in Arabic. For some reason, I felt as if Ahmed were saying, "I understand, I know exactly what you are talking about."

I checked my wristwatch and noticed that we were running late, so I grabbed my rolled papyrus and followed Ahmed out of the shop. We left Islam behind, looking down at "his" papyrus and muttering to himself.

We emerged onto the streets of Cairo as rush hour was approaching. I should probably mention that Cairo is tied with Naples, Italy, for the most chaotic traffic I have ever been in. There is no way to describe it. It's like thousands of scarabs going in every direction! In fact, on our pyramid tour the day before we got into a fender bender. There was a lot of yelling back and forth and then everyone went his separate way. It is the Egyptian way.

Ahmed and I crossed two lanes of traffic and were almost sideswiped by a speeding Land Rover as we made it to a traffic island where we felt safe. Ahmed kept studying the traffic. I was planning on following his lead. A small Egyptian man in a white crocheted linen cap and wearing a long, wide, ornately embroidered robe-like garment with wide sleeves appeared next to us on the island.

"What is the matter?" He asked in English.

"We are just waiting for an opening," Ahmed explained in his British accent.

Walk Like an Egyptian

"Hah, this is Cairo, you must walk like an Egyptian!" And off he went, magically weaving through the maze of moving cars.

"But I *am* an Egyptian!" Ahmed called after him.

The little man waved to us once he made it to the other side of the street. We were able to find an opening in the traffic pattern a little later and made it back to the hotel in plenty of time to join Dr. Kalib's guests for dinner and my performance.

During the question and answer session following my show, a man from Oman asked me what was the most extraordinary thing I had ever experienced.

"I experience the extraordinary all the time," I replied. "Just yesterday for example, I was at Giza with the Sphinx and the pyramids and visited Imhotep's step pyramid. Then today, I visited the Cairo Museum. What an extraordinary place!" I gushed.

"And then after the museum, Ahmed and I visited a small shop and heard the most amazing story," I continued as I looked toward Ahmed for confirmation. Was it my imagination or did he subtly put his index finger to his lips indicating that I shouldn't speak to this group about Islam's tale?

"Next question," I stopped in mid-story.

The "Ignite Your Intuition" session the following day was well received. I will never forget the sight of four Arab men moving a table about a dance floor at their fingertips!

Late that night, Dr. Kalib dropped me at Cairo International Airport for my flight to New York. I was going to miss Dr. Kalib and his family. The hospitality they had shown me was extraordinary, to say the least. I waved goodbye and headed to the check-in counter. When I handed the counter agent my passport, he flipped through it and frowned.

"I will return," he said as he disappeared into a room behind the counter. Thirty minutes later he was back, telling me that I could not leave Egypt!

"Why?" I asked.

"You left while you were here and went to Saudi Arabia. You violated your business visa," he explained pointing to a Saudi Arabian stamp in my passport.

Fortunately, I had become proficient in reading Arabic numerals, and I pointed out that the stamp was from the prior year, 1997, not 1998, and I would be leaving Egypt as planned. I was pretty firm. I think he was setting me up for a bribe, but I had learned my lesson on a camel at Giza and at Djoser's pyramid. It is the *Egyptian way*!

CHAPTER EIGHT

Three Houses, Part I

As you probably know by now, I make my home in Wheeling, West Virginia. Oftentimes when I'm traveling and someone asks me where I live I say, "near Pittsburgh," which is the truth. Pittsburgh is the nearest major metropolitan area to my home. Pittsburgh International is also my "home" airport. I've learned to say this because it helps the person I'm conversing with get a geographical fix on my hometown. If I say I'm from West Virginia, I'm almost immediately greeted with "I have friends in Richmond," or "I've been to Virginia Beach." Not the same state, not really even that close. I can drive to Manhattan in less time than it would take to drive to Virginia Beach and be in Indianapolis or Detroit before I could reach Richmond. I live in what's called the Northern Panhandle of West Virginia. It's a narrow strip of land, maybe a dozen miles wide, squeezed between Ohio to the west and Pennsylvania to the east.

BOO! Just wanted to refocus your attention after that geography lesson and before we begin an *extraordinary* three-chapter experience. This experience did not take place in some faraway land but just to the west of Wheeling, across the Ohio River in a quaint little town called St. Clairsville, Ohio.

In St. Clairsville, a stretch of four houses (all next to each other in a row) were owned by a single person. Galen was his name. Galen was a good man and appreciated the history of these four houses he owned. He and his wife lived in an old brick house (this one *wasn't* haunted); his sister, Trudy, and husband, Earl, lived in the white house east of theirs; his sister, Glenda lived two doors down to the west of his house; and he rented out the other house directly next door to his own place. All houses were very elegant, well built and *huge.*

Galen was only the second owner of this "set" of houses. The original builder was a well-to-do judge who utilized each of these abodes much as Galen did. The judge's family of sons, daughters, and in-laws surrounded him on both sides. The judge spared no expense when he built these structures full of crystal chandeliers, imported fireplace mantles, marble and beautiful wood floors. Normally, hardwood floors on the ground level were oak. Once you moved to the second and third stories of these Victorian-style houses, a lesser-quality wood was used such as pine or poplar. This was not the case for the judge. He opted to go with oak on the second level and even in the *attic* in some of these homes! The point is that these beautiful, large homes were not cheaply built. They were never rickety or falling apart.

However, if you stood on the main road and looked at all three houses, you might develop a lump in your throat or feel a chill run up and down your spine. Any *single one of these houses* could have been used in those horror movies focusing on that eerie "haunted house."

People would pass the houses and would swear someone was standing in the attic window looking down at them; but when they looked up, they saw just a curtain flapping in the wind. I realize the mind plays tricks, but there have been so many reported sightings that you have to believe there just might be something to it. I've had that strange sensation *too many* times. The *chills*, the *willies,* the anticipation of just walking by these houses was overwhelming. And there were stories. Oh, yes, there were too many stories from reliable sources and unrelated sources as well. You're about to hear some of those stories. Are the "three houses" haunted? You be the judge.

Galen's sister, Trudy, was getting ready to go out with her husband one winter evening to the Heart Ball, an elegant charity ball held annually at the Belmont Hills Country Club. They never missed this event. It was *first class,* with the women and men on display showing off their most expensive dresses and formal wear. The finest food was catered by the most renowned chefs in the area, and a fun evening with friends included dancing and stimulating conversation. They were really looking forward to this night.

According to Earl, Trudy seemed to be primping and preparing for the ball the entire day. Her hair and makeup had to be perfect. Every prominent person in business, law and politics would be at this event. She had to look her best. About two hours before they were to leave, Trudy was putting the final touches on her hairdo in her bedroom. She was sitting in front of her vanity when she felt a cold draft blow across her body. Was a window open? Certainly a fan wouldn't be turned on at this time of year. These thoughts may have crossed her mind for just a fraction of a second before she came to grips with the truth. She knew. She had always known. Although she and her husband had never discussed it, they were both aware of the "strangeness" and the weird aura that surrounded the place where they lived. A spirit or something like it was watching her. Trudy looked at her arms. Although very smooth and feminine, the small fine hairs were standing on end and she was completely covered with goose bumps. Then she looked up from examining her arms. The way the vanity was positioned in her room, she could see the hallway reflected in the mirror. As she glanced up, she saw him. Not necessarily *him,* maybe *it.* A tall figure was looking back at her reflection in the mirror. She made eye contact, but was not going to look directly behind her at him to see if he was really standing there. It was as if time stood still for a moment. She didn't move. He—*or it*—didn't move. A tall figure well over six feet and faceless, wearing a black cape, pin-striped suit, black shirt, black tie and a flat, black-rimmed hat stood there. The cape was blowing in the wind. This had caused the cool wind she had felt earlier; but now a sense of warmth overcame her. It was not that she was flushed or that she might pass out, but rather a warmth that completely comforted her. Although this intruder was an uninvited and intimidating figure, she did not feel threatened. In the blink of an eye, while Trudy was looking at this thing dressed in black, he was gone. Trudy, not feeling any sort of uneasiness whatsoever, got up from her chair and sprinted to the doorway. She peered down the wide hallway that was well lit and glamorous like the rest of their house, and immediately that same cool breeze hit her right in the face. As she looked further down the long hallway, she saw the tail of the cape make the turn at the corner and disappear down the steps. She took off to get a glimpse again. The hallway felt as if it was 30 degrees cooler than her bedroom. As she made the turn, Earl was heading up the same staircase to check on her "primping progress" that the ghost had just whisked down. Trudy was not afraid. She just wanted to see the "Man in Black" one more time. She nearly knocked Earl down the flight of steps. He could tell something was bothering her. Trudy just didn't look like herself; and why was she running? A strange thing happened at that point. Trudy and Earl shared their most intimate secrets with each other and were happily married; however, Trudy didn't mention the "sighting" to Earl. "Did you see him?" "Where did he go?" "Did you get a look at his face?" "Are you freezing to death like me?" None of these questions were asked. Surely Earl would have noticed this ghost flying right past him down the stairs, right? Maybe Trudy was losing it. No, *it* was real. She had seen this spirit, and it would be etched in her mind until she died. She told Earl a little white lie. "I thought I was running late." Looking at her watch, she composed herself and added: "It's only five o'clock and I thought it was six o'clock."

"We still have plenty of time, dear," Earl said. He laughed and walked with her back to the bedroom where she could finish getting ready for the dinner/dance. He seemed so collected as if he knew what she had seen. Had he seen the "Man in Black" too? If so, why didn't he panic? Why didn't he say something? Maybe she was imagining things. It was just so realistic.

The ball was perfect. It was great to see old acquaintances, meet new ones and just enjoy the evening. But Trudy couldn't shake the image from earlier that night from her mind. It seemed so clear, so vivid and *real*. Why didn't Earl see the "Man in Black" glide past him on the staircase? Or *did* he? Earl seemed in control, but Trudy could sense that he was just a little bit uneasy about something. He trembled when he walked her down the hallway which was not as cold at that point, but maybe it was just she who was shaking. He took care of her 24/7, but could he protect her from this ghost? Did she *need* protection? Trudy still felt safe.

Weeks went by after that strange evening of the encounter with the mafioso-looking spirit. But each and every day since that incident, she had thought about the ghost constantly. She truly believed that this was not imagined. About a month after seeing *whatever it was* she saw, Trudy and Earl were sitting in the parlor enjoying a cup of tea and a late night snack. She decided it was time. Trudy needed to share this with somebody, and that somebody just had to be Earl. He wouldn't ostracize her. He wouldn't mock her. He might not believe it, but she had to talk about this incident. Earl had his face buried in the evening paper. The *Times Leader* reported a local steel strike, a break-in burglary in Eastern Ohio and predictions of a late spring. "I saw something the night of the ball," Trudy said. *Nothing.* She spoke to the back of the paper again. "He was dressed in black, Earl. I think he was a ghost," she added. She heard a turn of the page and the ruffling of the paper. "Honey, you must believe me. I am positive that I didn't imagine what I saw," Trudy pleaded. *Still no response.* Trudy heard a loud bang in the kitchen three rooms from the parlor. Earl didn't flinch. She turned around when she heard her husband curse and apologetically announce that he had broken a few pieces of Trudy's fine china. She turned around toward the kitchen. Earl was in the *other room*! *He* was the one making the noise in the kitchen! He must have gotten up to get more tea when she was deep into reading her novel. She knew what she would see when she turned around toward the chair. She knew that the "Man in Black" was sitting in her husband's seat. She felt the cool air again. When she looked toward the chair, he slowly lowered the paper that covered his face—or where his face *should have been*. She was obviously startled, but that calmness was still looming around her. This was so surreal and unexpected; yet she still was not afraid or alarmed by the presence of the ghost. Same black pinstriped suit. Same black flat-rimmed hat. And that cape. It blew behind him as he floated toward the alternate archway away from the parlor and toward the staircase. There was no eye contact as he didn't have a face, but a sense of peacefulness and tranquility was the general mood in the room. Almost simultaneously, when the "Man in Black" left the room and when a distraught Earl entered, Trudy fainted.

When Trudy gained consciousness, she saw Earl standing over her fanning her with the same paper that the "Man in Black" had been reading nearly ten minutes earlier. She thought she had been talking with Earl and telling him her secret, but it wasn't *Earl*. She had spilled her guts to the same thing that had been literally "haunting" her for weeks. *Now* she was concerned. Maybe she was hallucinating. Maybe she should be transported immediately to the mental institution. She had never experienced anything like this before. There had been no signs of ghosts, goblins or ghouls in her house until the night of the ball. She had a headache. Trudy felt as if all of the energy had been drained from her body. While lying limp on the beautiful parquet floor, Trudy looked up to see Earl's gentle face staring down at her. "You'll be alright," he said. She couldn't speak. Tears welled up in her eyes. She truly loved him, and he was taking care of her once again.

"I…" Trudy tried to speak.

Earl touched her lips with his index finger to silence her. "You're going to be fine," he re-assured her. Trudy's eyes slowly drew shut as she focused on Earl's kind and understanding face.

She didn't remember how she had ended up there, but Trudy awoke the next morning in her bed. Although she was out of it after she fainted the night before, the encounter with the ghost was still crystal clear in her mind. She felt better. Her headache was gone, but she was still a little weak. Things were probably going to change from this day forward. In Trudy's mind, Earl, Galen and the rest of her family would most likely be visiting her in the

Three Houses, Part I

"loony tunes" house 30 miles from their now authentic "haunted house." She wouldn't and couldn't live like this. It didn't matter what Earl thought of her. She just *had* to tell him the truth. She was shaking. Trudy had to tell him. She already had told him once, but unfortunately, it was to the "Man in Black," not to her husband, that she had spoken.

Earl entered the bedroom. He had coffee, juice, cereal and the poor result of his valiant effort to make his beautiful wife Eggs Benedict. She didn't care. Trudy knew he would still love her even if she turned out to be a true blue nut job.

"Earl, I have to tell you what I saw last night," she announced. "I think... no, I *know* that our house is haunted," Trudy said. Earl didn't speak. "I know it sounds crazy, but it's happened before, too," she added. There was no word from her husband. *He does think I'm a lunatic* Trudy thought. "I saw a ghost, Earl, a real ghost. He looked like...."

Earl interrupted. "No face, black suit, black cape, black hat," he said stoically. Her headache returned.

"What did you say?" Trudy asked already knowing the answer.

"A man. In black. Faceless. I've seen him too, Trudy," Earl said.

"But why didn't you say anything before?" she asked. Trudy was shocked, but somehow knew that she might not have been so understanding as Earl if it had been he telling her that he saw a ghost in their house.

"I wanted to, but I felt that as long as we weren't in any danger that you didn't need to get yourself upset. And... you might not have believed *me*," he chuckled.

"I *do* believe you, Earl. And I agree with you. He's not here to hurt us," she re-affirmed. A sense of relief flooded Trudy's veins. She had shared her secret with her very own husband and not only did he believe her, but he had seen the spirit, too.

Ghosts, goblins and ghouls. It seems like a scary Halloween story, but these two individuals were not lying. There were too many collaborating stories to be a coincidence. Trudy and Earl were not the type of people to make things up, either. The descriptions were strikingly accurate and the confirmation of the cold breeze, pinstriped suit and the overwhelming agreement that this spirit did not intend to harm either of them was uncanny evidence that they were *both* telling the truth. There was no reason to lie about this "third resident" who lived with them.

It didn't happen often, but they both saw this "Man in Black" during the period they lived in their house. It wasn't until years later after Earl had passed away and Trudy was living in a long-term care facility that she ever spoke of the ghost to anyone but her late husband. It was a beautiful spring afternoon, and Trudy was sitting outside the nursing home in her wheelchair when an attractive young man and his significant other were cautiously approaching her. "Excuse me, they said you were Trudy," the young man said. She acknowledged that she was. "We wanted to ask you something," he stated. "We recently moved into the area and bought a home a few miles from here. We found out you used to live there," he added. "This may sound strange, but...."

Trudy, although feeble, weak and shaky interrupted the young man and said: "No face, black suit, black cape, black hat." The man just stared back at her. His wife did the same. They just stared at Trudy in the garden at the old folk's home. Then the stares changed to smiles. Smiles of relief. Smiles of affirmation. The young man and his wife were just thrilled they could share their "ghost story" with someone else. So was Trudy.

CHAPTER NINE

Three Houses, Part II

Weird stuff, huh? Well, more *extraordinary* stories are coming your way from this stretch of "haunted houses" in Ohio. Some are not so comforting as Trudy and Earl's "Man in Black" ghost. Unfortunately, a few of the other tales I'm going to share with you are more Freddy Krueger than Casper oriented. But before we get into the ghost stories that will give you the willies, let me tell you about another one of Galen's relatives who lived in the house two homes west of his.

Although not as elaborate a home as Galen's or Trudy and Earl's home, Glenda's residence was still a beautiful Victorian; yet, it was not as large as the other two. Glenda was Galen's other sister. She was the youngest of the siblings and the most reserved as well. She had never married and had always contemplated becoming a nun, but never did. She was a sweet person and lived alone with her dog, Roger. Glenda was always the leader in organizing all family dinners each Sunday afternoon, on holidays and for other special events that usually centered on food. Glenda was an excellent cook and was dearly loved by her entire family, especially her nieces and nephews. Glenda's house was always open to the children after school, and she had absolutely the *best* toys to play with. Most importantly, she offered free access to all corners of her home. The attic, basement, spare bedrooms, family room, all nooks and crannies, and basically, anywhere a "spirit" might hang out were never off limits.

The first time Glenda recognized that there was a "presence" other than herself and her canine in the home was just a few years after she moved into the family owned mini-mansion. Glenda never had trouble sleeping. She was always "out" as soon as she hit the pillow, and most likely if she had ever married, her husband would have said she was a loud snorer as well. This, of course, could not, nor ever would be, corroborated; however, a few neighboring family members could hear her sawing logs during the summer months when the windows were open. Actually, according to unnamed sources, the noise level from Glenda's bedroom sounded more like a lumber company rather than just log sawing. Anyway, the point is that she rarely, if ever, was disturbed in the middle of the night.

One evening, Glenda did wake up when she heard Roger barking frantically. Dazed and confused, Glenda quickly composed herself, put on her housecoat and hurried to the hallway to see what the commotion was all about. Remember, back in those days, it was virtually unheard of for anyone to be robbed or burglarized. There was very little crime in the small community where Glenda and the rest of her family lived. It never crossed her mind that a prowler might be in her house until she saw a movement at the end of the hallway.

Again with the haunted hallways! Although she was a small woman who lived alone, Glenda always had been tough and not easily startled or frightened by anything. That was just her nature. Her nieces and nephews called her "Thunderball" for her feistiness and fearlessness but mostly because they loved the '60s James Bond movie of the same title. As in the previous story, whatever the movement was at the end of that hallway was non-threatening to her—a gut-feeling if you will.

Roger was growling, barking and in attack position protecting his master. But what was he actually going to attack? There was definitely something at the end of the hallway, but Glenda doubted that if Roger lunged toward this "intruder" he could really sink his teeth into the apparition.

Glenda, a skeptical person by nature, was not necessarily nervous but rather "cautiously curious" when she walked closer to get a better look at whatever was moving at the end of the hallway. Roger continued barking and was poised for the attack. As Glenda moved closer to the silhouette, she could see that the figure was a woman—a beautiful woman—with the most gorgeous face and warm eyes. Her dress was flowing and waved gently in the wind. A peacefulness came upon Glenda such as she had never experienced before in her life. Although this woman did not speak, Glenda knew that she meant her no harm. Roger could also never be accused of being a wimp. He followed his owner closer toward the "ghost woman" and fearlessly intended to protect Glenda. But when both of them moved closer, they could sense that they were in no danger whatsoever. Roger instantly stopped his barking and growling and just stared at the woman. You could not see through this spirit, but there was a transparency surrounding her body. Eye contact and the general aura of the encounter eased the minds of both Glenda and her dog. Although the spirit did not speak to Glenda, her eyes spoke with the great prose of a classic author. Glenda knew that this ghost was friendly and for some reason knew that she had a connection to the very house in which she lived. But she also knew that this woman was almost "lost" in a way. Yes, Glenda sensed all of this at once, like a tidal wave washing over her. Oh yes, she was wide awake now, and this image was very real.

Glenda must have stood and stared for what seemed like every bit of five minutes. But there was something else, another sense was aroused by the spirit's appearance. There was a hint of perfume. It was a sweet-smelling aroma that Glenda could not describe. It was nothing like she had ever smelled before. It was pleasant and calming, with hints of flowers and scents of all four seasons. The aroma seemed a perfect combination of various olfactory-stimulating fragrances, indescribable yet etched in her memory for a lifetime. This beautiful smelling "perfume" the ghost emitted was not hypnotic in the sense that she wanted control over those who viewed her; but rather as another stimulus to assure peacefulness and that she would not harm those she came in contact with at any time. Roger was sniffing like crazy and Glenda almost noticed a slight smile on his face.

Once again, non-verbal communication was occurring between the mortals and their houseguest. The beautiful face, flowing dress, perfume and even the understood presence of calmness shortly offered a welcome addition to the spirit's visit. A white cloud surrounded the apparition. The cloud was not smoke or even of a nebula-type; rather it seemed more angelic, as if this woman was from the heavens and sent with a non-threatening message. What was this message, though? Why Glenda? Why in St. Clairsville, Ohio?

The "Smiling Angel" (as she would now be referred to by Glenda) may not have clearly defined the reason for her appearing every now and then, but Glenda felt that she was a lost soul who had unfinished business here on earth and was trapped between real life and the hereafter. I guess she thought of her as *The Sixth Sense* type of spirit. She may have been right. I really don't know, but what we do know is that these first two ghosts (especially the

"Smiling Angel") were not a threat nor did they try to drive out or haunt the residents of the homes they occupied.

This friendly spirit appeared every three or four months to Glenda, her nieces and nephews, and to Roger the dog. Roger, by the way, really warmed up to the "Smiling Angel" after her first couple of visits. I want to be clear about this and possibly even connect these first two stories in some way, shape or form. Were the "Man in Black" and the "Smiling Angel" husband and wife? Lovers? Brother and sister? Maybe, maybe not. Nobody will ever know, since ghosts don't care (or are flat out unable) to grant interviews. Glenda had the determination and perseverance to delve more deeply into this mysterious and unique situation. She researched previous owners of her home. This wasn't hard to do as there had been only two: her brother and the judge who built all three of the houses in a row. But what about the occupants? Also an easy task. No history of psycho relatives. Everyone was (at least on the surface) "normal" and would not seem to be provoked to stick around and haunt after they passed on. But she couldn't possibly know all of their personalities and deep-rooted secrets. Glenda just had that "gut-feeling" again. She looked through countless numbers of scrapbooks handed down through the years by her own family and even was able to get in touch with a descendant of the judge's family. You will recall that the judge had built the homes. Genealogical charts and graphs, family trees, and the name, rank and serial numbers of every single aunt, uncle, brother, sister, or in-law were provided to Glenda by the great-granddaughter of the judge. They became friends, and Glenda shared the story of the "Man in Black" and the "Smiling Angel" with her. The judge's great-granddaughter never had encountered any of these ghosts. Galen's family had purchased the properties before she was born, but she did remember some of the stories and encounters with the strange and supernatural being told by her grandparents. They were mostly stories of unfriendly and even downright scary run-ins. These stories were not just about ghosts and goblins, but strange and creepy things that would happen in the houses that were unexplainable and seemed to be intended to inflict harm or induce fear. (Please plan on reading the next chapter in this book about those "bad ghosts").

This information was very interesting to Glenda, but there was still something she was missing regarding the two spirits she was familiar with. They had to be connected in some way, but nothing the judge's great-granddaughter provided to her was the link she needed.

Years went by before Glenda stumbled by accident upon what she was looking for. She had always been a reader. Not just because she lived alone and was looking for a way to pass the time, but Glenda was a very intelligent person with the desire to better herself intellectually. She was educated and took that extra step to find more information on the subjects that she was taught.

For instance, Glenda always had taken a liking to weather. Storm fronts, floods, snowstorms, you name it, Glenda liked it. She never missed watching or reading the weather forecasts, and she educated herself above and beyond what she had learned in school about meteorology. Glenda basically earned a self-taught master's degree in this subject and others. She would bury her head in countless books for hours on end to learn more about a subject that was interesting to her. She explored the effects of clashing cold fronts, the greenhouse effect, global warming and other issues and how they related to weather. She was a bona fide expert in the field with minimal formal education in the subject.

Another example of how Glenda educated herself was the history of the Civil War. "Thunderball" was a daily visitor to the St. Clairsville Public Library. She would retreat to her private cubicle and immerse herself into the strategies, doctrines, battles and prominent figures of the Civil War era. Glenda was a human database when it came to the dates, individuals and significance of this period in our country's history. Here's where the bolt of lightning hit her and the connection was made between the two ghosts, "The Man in Black" and "The Smiling Angel."

During the Civil War, most of the battles were fought in the original South. However a lot of the activity, especially when it came to slavery, occurred in the Northern Territory. Many slaves escaped to freedom in this part of the country. The way they were hidden and moved toward the Northern Territory was through a system of tunnels called the "Underground Railroad."

That was it! The connection was from this period of time, not when the three houses had been built, but *before* they existed. She knew exactly what she needed to find to make the correlation between that period and the present. She had to literally dig deeper and deeper into the ground to find what was under her own house! Glenda had to locate the maps of the Underground Railroad system. She was sure that she could find out the history of the land from that information. Months of research, miles and miles of traveling to major cities and museums and numerous phone conversations along with mail correspondence finally led Glenda to the answer she was looking for.

A very wealthy northerner owned a huge farm with hundreds of acres surrounding his home. The man had two children, a boy and a girl who were twins. His involvement with the Civil War and the abolishment of slavery engulfed his life. He eventually liquidated his assets and used his fortune to assist with the Underground Railroad system not just in the Ohio Valley area, but all across the Northern Territory. His children stayed with their mother who was a loving wife and mother. Their home was one of the many in the area that had a lantern outside. When the light was on, it was a signal to slaves that this house was a safe, anti-slavery home, and that they were welcome to use the underground tunnels to travel. The wife and her children helped hundreds of slaves move north to freedom.

Unfortunately, the mother passed away, and when the father returned, he died shortly thereafter upon hearing the news. Most likely he was overwhelmed with grief and regret that he hadn't been there for her and his children. The twins had no other living relatives that they knew of and had been taught to live off the land at a very early age. They were now in their late teens and by default stayed in the house they grew up in and learned to take care of themselves. One night, close to a year after their father had passed away, a fire engulfed the twins' house, and they both perished. Their deaths were significant since they had continued their parents' legacy and even as teenagers operated the Underground Railroad out of their home. The house was gone, but the tunnels remained intact. This part of the system was exposed and eventually was shut down. By then, the end of the war was approaching, President Lincoln signed the Emancipation Proclamation, and there was no further need for the slaves to secretly escape to the North. Their freedom was granted and legal.

The tragic deaths of the twins may have explained why their spirits continued to live within two of the three houses. You see, although there were no other structures built near the farm house that was destroyed during the Civil War era, the Underground Railroad still existed. Those tunnels still remained underneath the structures that were erected near the late-1800s, and included two of the three houses built on that land. That's right. Trudy and Glenda's homes were unknowingly built over the Underground Railroad tunnels which was "sacred" ground, so to speak. What an extensive research project initiated by Glenda!

Mystery solved, or sort of, anyway. We may never know what kind of trapped existence the twins ended up in or why, but good old Glenda found out another tidbit of information about those twins. You guessed it. The boy used to meet secretly with leaders in the community who were abolitionists and would arrange to assist the slaves who needed their help. This was very risky, and the boy gained well-deserved respect for risking his own life (and his sister's) to help others. When traveling to these secret rendezvous', he would dress in (no surprise here) all black to discreetly move in the dark. His sister would greet those in need in (once again, not a shock) full formal dresses that used to be her mother's. Once she became older and outgrew some of her own clothes and was too busy to make her own outfits, she wore her mother's gowns that were left behind after she passed away.

It probably wouldn't be too bold to assume that the scent of "The Smiling Angel" had to do with a combination of the perfume her mother had worn and the fresh aromas found on the farm where they resided. What about the "cloud" that surrounded her? We can only assume it represented memories of the fire.

CHAPTER TEN

Three Houses, Part III: The Final Chapter

Now, the "Nightmare on MAIN STREET" stories… I mentioned earlier that some of these tales might not actually be the "feel good" ghost story of the week. Well, here's one that isn't.

Although the previous two "extraordinary" stories were kind of weird, at least there was a common tie they shared: the spirits were not out to harm anyone. Maybe they were in a transitional state; or maybe they just didn't want to leave the neighborhood. At any rate, this third house was the one with the proverbial black cloud that had hung over it ever since it was constructed.

As previously mentioned, this was the house that was always rented. No *family* member ever lived in this structure. Throughout the years, numerous families rented this house, and nearly every tenant experienced something disturbing, frightening or just down right bone-chilling-spine-tingling-scary.

The rumors were prevalent about all three houses, but there was always a fear in the community concerning this specific home. Galen and family heard them all. Most were consistent. Most involved a group of spirits. All of these ghost stories were disturbing.

Three Houses, Part III

This story concerns a family that rented from Galen. The father was originally from the Ohio Valley area, but had moved to North Carolina for a few years. He missed the place where he had grown up, and loved the Valley. He was fortunate enough to land a good job with a coal company, and he, his wife, six-year-old son, and Boston terrier moved back "home."

The house was perfect for this particular family. There were three bedrooms, plenty of space and a lot of land for the dog to run. It looked good on paper, but later they found out there were a few other residents that lived there as well.

The first indication that there might be trouble was with the dog. Although a relatively hyperactive breed, this particular pet was very tame and rarely barked or made too much noise. Within hours after getting settled into their new rental house, the pooch was in the kitchen and froze in his tracks at the bottom of the butler's staircase. At first, the dog didn't even blink, but after about a minute he growled and started barking uncontrollably... at *nothing*.

This seemed strange to the mom and dad; so they ventured toward the steps to see what was wrong. The dog started jumping up and down and got between both of them so they couldn't walk up the stairs. Being a little dog, the mom finally grabbed him in mid-air so the dad could finally get past their pet. Described as a feeling of "unbearable coldness" and "complete despair," the dad stopped after about three steps. A feeling of utter sadness more than fear overtook the dad. The mom, still holding the hysterical dog, looked at her husband in the shadow of the back staircase. What she saw was not necessarily in human form, but rather a transparent figure. From her angle and in the dim lighting, she witnessed a pale, pitiful figure. Although the husband was still frozen and absolutely terrified of what he was feeling, he was not able to see this pathetic apparition. The mom screamed, dropped the dog and grabbed her husband's hand to pull him off the stairs and back down into the kitchen. The dad snapped out of his trance and was standing in the kitchen holding his wife close to his body. He was totally drenched with sweat, but was cold as an ice cube. It was almost as if he had had a fever and it had broken. He was beyond terrified by just the feeling he had experienced that had caused him to break out in a cold sweat. His body temperature had dropped so much that he was shivering uncontrollably. His wife looked toward the staircase, and the transparent figure literally vanished into thin air.

"What on earth happened to me?" he asked his wife. "I felt so cold, and my heart physically ached from sadness," he added.

"Didn't you see it?" she exclaimed. "He was hovering right next to you. A very pale figure with no expression."

"What are you talking about? There was nobody near me. I didn't see a thing," said her husband.

Out of nowhere, they heard a voice: "I did." Their six-year-old son was standing ON the staircase. Apparently, all of the commotion made by their dog had awakened the boy and he had come down the butler's staircase from upstairs. He said he had seen the same man as his mother "flying" near his father on the staircase. Strangely enough (and maybe because of his age and his not knowing these phenomena are very uncommon), the boy was not upset or bothered by any of these strange visions, waves of coldness and feelings of sadness.

Since they all had just moved in that same day, boxes of pots and pans, dishes, toys and suitcases of clothing were piled up everywhere. Without saying another word, the dad rummaged through a few suitcases and found one of his shirts. He took off the sweat-drenched shirt he was wearing, put a dry one on, grabbed the car keys and left with his wife, son and dog to go to a relative's house about ten miles from his newly rented house. Nothing was spoken about that night except that "the place isn't going to work out for us as we expected."

Although they had signed a lease, Galen was kind enough to let them out of the agreement. The dad said that the house was going to be too much for them to handle, but unbeknownst to her husband, the mom had told Galen the *real* reason. Galen confirmed that he had heard similar stories over the years from other tenants, but nothing so explicit and detailed as their experience. "You have been straight forward with me; so I wanted to let you know that you weren't the only family to have a strange experience in that home. You are NOT crazy, and I believe you. I will not make you pay rent to me if you don't want to live in this house, and I understand your concerns," he told the woman.

The house was very nice and wasn't difficult to rent. Another family would move in almost exactly thirty days later without a problem. The mom, dad, six-year old son and dog did not spend a single night in that house after they moved in.

Three different tenants lived in that home after the spirit appeared on the butler's stairs. None of them complained to Galen about being harassed by a ghost. Maybe they were bothered, but didn't want to speak up because he might think they were crazy; or maybe the spirit just didn't make his presence known. Nonetheless, the third family who lived in the house found something very interesting while putting their Christmas decorations away in the basement.

If you are familiar with old homes, you know what the cellars look like. No family room or big screen televisions will ever occupy these cramped, low-ceilinged "dungeons." Most of the old homes had either dirt floors or nothing better than concrete. Knob and tube wiring systems were visible on the support beams. There was not much potential to remodel or use the basement space for anything other than storage and a furnace room.

While the mother of the third family was storing the decorations after a fun-filled holiday season, she noticed at the far end of the "dungeon" a faint outline of a door, but no handle. Curiosity got the best of her and she proceeded to clear the dirt buildup out of the outline with a screwdriver and tried to pry the door open. It wouldn't budge. After being sidetracked, she realized that she had been working on getting this "door" open for nearly two hours. The kids would be coming home from school soon, and she had to get supper ready. She decided to finish storing the decorations and get to the kitchen soon. Although she wanted to see what was behind the possible opening, it could wait until later.

She forgot about the "door" for a few days, but a loud noise in the basement late one morning immediately triggered the memory of her discovery just a few days ago. The basement. What was that noise? It wasn't the furnace kicking in, the heat was already on. No, it sounded like a crash, as if something had fallen off a shelf or maybe some of the Christmas decorations had toppled over since they weren't stored properly. Although old basements are kind of creepy, she was never afraid to venture downstairs. The "dungeon" might have been a little dusty, but she had no fear until she reached the bottom of the steps. Coldness swept over her entire body and a feeling of overwhelming sadness made her gasp for breath. Once she had composed herself, she saw something that would change her life forever. The outline of the "door" was open! Although not completely ajar, she could see that it was indeed a door and could be opened. Was that where the noise had originated? Was someone in the house with her? Every single sensible thought she had told her to run back up the stairs, deadbolt the door, call the police and get out of that house. But she couldn't. She was drawn toward the door, and although the feelings of coldness and sadness frightened her, she somehow knew that going inside the secret passageway would be fine.

She was able to pry the door open far enough to peek inside. It was dark, but lighting from the main section shone directly on a light switch right by the inside of the secret door. She flipped it and it turned on a single bulb that hung from the ceiling. The room couldn't have been more than four feet by four feet. Possibly, it was an old coal chute room. She saw something immediately toward the back of the room. A chair was upended. Was that the sound she had heard upstairs? As she approached the chair, she let out a blood-curdling-horror-movie scream when she noticed a rope and noose hanging from the rafters. There was also a single piece of furniture next to this toppled chair. It was an old Victrola, a four-foot tall record player. It was covered with dust but she could see that it was in pretty nice condition. She lifted the lid and (you guessed it), the record started spinning and the music started to play! It was a strange 78 r.p.m. Irish record that sounded like a Leprechaun singing the lyrics to a demonic jig. Although 99.9% of us would most likely have bolted that scene as soon as we reached the bottom of the steps, she still stayed in the room! She shut the lid and the music stopped. Out of the corner of her eye, she saw a piece of worn parchment protruding from the side of the record player. Had she jarred something loose when she shut the top? It was a letter. Not a shopping list or a love letter, but a *suicide note*!

This true story of finding the suicide note tied all of the events together at the haunted rental house. The note was written by the younger brother of one of the tenants who had lived in the house in the early 1900s. Nobody even knew that he had lived there with his older brother. In those days, treatment for depression or psychosis was obviously different from what it is in this current day and age. The younger brother was taken in and basically "hidden" from society. I suppose the logic was that the older brother could keep his younger brother in the basement to possibly have a better life than that of being subjected to treatment in a turn-of-the-century mental facility.

The younger brother's note was very simple, yet disturbing. It read: *I have been a burden to you, my very own brother, and know something is not right in my mind. I never wanted to be this way and live in fear everyday. I am sorry for causing you pain and I have no other option now but to say goodbye.*

The woman stood near the opening of the door near this small room where a very depressed man most likely had hanged himself after a long battle with his own demons. Her mood was somber, but unlike the coldness and sadness that had engulfed the family on the butler's staircase, a sense of serenity and even a sweet smell that was like a mixture of aromatic spices/perfume floated right under her nose. Without hesitation, she turned off the light switch and closed the door. She felt that the spirit of this depressed man could now move on once the truth was known and that he was "released" from the tortures he had encountered during his life (and possibly death).

The confusing part about this experience to her was that there were no remains. Where was the skeleton of this man who had hanged himself? Did any other family member besides his brother know about his *existence* let alone his mental condition?

She kept this entire encounter to herself for nearly a year. When she was retrieving the Christmas decorations the next holiday season, the memory was triggered again. The woman did not notice it the first time, but when she ventured into the basement on her second trip to get the garland, she noticed the outline of "the door" had been sealed. Just a very faint trace of the outline existed. She approached and saw that the crack had been sealed tight but not with mortar or caulking. This seal was "natural," as if nothing ever had existed there before. *Well, I'm not surprised,* she thought. She was not afraid, but wasn't in the mood to decorate due to the sight of this "self-sealing" door. The combination of keeping all of this inside and the creepiness of the suicide ghost led her upstairs to the kitchen where she made herself a drink. No Kool-Aid, but a stiff gin and tonic to soothe her nerves. The reason wasn't clear, but after she downed the first drink, she made herself another and headed BACK DOWNSTAIRS to the basement! She stood merely sipping on the second cocktail this time and stared at the sealed door. She slowly raised her glass, said a silent prayer for the man who had taken his own life and just stood there for a few minutes overtaken by disbelief and sorrow. Just as she was ready to head back upstairs, the same spice/perfume aroma filled the air and then quickly disappeared. "Peace at last," she said aloud.

She told her husband the entire story that night. At first he might have questioned her drinking during mid-day and she could have been hallucinating; but he, too, had experienced numerous strange encounters over the years they had lived there as tenants. He believed her—always had, always would.

About four months later, she was planting flowers in her front yard for the spring and needed some stones to surround her flower bed. The backyard of the rental house was about three acres and was a very steep, uninhabitable tract of land. It had once been an old "landfill" not too far under the surface of dirt you might find different "treasures" such as old medicine bottles, ceramic collectibles and other items. She found some stones nearly two acres deep into the property behind her house and was getting ready to push her wheelbarrow up the hill to finish her project when she noticed a large white bowl or something sticking out of the ground. She knew that some of the past tenants and owners of the land would occasionally set out on an "archeological dig" on this property looking for old glass bottles, etc. She headed toward this "bowl" and immediately realized that it was nothing close to what she had thought it was. It was a skull. A HUMAN skull.

After contacting the authorities, an investigation began. They were not able to use DNA like they do in these modern times; and the *CSI:Miami* team of detectives did not show up at the scene. These remains found were from a human years ago. Technology wasn't running rampant at the turn of the century, but one thing did exist—*dental records.* The investigation took nearly a year-and-a-half, but they eventually found out that the skull was the body of a mental patient who was housed in nearby Cambridge, Ohio for a year in 1905. The man was released (after unsuccessful shock treatments) to the custody of his own brother. The caretaker was unable to properly tend to his sibling's needs (physical or psychological). It was just too hard for the older brother, so he kept his insane brother out of sight in the basement of the house. When the younger brother was discovered by his older brother in the basement hanging from a noose, he most likely panicked and hurriedly buried his own sibling behind the house in the woods. Who would ever find this out? Nobody even knew that the insane brother even lived there! The guilt the older brother felt because of the years of helplessness in caring for his sibling, coupled with him not even giving his younger brother a proper funeral drove him to the brink... This was way too much for the older brother to handle; so he, too, took his own life. It was a double suicide; but at the time, only one body (the older brother) was found in the home—the younger brother's body was discovered nearly seventy-five years later.

Two ghosts in this haunted house. One brother with a mind that took over his life and soul, now at peace. Another brother who tried to care for his own flesh and blood; but he, too eventually went mad and took his own life. Was *he* the spirit on the butler stairs? Will he *ever* find peace?

When the tragedy became exposed and the mystery had been solved, the woman again ventured into the basement almost the same time as the year before when she had had a toast and prayed for the man who had committed suicide in the basement. She, and her husband who was with her this time, both lifted their glasses in remembrance of BOTH brothers. As she turned to head back upstairs, her husband noticed a faint light behind an old outline of a door and asked what kind of perfume his wife was wearing....

CHAPTER ELEVEN

Bigfoot, Marmots and Mormons

I have always enjoyed Spokane, Washington. The city just resonates well with me. It's not too big, not too small. The downtown area is still alive and vibrant. Riverfront Park developed from the remnants of the 1974 World's Fair, Expo '74, is a centerpiece of downtown with a bit of a European feel to it. Then there is Spokane Falls, beautiful waterfalls cascading through the middle of town. You can walk across a series of bridges and marvel at the raging whitewater rapids. I've been traveling there since the mid '80s. I've done corporate presentations at the beautifully restored Davenport Hotel, and I've played many of the nearby colleges a time or two. I most frequently fly into Spokane to play Eastern Washington University in nearby Cheney. I've played there at least a half-dozen times over the years.

I actually love the Pacific Northwest in general. I've had some of my best day hikes on the Olympic Peninsula in Washington and along the Oregon Coast. Still, some of my best memories are of Spokane. I remember being there in January one year. It was bitterly cold, and I had the weekend off. I went to the Spokane Zoo, which sadly is no longer there. I think I was the only visitor that day. I would go by the concession hut to warm up and fill up on hot chocolate and then wander around the zoo. Since it was winter, and a very cold one that year, the animals weren't used to seeing anyone in the zoo. This was a plus for me. You know how it is, you go to a zoo, walk up to the tiger cage and try to spot a tiger's tail poking out from behind a rock. Well, on this winter's day, the animals came to me. A tiger padded down a path in his enclosure coming right up to the fence! I walked up to the bison pen and a large bison came right up to the fence, eyeing me! After a few minutes of this staring contest he started to snort and sounded pretty perturbed; so I backed away. It took me a while to realize that the animals were reacting this way because the only person they saw this time of year was a zookeeper who fed them. They weren't accustomed to a freezing, hot chocolate drinking tourist wandering around.

One year, I was on what seemed to be a month long college tour throughout the Pacific Northwest. I believe it was 20 shows in twenty-five days. I had some time off. Early in the tour, I was finishing up some work in the Seattle area, and I mentioned to my contact at the school that I would be heading over to Spokane a day or two early. He wanted to know why I didn't spend the time off in Seattle. And while I love Seattle, Spokane was calling my name. It's hard to explain, especially to someone from Seattle.

Charlotte was going to join me at the end of the tour. We were going to spend some time in Seattle and some time in Spokane. The two or three days in Seattle already had been planned: dinner at the top of the Space Needle, shopping in Pike Place Market while watching those crazy fish tossers at the Pike Place Fish Market, then watching live fish at the world class Seattle Aquarium. We would stay at a downtown hotel close to a monorail system that would get us everywhere we needed to be. On our way over to Spokane, about a four-hour drive, we planned to overnight thirty minutes outside of Seattle at The Salish Lodge, one of my all-time favorite hotels. It's a boutique hotel with a wonderful spa and sits at the crest of Snoqualmie Falls in the foothills of the Cascade Mountains. When Charlotte joined me later in the month, we had a wonderful overnight stay there including a hike to the bottom of the falls, a great spa session and one of the best breakfasts we've ever had—I think it was a six course meal.

But back to Spokane... I was on a mission to locate a nice hotel for Charlotte to stay in. I would be there too, of course, but back in those days when I had time off I rarely, if ever, treated myself. I would just find an inexpensive motel and bed down for the night. However, with Charlotte along this was turning into a vacation, and we really wanted to enjoy ourselves.

At the time, there was a company called Cavanaugh's that seemed to have a monopoly on any nice downtown hotel in Spokane. There was

Bigfoot, Marmots and Mormons

Cavanaugh's on the River, Cavanaugh's in the Park, etc. I was exploring these properties, checking out the rooms, the amenities and the grounds when I had my first encounter with a marmot.

I had left the lobby of Cavanaugh's on the River and walked around to the riverbank at the back of the hotel. Suddenly, I saw a half dozen furry little heads pop up over the riverbank. Within seconds, I was surrounded by a dozen or more animals I thought were prairie dogs. I love animals, but I was a bit frightened by the sudden onslaught of these curious creatures. They ran right up to me and stared at me while twitching their noses. After my initial surprise, I deduced that they must be pretty tame and they were probably looking for food. I have my mother's gene when it comes to wanting to feed every animal I come in contact with; so I left the hotel and headed to a nearby drugstore looking for some trail mix.

While at the drugstore, I was told that these animals were marmots which are basically large rodents, but they are so cute! When I arrived back in Marmotville with my trail mix in hand a feeding frenzy ensued! They would come right up to me and take the raisins and peanuts from my hand. I could pop a tasty treat right into their mouth. It didn't take long to get rid of two bags of trail mix. I also noticed that some of the animals preferred certain treats more than others. For example, there was a rather large "Momma Marmot" and she loved the raisins, ignoring a peanut until a raisin came her way. Others were partial to the peanuts and didn't care for the raisins while still others wanted to feast only on sunflower seeds. It may sound odd, especially if you're not an animal lover, but I had so much fun!

To this day, whenever I'm in Spokane and have some free time I usually have a late lunch at Clinkerdagger (the Cajun chicken pasta fettuccini is my favorite) which overlooks the falls, and then I head down to the river to get in touch with my inner marmot provided it's not their hibernation period. I was so sad when I found out the marmots hibernate, and there are some trips I have to make to Spokane that are destined to be marmot-less.

A day after my initial marmot encounter, I was performing at Eastern Washington University. After the show, I was talking with a group of students. Out of the corner of my eye, I noticed a large, bearded man in a flannel shirt, worn blue jeans and dirty hiking boots rocking back and forth on his heels and staying just within ear shot of my conversation with the students, but obviously choosing not to participate.

A bright eyed blonde freshman from California was quizzing me about the show and then bemoaning the fact that she left SoCal to come to Cheney, Washington, to attend school. She had yet to visit beautiful

119

downtown Spokane; so I tried to tell her how wonderful I thought it was. At some point the conversation turned to marmots. However, a curious thing happened. There was a communication breakdown between us. As I began to tell her about my marmot experience, she thought I was saying *Mormon*, and every time she said Mormon, I thought she was saying *marmot*. We figured it out, but it was definitely a strange conversation, especially for her. To give you a better idea, it went something like this:

"I love Spokane. Did you know that you can go down by the river and feed the *marmots*?"

"Really, there are *Mormons* down by the river?"

"Oh yes, whole families of *marmots*! I get trail mix and feed it to them. They love it."

"You mean these *Mormons* live by the river?"

"Yes, I've never seen so many *marmots* in one place. The first time I went down to the river they all came running up to me, begging for food."

"You're kidding. There are families of *Mormons* living by the river who beg for food?"

"Not only that but they like different kinds of treats. For example, yesterday, I was feeding a big momma *marmot* raisins only, she loved them and would turn her nose up at a peanut or sunflower seed."

"That doesn't sound like the *Mormon*s I know."

"You know *marmots*?"

"Sure, that's not that unusual, I went to school with several families of *Mormons* in California."

"Now, you're the one kidding me, *marmots* don't go to school, not even in California."

"How can you be so prejudiced, just because you don't understand someone's religion doesn't mean you have to be so ignorant and judgmental!"

At that point I knew something was wrong. We traced back the conversation and discovered the problem. Everyone had a good laugh.

After the *Mormon — marmot* incident, the students disbursed and I began packing up my show props. I couldn't help but notice that the bearded man was still in the ballroom. He started moving toward me. It was obvious he wanted something, but what?

"Excuse me buddy," he said as he approached.

"Yes sir, what can I do for you?" I replied.

"I loved that marmot story! They are feisty little creatures, tasty too, if you get the spices just right!"

I thought he was kidding, but then I looked in his eyes, realized he wasn't, and I cringed.

"That was a good show you put on tonight. Amazin' stuff. If it wasn't for something that happened to me a while back I would say it was the most amazin' thing I ever saw."

"Well, thank you, I appreciate it."

He just stared at me and then it hit me that he wanted me to ask him what had happened "a while back." I was curious, but I was also tired. I gave in, and I'm glad I did.

"What happened to you?"

He looked over his shoulder then looked back at me and whispered, "I came face-to-face with Bigfoot."

"Really?" I asked. "You mean Sasquatch?"

"That's the one," he answered.

Of course, I was familiar with the legend of Bigfoot, a large, hairy primate wandering the deeply forested areas of the Pacific Northwest, from Northern California to British Columbia. Its "cousin," the Abominable Snowman (or Yeti) was also said to exist on the other side of the world in the Himalayas. I was also aware that very few people had ever seen the creature. The major evidence for its existence were huge footprints found in isolated areas throughout the Pacific Northwest. I had done a show at Spokane Community College during this particular tour, and I recalled seeing a statue of Bigfoot in the hallway of the student center. The school had adopted the mythical creature as its mascot. I was definitely in Bigfoot country.

"First things first, my name's Ben Robinson, but you can call me Big Ben," he said. "You know, I've made a study of these things. Seein' one can really light a fire under you to find out what they're all about.

"They accept 'em as fact in Tibet. Big, hairy wild men, whole tribes of 'em wanderin' around in the mountain snows. There are reports from the late 1800s from Europeans tellin' about 'em. In the early '20s a climbing team from England was goin' up Mount Everest and at about 17,000 feet saw these big shadows ahead of 'em on the mountain. When they got to where the shadows were, no one was there. But, there were these humongous footprints in the snow.

"In the '50s these other explorers were checkin' out routes to climb Everest and at 18,000 feet they found fresh tracks which they followed for a mile. I believe these tracks were about 13 inches long and eight inches wide," Big Ben educated me.

"Other people have seen smaller versions of the creature and spotted smaller footprints. All the prints look pretty much the same, five toes, like a human, but the foot is usually wider. You got your ginormous prints and your little prints. I think there's more than one creature, whole tribes of 'em in fact—males, females, big ones, little ones, young ones and old ones just like your marmots," he went on.

"Know what else?" he asked. Without waiting for my reply he jumped right in. "In Mongolia, there are these hairy manlike creatures called Almas. The locals take 'em for granted, know they exist and accept 'em. Now they're not big like my Bigfoot, more human size, maybe even a little on the short side, covered in hair with long arms, human hands and fingers, and they can run like the devil."

This Almas species was a new one to me, but I have to say, Big Ben was spot on with his history. Everything checked out when I looked into it later. Big Ben was a true aficionado of the weird, wild and wonderfully strange creatures that may or may not inhabit our planet.

"Then there was Zana," he said.

"What's a Zana, is that another species of Bigfoot?" I asked.

"Nah, Zana was an Almas. I believe it was the late 1800s when she was captured. A farmer kept her in a stone pen for years. She was ornery, mean, violent. She was scary lookin', all hairy, great big teeth, big ass jaw, flat nose, high cheekbones and red ringed eyes. They would just toss her food into the pen. No one dared get near her. She dug a hole in the dirt and slept there. After several years, she seemed to calm down. They got her out of the pen and would tie her to a post, like a dog.

"Then she started doing chores around the farm. She couldn't stand being inside, got too hot. They tried to teach her to talk, but she never did learn. She would communicate in a way though, mainly through grunts, like a caveman.

"Do you believe all this?" I asked.

"'Course I do. You would too if you saw what I saw. An experience like that can change your mind in a heartbeat."

"But what did you see?" I pushed for him to get on with his personal story.

"I'm comin' to that. I just figured if I filled you in on the history of these creatures, you might find my story more believable," he replied.

"I'm not some crackpot ya know. For example, those little Indian fellas that guide the mountain climbers, the Sherpas, they say that so few people have seen a Yeti 'cause it can turn itself invisible at will. Now that's just plain ridiculous! I don't think these things are supernatural beings. I think they're caught between monkey and man on the evolution chain. Simple as that," Big Ben explained.

"OK, tell me more about Zana," I said.

"The weirdest part of this Zana story is that she had babies, half human and half Almas babies!"

"That's a bit far fetched," I said and then realized how ridiculous that sounded based on the conversation Big Ben and I had been having.

"Not at all, " he replied. You've heard of lonely farmers getting friendly with sheep, right?"

"Well, I am from West Virginia and I've heard stories. I like to believe it's all an exaggeration," I answered.

"Well, it ain't. Sheep aren't the only animals neither. Now think about this, you got this almost human creature who is really a slave. You got a lonely farmer and his friends. Put two and two together. I mean we're talkin' late 1800s Mongolia here, not 20th century Spokane," Big Ben said.

"I think she had four babies that lived. She lost the first few babies. She'd get pregnant, deliver the baby on her own and then take it to the river to wash it. She'd end up drowning the baby by mistake. After this happened a couple of times, the villagers would take the babies away and raise them with human families."

"What were they like, these half-human, half-Almas children?" I asked.

"Not much different than you and me. Came out more human than Almas. They could talk. Dark skinned though, and unruly. They were very strong. In the '60s this Russian scientist went to Zana's hometown to investigate all the stories. People live a long time in those mountains. He said he talked with people who remembered Zana, even went to her funeral. He talked with some of her grandchildren. One of 'em gave a display of strength for him. He had a man, a man mind you, sit in a chair. Then he picked up the chair, with the man in it, using nothin' but his teeth!" Big Ben went on.

"Wow, that is some story," was all I could say.

"So you have these things spotted in the Himalayas and Mongolia," I stated, trying to keep the geography of the story straight.

"China too," offered Big Ben. "They're called Wildmen there. Those things are more like my Bigfoot."

"So tell me about your Bigfoot," I said.

"The American Indians were the first to encounter Bigfoot. That's where the name Sasquatch comes from. It's a Salish tribe word meaning wild man of the woods," Big Ben began. I felt as if I had just enrolled in *Bigfoot 101*, taught by Professor Big Ben Robinson.

"In 1811, the first tracks were sighted by a white man. Canadian trader name of Thompson saw 'em in the mountain snow near Jasper, Alberta. In 1884, there was a report of a little one being captured but he escaped. A bunch of 'em were said to have attacked a prospector's camp. Sightings continued here and there from 1811 'til today, but it was the stories of the Yeti comin' out of Mount Everest in the '50s that really caused people to take a hard look. People reckoned if scientists were takin' an interest in the possibility of a giant man-beast in that part of the world maybe there was something to all the stories coming out over the years in this part of the world."

"Makes sense," I said.

"A fella named Green and a fella named Dahinden started lookin' for Bigfoot. They were obsessed. They collected every story they could find and they found some doozies! Real life, face-to-face encounters. Like this trapper named Roe up in B.C. He thought he stumbled on a grizzly bear in the woods messin' around in the bushes, but then the darned thing stands up on its hind legs and looks right at him. It was a female, breasts and all. He said the thing was about six feet tall and about 300 pounds, all covered in dark brown hair. He said that when the thing saw him she showed surprise on her face. He almost peed his pants! He thought about shootin' it but he said he couldn't even raise his rifle 'cause it was so human like. Anyway, she just turned her back on him and walked away, deeper into the forest. And you know what?" Big Ben asked.

"No, what?" was all I could come up with in reply.

"The damned thing lifted its head back and laughed!"

"Really?"

"Yep, that's what Roe said. Another fella named Ostman was kidnapped from his camp by a family of Bigfoots and held captive in a canyon in 1924. They grabbed him while he was asleep in his sleepin' bag and carried him 25 miles to their home. There were four of 'em. A big 'ol eight-foot male, a seven-foot female, a seven-foot young male and a smaller, younger female. He said they never tried to hurt him, but they kept him for six days. He escaped by giving the big male a can of snuff. Made him sick, and in all the confusion he bolted. He never told no one this story until 1957 when he met up with Green. He was glad that someone was takin' the Bigfoot thing seriously. He thought anyone else would think he was crazy."

"Yeah, I can see that," I said.

"In the late '50s they were building a road into the forests around Bluff Creek in Northern California. About every day a guy named Crew would come out to start work on his 'dozer and he would find these big tracks in the mud all around the machine... 16 inches long—Bigfoot. They would follow the tracks into the woods but then lose sight of 'em. It seemed like the Bigfoots were checkin' out the machinery at night and then sneakin' off into the woods before sun up.

"'Course Green got wind of this and headed off to Bluff Creek. Whole bunch of tracks were found by Green and others. One set of tracks led to a 55 gallon drum of oil, 175 feet from the road. It was like a Bigfoot got hold of it and carried it off. You know how heavy a 55 gallon drum of oil is?"

"Pretty heavy," I answered.

"They did the same thing with a 250 pound truck tire. These things are strong. They traced tracks up and down terrain that man couldn't navigate."

I wanted to ask him how man could trace the tracks if man couldn't navigate the terrain, but Big Ben was on a roll.

"Walkin' stride of four feet, runnin' stride of ten, big suckers. Hundreds of tracks were found. People seen actual Bigfoots too in Bluff Creek—doctors, hunters, outdoorsmen. Some reporter asked a Huppa Indian what he thought the creatures might be and the Indian said, 'Good Lord, have the white men finally gotten around to that?'

"See, people who been in the woods a long time or livin' in the mountains be it Mount Everest, Mongolia, China or right here, the ones that should know the best, know these things exist. They are real. I know now too," he stated, making me more curious to hear of his personal encounter.

"'Bout ten years after the first track sightings at Bluff Creek, we're talkin' late '60s, another Bigfoot hunter came to the area. This guy's name was Patterson, and he got a movie of the thing!"

Now this I was familiar with. I had actually seen the film during a theatrical documentary on Bigfoot. It was interesting. I tried to tell Big Ben this but he was difficult to successfully interrupt.

"Patterson and his buddy were out on horseback lookin' for Bigfoot. They were ridin' right along side Bluff Creek when all of a sudden they came up on a big female. She spooked the horses. Patterson's horse reared up and threw him. He was freakin' out. Still had the right mind to grab his camera

125

and run after the Bigfoot. She wasn't hostile. Just seemed a little startled with the horses and men up on her all of a sudden like that. She loped off into the woods with Patterson followin', filmin' her. Then he ran out of film, and the Bigfoot was gone, vanished into the woods. The men's horses had run off, and they had to go find 'em. They got the animals and brought 'em back to where they saw the Bigfoot. Got a beautiful set of plaster casts of footprints and the movie. You should see it," he said.

"Oh, I have. It was very convincing. Kind of jerky as you would expect a terrified man-on-the-run's camerawork to look like, but impressive nonetheless. I guess it comes down to belief. If you believe it to be real, there's your proof. If you think it was a hoax, which it certainly could be, then it means nothing," I said.

"Yeah, I know what you mean," Big Ben replied. "It's personal experience that counts. I believe most of the stories, 'cept for the Sherpa's invisible Yeti one, but I wouldn't have believed 'em before I had my own experience. I would have probably thought they were all just hoaxes or tall tales. Now I believe each and every one because they all seem possible to me because of what I experienced. Hey, wait a second, where did you say you were from?" Big Ben suddenly asked.

"West Virginia but the northern part of the state. I live an hour outside of Pittsburgh, Pennsylvania," I responded.

"Well there you go! Normally, I wouldn't have told you this, but do you remember a series of Bigfoot sightings near your home back in the '70s? Happened around a town called Greensburg," Big Ben wanted to know.

"Not that I can remember. I know Greensburg, it's less than an hour-and-a-half from my home. Tell me more."

"Well I think this is all pure bull. I'm only tellin' you this 'cause I want you to see that while I believe most of the Bigfoot stories, I know some just gotta be made up. I think it was '73 and Bigfoots were popping up all over western Pennsylvania. But the weird thing is, these creatures were always seen during UFO sightings. UFOs were big back then, sightings every week. Anyway, these three kids saw a UFO land in a field and went to investigate. Two big, gray colored, eight-foot tall hairy apelike creatures came out of the UFO and approached them. One of the kids fired a rifle over their heads but they kept a comin'. Then he shot one! The thing cried out in pain, the UFO took off, and the creatures went off into the woods. The police came and investigated but found no evidence of any UFO landing or the creatures. It did stink though, sulfur smell that made everyone sick. The new theory is that the Bigfoots materialize 'cause of the UFOs. Either they're space creatures, or—here's the kicker—they come into our world through the energy of the witnesses. The UFOs suck out the energy from the people and that allows the Bigfoots, or whatever, to enter our world through some other dimension. Or, get this, the UFOs are some kind of electromagnetic energy that gets released geologically and this energy then plays tricks with the witnesses' minds, hypnotizes 'em into seeing things like UFOs and Bigfoot," Big Ben explained.

"Now, that is farfetched, I'm not even sure I understood what you just told me," I said.

"See, isn't it easier to believe that these things are really just a kind of missing link? They're rare, they stay out of sight, live in remote areas and are rarely seen. But, they are seen, I'm proof," Big Ben added.

"OK, Big Ben, tell me, what happened to you."

"You know Walla Walla?" he asked.

"Sure, the city so nice they named it twice! I play Whitman College down there."

"Well, we're talking mid '80s. In '82 this guy from the National Forest Service, Paul Freeman, was trackin' some elk along an old loggin' road when he saw a Bigfoot comin' down a hill no more than 60 yards away from him. The thing saw Freeman and ran. Freeman investigated with some other forest guys and they found 21 footprints. They did the usual, made the plaster casts. About a week later, Freeman was back on the loggin' road and found some more tracks; so they made more casts. When this scientist, anthropologist, is that the right word?"

I nodded yes.

"Anyway when this anthropologist, Krantz, got to lookin' at 'em he decided the tracks were from two separate Bigfoots and when he really got to lookin' at 'em he discovered all those swirls and rings in the footprints, you know, like fingerprints. He even found sweat glands, you can't fake that. Krantz thinks there are maybe a half dozen Bigfoots roaming around Walla Walla."

"So, is Walla Walla where you saw your Bigfoot?" I prodded.

"Yep, in the Blue Mountains, near there. I was hikin', huntin' and campin'. I'm kind of a lone wolf. I had been out for about three days. It was nighttime and I was bedded down. All of a sudden, I hear some noise. Sounds like someone is messin' around my campfire. I poked my head out of my tent but didn't see anything. I went back to sleep and then I heard noises again. This time, I grabbed my rifle and burst out of the tent. Nothin'. There was a smell though. Not as strong as a skunk but that's what it reminded me of. Between the smell and the scare, I had a hard time going back to sleep, but I managed. The next morning, I found these big tracks around my campfire. I measured 'em, 17 inches long by ten inches wide. Hair stood up on the back of my neck, creepy," Big Ben said.

"Now, I knew about Bigfoot of course. Can't grow up in these parts and not be aware of him. I had no explanation unless someone was trying to play a big joke on me, but who would go to that trouble? Track me out into the woods, make big fake tracks and not leave any of their own. I mean I can see a guy walkin' around the fire with big fake shoes on, leaving big fake tracks, but why? Why way out there and why me?" Big Ben went on.

"I thought about packin' up and leavin', but something told me to stay; so I did. I spent another day in the great outdoors doin' my thing, and then it was time to call it a day. I have to admit, it was hard to go to sleep. About two in the morning, I hear noises again. This time, I'm ready. I got my flashlight and my rifle and I'm all quiet. I lifted the flap of my tent a bit and I could hear better, smell better too—same smell as the night before. This time, the noise wasn't comin' from the campfire but farther off, into the woods. I snuck out of the tent and hid behind a tree, just watchin' and waitin'. It probably was just a few minutes, but it seemed like hours, and all of a sudden the noise starts gettin' closer. Something or someone is right there with me, just off the camp site. I didn't want to turn on my flashlight just yet, and I was hopin' that whatever it was would come close enough to the campfire so that I could see it." Big Ben was getting visibly excited as he continued his story.

"Then, BAM, there it is, in the light of the fire. First, it was just a shadow, then I could plainly see it. Big, 'ol hairy thing. I swear, it had to be close to seven-feet tall and it was all hunched over, big 'ol head, didn't even seem to have a neck, long danglin' arms. It was a dark brown color. I had to get a better look; so I turned on my flashlight, makin' sure my rifle was still right next to me. I shone that light in its face and it looked shocked. Just kind of stared at me for a second, then it threw its arm up to cover its eyes. I don't know why, but I started to approach it. He turned around, ran off, very fast and just as fast as that, he was gone.

"Do I have to tell ya, I didn't get any sleep the rest of the night. I did find fresh tracks in the morning. I was goin' to pack up and head out, but I wanted to stay, too. It's hard to describe how I felt. Stay, I did, for two more days. I spent most of the daylight hours lookin' through the woods, tryin' to find a trace of Bigfoot. And I spent the nights awake in my sleepin' bag waitin' for his return. But he never came back. Finally, I packed up and left."

"What an adventure," I said.

"You believe me, don't you?" he asked.

"I don't know, I guess so. I mean to be honest Ben, I don't know you and you've told me more about Sasquatch in the last few minutes than I've ever known; so I do want to thank you for the conversation and the education."

"Well magic man, I don't know if I believe you either. I mean you did some fancy tricks, some of 'em could be real, but you could be a big hoax too."

I had to laugh and then agree with him, "Yes, I certainly could."

At that point, the custodian came into the ballroom to shut off the lights and lock up the student center. I looked around, and sure enough, some time had passed. The chairs were all put away and it was just Big Ben, the custodian and me in the building. Big Ben and I said our goodbyes and parted ways, him wondering about my stage show and me wondering about his experience with Bigfoot.

Cryptozoologists, scientists who study previously unknown species of animals, theorize that if the likes of Sasquatch, Yeti and the Almas do exist they are most likely some type of "missing link" just as Big Ben surmised. The fact that there are only sightings and footprints to go by, no real physical evidence, doesn't deter many people's belief in at least the possibility of a breed of hairy hominoid roaming the planet.

Cryptozoologists, who are potential believers in Bigfoot, will be quick to tell you that an unknown species of shark (Megamouth) was found in Hawaii in 1976, and another was netted in California eight years later. Then there is the story of the coelacanth, a large, armored covered fish with big bulging eyes. The fish was known to zoologists but was thought to have been extinct for seventy million years. When a coelacanth was caught off the coast of Mozambique in 1938, the textbooks had to be rewritten. The giant Komodo dragon has been around for one-hundred-million years but has only been recognized by science for a century. The giant panda, found only in China and Tibet, was first seen by a Westerner in the early 1900s.

What do I think? I really don't know. There is some convincing evidence, thousands of footprints, thousands of sightings. The Patterson film has come under fire. While Patterson died in 1972 and swore on his deathbed that the film was legitimate, a man recently claimed to have made the Bigfoot costume and sold it to Patterson. Two other men claimed they wore the Bigfoot suit. However, no one can offer any proof, and you have to be just as skeptical of these claims as you have to be of Patterson's claims. I mean, why wait this long, and where's their proof? Couldn't they just be seeking publicity like they said Patterson was?

I can tell you one thing. A year or so after my encounter with Big Ben, I was hiking in Oregon in the Umpqua National Forest, heading toward Salt Creek Falls, the second highest waterfall in the state. After I viewed the falls, I headed off into the woods, deeper and deeper. The foliage became very heavy and it was dark. I stayed on well-marked trails and was out for about four hours. Not once did I see another person and the forest seemed to go on and on forever. At one point, a large bird of prey, swooped down right in front of me, soared over the trail and into the canyon off to my right. I didn't know if it was a hawk or an eagle, but it was startling. As I hiked on, I started to calculate how long it would take to get back to my car. Then I started thinking about Big Ben. Then I started thinking that no one knew I was hiking in the forest. All this thinking unnerved me to the point that I cut my hike short and headed back to my car early. Could a Bigfoot-like creature live in this kind of terrain and only be spotted occasionally? It certainly could.

CHAPTER TWELVE

Out of Control on 9/11

Control. I've always striven to grab the reigns and charge full steam ahead—with *me* calling the shots. This is not out of vanity or a deep inner desire to build up power, but rather to not have to place blame on anyone but myself. When you travel as much as I do, you obviously have to let go of that feeling of control when you're flying (unless, of course, you're John Travolta).

Through day-to-day experiences, we tend to realize that we can't always have it the way it's mapped out on the "how-to-live-your-life" game plan. September 11, 2001 was one of those days.

On September 11th, I was at Boston's Logan Airport, scheduled to fly to Denver aboard United 505 which left at 8:00 a.m. My plane left two minutes later and from an adjacent gate to the ill-fated United 175, which hit the south tower of the World Trade Center sixty-three minutes later, at 9:03 a.m.

Cruising at 35,000 feet, I had a bulkhead seat in the "economy plus" section, and I was just taking off my shoes and reclining my seat a bit when the pilot's voice came over the intercom, "Attention ladies and gentlemen, this is your captain speaking. Something unusual has happened. A terrorist act has been committed. The FAA has ordered all aircraft out of the sky. We are not in any danger, but we have been diverted to the nearest major airport,

Detroit. We'll be landing in approximately thirty minutes. Once we're on the ground, you'll be given further information."

Oh great! I thought. *What's really going on? The FAA isn't going to order every plane out of the sky. There must be a bomb threat concerning a Boston flight and we'll have to land in Detroit, have the plane swept for explosives and then we'll be back in the air. It may be a two-hour delay, but I'll still make the show in Colorado Springs!*

As we landed in Detroit, I could hear some of the passengers talking on their cell phones and I could hear people sniffling as if they were trying to hold back tears. We were instructed to head to baggage claim to retrieve our luggage. I still thought the bomb threat was the most likely scenario.

As soon as I got off the plane, I called Charlotte. She answered in tears.

"Oh honey, you're all right, thank God!"

"What's going on Char?"

"Terrorists, they crashed a plane… two planes into the World Trade Center and a third plane into the Pentagon. It's unbelievable, I can't take my eyes off the TV, and the images are so horrifying."

"Oh my God," I said to my half-hysterical wife.

"They haven't identified the planes that hit, only that they came from Boston. I was so worried."

"Well, I'm OK. I'm in Detroit. I'm headed down to get my bags, and they said we would get further instructions. I'll call you back. Don't worry honey, I love you."

"I love you too, come home soon," Charlotte said as our signal dropped and the call failed.

Everyone in baggage claim was gathered around a few TV monitors watching those images of the Twin Towers that have become permanently etched into all our minds. That's when the enormity of what happened started to sink in. I immediately thought of our friend, Stan, who worked at the Pentagon. Was he OK? It seemed as if the world had gone mad.

I soon found out that I wouldn't be going anywhere, anytime soon, via an aircraft. Detroit is only five hours from my home; so I thought I better try to get a rental car. It was nearly impossible to get a cell signal due to the high volume of calls. I finally got through to Hertz and made a reservation for an immediate pick-up at the Detroit airport location for a one-way rental with a drop in Pittsburgh. It didn't appear as if my bags were going to come anytime soon; so I boarded the rental car bus and headed over to the Hertz lot.

It was pandemonium at the rental car lot. I'm a Hertz #1 Club member, and as I walked up and prepared to join the line which snaked around the building, I thought I might as well check the #1 Club board just in case they had been able to process my rental in the short amount of time since I had made the call. To my surprise, my name was on the board! I went over to my car, took the rental agreement and the keys and then headed back to the bus to return to baggage claim in order to retrieve my luggage.

On the way back to the airport, I phoned Charlotte and got through on the third attempt. I let her know I would be at the Pittsburgh Airport in five to six hours time and she said she would meet me there. Then she said, "Another plane went down."

"You're kidding?"

"Of course I'm not kidding. It crashed in Pennsylvania, close to Somerset. They think it was headed to D.C. or Camp David."

"How many more are up there?" I wondered aloud.

"That's why they ordered every plane out of the sky," Charlotte replied as the horrible, potential possibilities flooded my thoughts.

I just wanted to get home and hold Charlotte. I made it. Charlotte had called the next date on the tour, Lander University in South Carolina. She asked if they still wanted me on campus. They immediately said yes. The student activities people really wanted the students to have a distraction from the horrific events of 9/11, if only for an hour or two. We made the overnight drive to South Carolina.

Next stop, Teikyo Post University in Connecticut. They wanted the show too. We made another overnight drive. In Connecticut, you could really feel the effects of 9/11. Many of the students were from the New York City area, and many of them had friends or relatives who worked on Wall Street.

I secured another rental car in Hartford, Connecticut, as Charlotte headed back home. The news media continued to announce that air travel would resume in twenty-four hours, but it was now two days after 9/11. I drove to Maine for a show and then down to New Hampshire for another. Four days after 9/11 and air travel had still not resumed. I was off on Sunday, September 16th, and I remember that that was the first day I saw an airplane in the sky. It was a strange sight as the skies had become so open, so quiet, and so lonely. I was sitting atop Kearsarge Mountain as I watched the lone plane fly overhead. I decided to hike in an effort to clear my head and get a grip on what the world had become and what the ramifications of this terrorist attack would be.

On Monday, September 17th, I played another college show, this one in Massachusetts. This was the fifth show I had done since 9/11. It amazed me that the schools didn't want to cancel, but on the other hand, it made perfect sense. Everyone needed a distraction, a laugh, something else to focus on. I was happy to have the work. It kept my mind on something other than that terrible day.

I had an e-ticket reservation for a flight from Hartford to Columbus, Ohio, on Tuesday, September 18th, a week following the attacks. My plane was scheduled to leave on time. It was very eerie in the airport. There were very few travelers, and everyone was so quiet. After our departure from Hartford, we flew over the Manhattan skyline. I remember it was an absolutely beautiful day, the Twin Towers, or the site of the Twin Towers, was still smoldering, smoke billowing into the clear, blue sky.

I was seated next to a man on this flight. We were both very quiet at first, but then we started to talk and, of course, our talk revolved around what had happened the week before. I was wondering what the future would hold and if I would ever have control over my travel again. My seatmate, I'll call him Henry, ended up helping me understand that I don't have to have control over every situation.

Henry was in Boston at the same time I was on 9/11. Like everyone else that day, we were all stunned, angry, confused and yes, *afraid.* This is Henry's remarkable story of an encounter he had that day at the airport:

"Dozens of stranded passengers and airline personnel were gathered around the televisions in the Crown Room at the airport," Henry told me. "I was standing while listening and watching when a pilot at a nearby table asked if I wanted to have the empty seat next to him," Henry said.

"There's a chair here with your name on it, buddy. Take a load off and relax," the pilot said to Henry.

"We introduced ourselves; however, that was about the extent of my involvement as Captain Trent Schuler began to describe an event that had happened to him, that undoubtedly impacted my own life," Henry explained.

"The pilot did not intentionally monopolize the conversation nor was he being disrespectful in not attempting to find out about me. I suppose he knew that I was just the person who needed to hear this incredible story about accepting that some things that happen are just plain out of your control," Henry added.

I feel your pain, Henry, I thought to myself.

"Pleased to meet you. My name is Trent," said the pilot.

134

"Actually Capt. Trenton G. Schuler according to both his security identification badge and nametag. Captain Schuler began to tell his tale within a nanosecond after I said, my name is Henry," my seatmate informed me.

"You know, Henry, I have logged thousands of miles at thousands of feet in the air all over the world. But I must admit, that if there was ever a life-altering experience that would end up bringing my own personal faith to the foreground, then *that* was the day," Captain Schuler testified.

Henry said to me, "Craig, you've always heard stories begin how it 'was a dark and stormy night,' or that 'there was something in the air that evening—you just felt it.' By gosh, if Captain Schuler didn't use *both* of these dramatic intros to begin his amazing story!"

"We got the weather report from the tower, and my crew didn't look too happy. I wasn't thrilled with the news either, I suppose," Trent told Henry.

"Our 727 was being de-iced as we waited on the runway for takeoff. Our flight was delayed for forty-five minutes because of the snowstorm developing in central Colorado prior to our trip from Denver to Seattle. I had a very strange feeling like something could go wrong, Henry," the captain continued.

"Trent recalled that all pre-flight checks were all cleared and there was nothing out of the ordinary that he or his crew found peculiar. But they just *felt* it," Henry told me.

"The flight pattern would take 148 passengers due west and then north to elude any turbulence and danger caused by the storm. The hardest part about the ascent in any type of bad weather is initially the visibility factor. Once you're above the clouds, you are usually pretty comfortable until the approach. With the advances in technology and communication, the human factor in flying a plane is minimized," Schuler continued.

My thought: *Yeah, it seems like a breeze maneuvering a two hundred ton hunk of metal off the ground to 30,000 feet and then gently floating it back to earth.*

"But I never liked the ascent," Trent re-confirmed.

Henry continued to tell the story Captain Trent Schuler shared with him that day in Boston: "Take off. No problem yet. Visibility was surprisingly clear, but within the first hour of the initial westward pattern every single person sealed within the metal tube with wings would be challenged to put aside their fears and literally 'let go' of the common human reaction to seize the moment or control the situation," Schuler said.

"Engine one sputtered and shut down without warning. Like a pickpocket on the street, a casual, unintentional bump goes unnoticed, and then you find out your cash is gone moments later. But you probably couldn't have controlled what happened anyway," Schuler explained to Henry.

I thought, *There's that word "control" again.*

"It seemed strange, but for some reason I expected the reaction," Schuler explained to Henry. "A sense of calmness not only among the crew members, but with the passengers as well. We experienced an immediate drop in altitude after the engine went out, but promptly regained control and leveled off at our safe cruising level. The main concern was clearing the mountain ranges during the crucial ascent period after takeoff. To add fuel to the fire, visibility was worsening," Schuler added.

"The way Captain Schuler had described the engine shut down it became very obvious that everyone on that aircraft was aware that there was definitely a major problem," Henry explained to me. He conveyed that Schuler told him that the calmness displayed by all passengers could have been interpreted in one of two ways: either these individuals *knew* that their fate had been sealed and were paralyzed with fear keeping them silent; or, a tranquil, peaceful reaction to the situation overtook their minds and bodies. "I had no doubt that it was the 'peaceful' reason, Craig," Henry said to me.

"That feeling of time standing still… like the silence of a snowfall, yet you hear the noise, an out-of-body experience that gave them a sense that they were watching the entire situation from their family room recliners, but the remote control was out of reach. Yes, there was only one channel broadcasting right now and it was listed in *TV Guide* as a horror movie; however, the spirit of the group was one of relaxation and confidence that everything would be OK one way or another. No screaming, not even a peep. To make matters worse, ground communication was inoperative." Schuler told Henry.

But of course, I thought to myself.

"As I reached for the intercom, to inform our passengers about the engine failure, I glanced at the instrument panel and noticed the altitude at 7,777. That just stuck with me because of the repetitiveness. Kind of like waiting and watching and sometimes speeding up to see your car odometer hit a major mileage landmark," Schuler said. He addressed the passengers and staff over the intercom: "This is your captain speaking. We are currently addressing an engine malfunction and ask that you continue to remain calm. Our ground control communication has been temporarily cut off, and we are attempting to regain contact as well."

"Still not a clamor or even whispering about the bad news," the captain said to Henry.

Schuler continued with his address to all those aboard his flight, "We will attempt to make an emergency…."

Sputter, bump, total silence.

"Henry, I've got to tell you again. These people were totally motionless. I'm re-emphasizing to you that anyone could have heard the proverbial pin drop and we had **no engines running at all**! The descent was nauseating even for a veteran pilot like myself. Well, I suppose I really wasn't trained in Losing-Both-of-Your-Engines-and-Crashing-an-Airliner-101. My initial reaction along with my co-pilot was to level off the plane to avoid the rapid descent. Remember, we had no engines. I guess it's kind of like turning the light switch on during a power outage. It's just a reaction. This all happened so fast. I would have been just as effective if I had gotten up and walked back to business class, found a seat, buckled up and started reading the crash information card. But I stayed put. And I will admit to you that it didn't really scare me. We were heading straight back to earth and I was hoping that I might be bouncing back to heaven after that," Schuler said. Henry had been captivated by this story and was virtually speechless until both he and Captain Schuler said simultaneously "but then…"

"But then…," Schuler continued. "The most life changing experience anyone could ever encounter happened to every single passenger on our plane. Since becoming airborne and losing the first engine, it had been nearly one hour. It had been less than sixty seconds since the second engine stopped. All of a sudden, both engines became functional and we were immediately able to level off the plane and begin a rapid ascent. But it seemed more than just mechanics, Henry. It seemed like the plane was being guided by strings, (kind of like those old model airplanes that you would spin around in circles), but instead, we were being pulled straight up to a safe cruising altitude. Yes, the engines were working again, but I am telling you straight forward, that there was no way we should have, or could have, recovered so quickly from our potential perilous demise. And here's the strange part," Schuler told Henry.

Oh man, it gets even freakier, I thought to myself again.

"Still no noise my friend. Still no screaming, crying, laughing, clapping. Nothing. We're talking close to 150 people on board who should have crashed and burned, and *not a sound* I tell you!" Schuler explained. "We knew at this time that we were probably going to make it. The plane was still climbing to a higher altitude, although we still did not re-establish ground control contact," the captain continued.

Schuler eloquently described the "strangest" part to Henry: "Just about one hour into the flight. Still heading due west. No communication yet. Then the most spectacular thing happened. The snow stopped and the afternoon sky literally opened up into the most magnificent sunset that you could ever imagine. Dusk was approaching and the view was serene and spectacular. Reds, oranges, purples and blues were streaked through the horizon and every single soul on our plane was humbled and appreciated life more than anyone for that brief moment," Schuler said.

"When he was telling me this story, Craig, he got really choked up. The captain was intelligent and an obviously strong man but had to pause for a moment and compose himself. He was overtaken emotionally and was truly certain that a miracle of some sort had taken place during this flight. The captain composed himself and apologized to me for getting emotional," Henry told me.

Henry said that Captain Trent Schuler looked at him right in the eyes and said, "Henry, I don't really know who else saw what happened next, but I know what it was!"

"The most beautiful and spectacular image that I have ever seen or could ever imagine appeared in the middle of the pastel painted sky and brought a sense of peace into my heart that warmed me like... I really can't describe it. It was a feeling that was almost non-human. Kind of like I was personally given a gift while still alive that I didn't deserve, but you'll never hear me complain or try to give it back. An angelical face with caring eyes and a delicate smile that made me feel like I was and will always be protected and looked after. A flowing robe with a brilliance and splendor hovered within feet of the cockpit window. No words needed to be spoken to me. I knew at that moment that our lives on earth are precious and that we don't have a lot of time to make an impact on other lives. It was real, Henry. It lasted for only a few seconds, but the overwhelming impact would never leave my human body. It was truly a gift. My life was spared, and I had to give something back. I had already made the decision that I would help others and leave my mark on this earth by doing something useful. Not that being a pilot made me a deadbeat. I just knew that in the few years that I have left, that I wanted to use this second chance at life to assist those who need help and guidance," Schuler explained to Henry.

"I have another thing to add, Henry," Schuler said. "Remember the number, 7,777, that I told you that I saw on the altitude gauge when we were having the engine trouble? Well, after the flight, I mapped out our course and calculated at that time that we were smack dab in the middle of the Mount Lamborn range. Not a single mountain, hill or peak under 10,000 feet. And that's a fact," the captain added.

Trent Schuler again looked deep into Henry's eyes with a piercing yet concerned gaze and spoke: "I hope that this story helps with the struggle that you're experiencing at this time, my friend. You cannot *control* everything. That is the moral of my story. There are stronger forces out there, Henry, and you are not expected to solve all of these issues. Live your life as a good man, husband and teacher. That's all you can be asked to do. You can call it faith. You can call it trust. You can call it anything you want, but you have to know that you're not alone. You'll be guided and you don't have to take all of the responsibility on all by yourself," the captain explained to Henry.

"I was visibly stunned and still speechless. What a story! What a lesson! What timing! What a special person!" Henry said to me.

"The airport was still full of stranded passengers and most were still in shock about the tragedies caused by the terrorists earlier that morning on 9/11. Captain Schuler stood up and shook my hand," Henry said.

"I have to be leaving now, Henry. I enjoyed the time spent with you and wish you well in life," Schuler told Henry.

"My jaw was wide open in amazement, and I couldn't even respond to him, Craig," Henry told me.

"I watched as this tall man with an extraordinary presence limped away, opened the Crown Room door and exited. Within seconds I composed myself, gathered my belongings and took off after Trent, at least get his address, find out where he lives, anything to remain in touch with the man who just made such a serious impact on my life," Henry said to me.

"As I ran out the Crown Room exit, I assumed that I would be able to find him with relative ease since his handicap limited him to walking fast. I looked left. Not a trace. I looked right. No Captain Schuler. Which way? I chose right and did the O. J. Simpson run through the airport corridor. No Captain Schuler. How about the nearest restrooms?" Henry continued.

"The restrooms were checked—no sign of Captain Schuler," Henry explained.

"No worries... I could check with my friend who works for the airline in Hartford to check on Captain Trent Schuler," Henry added.

"I finally was able to leave Boston the next day. I also got in touch with my wife and kids to let them know that I was OK and would be home as soon as possible. I was sad, and grieved with 260 million other Americans for the loss of innocent lives. I still do. But I had developed a calmness about what I can or cannot control, and I owe this change to Captain Trent Schuler," Henry told me.

"This morning, I arrived a few hours earlier than I needed to so I could meet with Frank, my contact at the airline office. I told him about the fascinating man who had impacted my life at the Crown Room in Boston. I wanted to find him and thank him for the inspirational story he shared with me. I envisioned us keeping in contact, eventually becoming friends, possibly visiting each other. I knew Frank could help me. He had all relevant personnel information at his fingertips. I just wanted to get Trent's address," Henry said.

"Frank went back to his office for about fifteen or twenty minutes. I waited patiently in the lobby and scanned through a few year-old *Sports Illustrated* magazines. When he returned, he had a strange look on his face. Almost a 'what drugs have you been taking' gaze," Henry said.

"Did you find his address, Frank? Where does Trent live?" Henry quizzed his friend.

"You mean where *did* he live?" Frank responded.

"What in the world are you talking about?" Henry asked.

"Henry, are you sure we're talking about the same Captain Trent Schuler?" Frank retorted.

"Of course! I saw his security I. D. tag and his gold plated pin. What did you find out?" Henry asked his friend again.

"Come back to my office, Henry," Frank said.

"We walked into the room and he motioned me to step behind his cluttered desk. Without divulging any personal information yet, he scrolled up to show me a picture on his computer screen," Henry explained to me.

"Is this the guy, Henry?" Frank asked.

"Yes, 100%," Henry confirmed.

"Frank's face contorted into a puzzled and disturbed expression that almost seemed comical," my seatmate described his friend's reaction to Henry's positive identification of Captain Trent Schuler.

"Captain Trent G. Schuler is deceased," Frank said.

Complete silence.

"Are you positive? It's impossible. I just sat down and had a two-hour conversation with him a week ago," Henry broke the silence as he couldn't believe what he was hearing.

"Frank seemed skeptical but I felt that he knew I was telling the truth. Frank provided explicit details about Captain Schuler's life after he resigned from being a pilot. He literally packed a few necessities and took off for Africa and assisted delivering supplies to small communities in a small, outdated cargo plane. While in Kenya, he was making a delivery for the Red Cross and actually swerved to miss a gazelle on the dirt landing strip and crashed. He did not die from the accident, but he did hurt his leg. Infection set in, and since medical supplies were virtually non-existent in this small village, Captain Schuler passed away," Henry explained.

"I didn't need to ask which leg it was. I knew it was his left. I saw him walk after the accident—one week ago," Henry added.

"Oh, another thing, Henry—can you believe it? He died on September 11th, 1991, ten years to the day *before* you met him," Frank said.

"I did meet him on 9/11. I did believe his story. And so did the co-pilot. I found the seventy-eight-year-old ex-aviator, and he rehashed the same story *verbatim* to me. Yes, Captain Trent G. Schuler certainly made an impact on my life," Henry said to me.

Mine, too, I thought.

CHAPTER THIRTEEN

Wanna Bet? (A Gift)

Gambling. Showgirls. Booze. Tom Jones.

Whether or not you like these aforementioned persons or events, they are still vices that are undoubtedly affiliated with "Sin City," otherwise known as Las Vegas, Nevada.

Yes, it was just a matter of time before we came up with an "extraordinary" story about this quiet little town. Sorry it took so long.

I love Las Vegas! I'm fortunate enough to travel to this one-of-a-kind city multiple times a year for corporate appearances. Over the years I've performed on "The Strip" at the Wynn, Encore, Venetian, Mirage, Caesars Palace, Bellagio, Bally's, Paris, Planet Hollywood, Rio, Las Vegas Hilton, Alexis Park, MGM Grand and Mandalay Bay. I've also worked off the Strip at the Green Valley Ranch Resort in Henderson and at the Loews Lake Las Vegas Resort.

If you go to Las Vegas, you really should do it right. Stay on the Strip at one of the mega-resorts. Skip the buffets and have a wonderful dinner at your choice of some of the best gastronomic experiences available in the country (Alex at the Wynn, Le Cirque at the Bellagio or Valentino at the Venetian). Enjoy world class shopping at the Grand Canal Shops at the Venetian, the Forum Shops at Caesars Palace or the Wynn Esplanade. Hit a hot club like Rain in the Desert or the Ghostbar at the Palms (actually the

Wanna Bet? (A Gift)

Palms Casino Resort is pretty much one big party) or check out XS at Encore or Studio 54 at MGM. Vegas has so much packed into the less than three miles that separates Mandalay Bay from the Wynn/Encore complex that you can't possibly get bored, and at night Vegas lights up like the Fourth of July. It's a neon explosion.

Oh, there's gambling too. I'm not a gambler. It just doesn't excite me, but plenty of people are. I sat next to a friend of mine at a Bellagio blackjack table and watched him play against the dealer for about fifteen minutes. He lost a couple hundred dollars. It was just him and the dealer. The cards were flying by so fast I don't know how he kept up with the action. It's just not my thing.

And don't stay more than three days! Vegas has a way of burning you out. If you want a slice of life to remind you of where you are, put on your sunglasses and walk the Strip. It's a bit like walking through hell (especially if the temperature is 100 degrees or more)! You'll see intoxicated people stumbling along with a beer in their hand or perhaps a margarita in a yard-long, custom container from one of the bars. There will be parents dragging their kids in and out of casinos. Las Vegas is no place for children, trust me. Don't even try to rationalize it by saying but we can see the Grand Canyon and Hoover Dam. There was an attempt a decade ago to make Sin City "family friendly." The MGM even built a massive amusement park to help attract a family crowd. It didn't work. On the streets there are endless lines of "snappers." These guys are just lined up, one after the other snapping photos of naked women in your face. They're advertising escort services, and some of the snappers are wearing T-shirts promising service to your hotel room within twenty minutes. Will Feisley, a young friend of mine, on a first time visit to Vegas asked one of the snappers, "If she's not there in twenty minutes, do I get her free, like Dominos?" The humor was lost on the snapper because he didn't speak English. In addition to the naked lady photos, you'll also see nearly nude young (and not so young) women roaming the streets. People let their hair down in Vegas.

But most of all catch a show... a *good* show. There are entertainment spectaculars in Las Vegas the likes of which you won't find anywhere else in the world, and there are so many options. I am a huge Cirque du Soleil® (Circus of the Sun) fan. If you've never seen one of their shows, you can't go wrong by buying a ticket to *Mystère* at Treasure Island. If you've seen one of the French Canadian Cirque du Soleil's creations but haven't seen *"O"* at the Bellagio, you won't be disappointed. It's the best of Cirque du Soleil®, with acrobats, synchronized swimmers and divers performing in, on and above the water to create an unbelievable experience. I liken it to watching a giant piece of art unfold before your eyes. Maybe you don't like the circus. Do you enjoy music? *Love* at the Mirage is a celebration of the Beatles done through the artistic eyes of the Cirque du Soleil® team. It doesn't feel like a typical Cirque du Soleil® show, and it is a wonderful production.

I am, naturally, a big fan of magic. Penn & Teller hold court at the Rio in a venue that is more like a modern performing arts center than a Vegas showroom. Penn & Teller are really performance artists as much as they are magicians. They make you think. If you're in the mood for an amazing, quirky, thought provoking and funny show, P&T could be the right choice for you. Lance Burton presents a classic, magical illusion show at the Monte Carlo in an opulent theater that is an experience in itself. And, you will often find David Copperfield, one of the most influential magicians of the 20th century and one of the greatest illusionists of all time appearing at the MGM Grand in a relatively intimate 800-seat theater.

I had just performed at the Paris as the closing general session for a national trade association's convention. It was a late afternoon presentation and that meant my evening was free; so I headed over to the MGM to watch David Copperfield perform his magic. Copperfield had just introduced an illusion called "Portal" into his show during which the master illusionist magically transports himself and an audience member to a remote, tropical island location where the audience member is reunited with a long-lost family member in an emotional finale as Copperfield reappears onstage. There is a live TV feed to the island, and while logic dictates that this just can't happen (remember, it's magic) it seems so very real. As part of the presentation, the illusionist asks his audience to close their eyes and think of a special place (his special place was the remote, tropical island) a place they would like to be. I closed my eyes and envisioned myself on the flagstone terrace that spans the back of our home in West Virginia. There was a fire in the stone fireplace and Charlotte was with me. We were each drinking a glass of red wine. The terrace faded, the fireplace faded and the wine was gone. All that was left in my mental image were Charlotte's big, blue eyes. It was obvious I was homesick. I had been on the road for a very long time. After this visualization exercise ended, Copperfield presented his "Portal" illusion much to the delight of the audience.

As I filed out of the theater, I couldn't help but notice that a large crowd had gathered around a craps table. The crowd was witnessing one of the *luckiest men ever* in action.

Wanna Bet? (A Gift)

John (we'll call him that in this chapter to protect the innocent) started the night with $500 in cash. He knew the specifics of the entire evening to a tee. He knew which table to head for, where he would stand, the precise time he would begin gambling (although his venture would be a "sure bet") and how long he would be there. He also knew the woman to the right of him and the man to the left of him... well, not really "knew" them, but rather he knew that they would be there. He had never met these two people who would become a big part of his evening, but he knew what they looked like before even setting eyes on them.

I couldn't resist. The aura that drew me to this table was a force acting as a tractor beam. I sensed something amazing was going on, and I was right.

It doesn't take long when everything goes your way. Your everyday common gambler in Vegas will usually be playing with $5, $25 or sometimes $100 chips. The standard red, green and black, respectively. I don't know if John had five black chips to start with, but what I *do* know is that when I glanced at the long vertical stack positioned in front of him I saw some weird looking chips. I'm talking about the pink polka dots with stars and racing stripes. These are the denominations that most of the "common folk" don't even get a chance to touch. Well, John had these kinds of chips right in front of him — a lot of them — and he was betting like a madman.

It was his roll again. The point was number nine. As long as John didn't roll a seven before he rolled the nine, he was still in good shape. The bets were big, the payouts were bigger. Four rolls and John was killing the casino. Before he rolled the dice again, John asked the dealer to *remove* all bets he currently had on the table. His "pass bet" had to stay, but just about every polka dotted chip was given back to him upon his request. John took the dice and rolled for the last time. Seven. Out.

It was very odd to see someone ask to remove all bets, but it was even stranger to see someone do it before, *right before,* they lost.

Before the man on his left picked up the dice, John asked for the pit boss. He wanted to ask him an important question before the roll began. "Sure. No problem. You've made everyone at this table so much money tonight, that I guarantee you won't hear anyone complain about waiting," one of the gamblers gleefully answered without authority.

When the pit boss arrived, he asked John what he could do for him. John said simply, "I want to place all of my chips on the come out roll, and then I'm going to cash them in and leave."

The pit boss said he would be right back and made the phone call. When he came back with the approval, the dealer sorted out all of those "pretty" chips and tallied up the final number. John had over $70,000 worth of chips. He asked to place $50,000 on the pass line and left the other $10,000 on the table but was not betting with that stack of money.

The crowd grew larger. The pit boss was perspiring. John was as cool as an arctic breeze. He just knew.

The man to the left seemed concerned, as well. If he rolled a two, three or 12, then John was out $50,000. He picked up both dice and an anticipated "new shooter coming out" was heard in the background above the excited murmurs and quiet comments.

The dice rolled from one end of the craps table to the other, and the red cubes seemed to pause in mid air before landing. One had five dots face up; the other had one more than that. Eleven. The table went nuts. The new "crowd" that had formed went nuts. I was cheering myself. John was smiling, but really didn't seem that surprised that he had $110,000 sitting in front of him.

As promised, he asked to cash out. The chips were gathered, and someone assisted John toward the cage to make change.

Before he left, the stack of chips that was sitting on the table was going to be counted, but John insisted that they be used as a "tip" for bringing him good luck. All were graciously accepted.

High-fiving and handshaking ensued while John was walking to collect his winnings. Oddly enough, he nodded in my direction and smiled.

How did he know to pull his chips off the table right before his last roll? Why did he risk exactly $50,000 on one roll of the dice? Was he a millionaire? Was he a professional gambler? Was he insane?

It was quite remarkable to watch. I couldn't stop thinking about the entire event for the rest of the evening. *Maybe I could do that too! Charlotte would be pretty happy if I brought home $100,000. Yeah, right.*

The next day, I checked out of my hotel and headed to McCarran International Airport for my flight back to Pittsburgh. I was just sitting and waiting for my flight when I noticed John across the hall checking in for his flight to Chicago, Illinois. He sat down and opened up a *USA Today* newspaper. I was one of the few who knew that he *could* be carrying $100,000 on his person.

My flight was delayed and wouldn't be leaving for another hour. I considered venturing over to John with a notepad and pen to ask him to explain to me the ultimate secret of winning big. Determined to at least discreetly congratulate him, I approached John and introduced myself. I told him that I was impressed with his good fortune and amazed by the timeliness of his betting procedure. He pointed to an empty seat directly across from him. "Have a seat and I'll tell you a secret," he said. *Get ready to take some notes.* I said to myself as my mind instantly displayed " retirement" in neon lights. "That wasn't the first time and it won't be the last," John explained.

"About two years ago, I was thirty-four-years-old, and I was in an automobile accident. I was unconscious and lay in a coma for one full month to the day. During that time, I had a vision. This seems very strange, but it was a vision of ping-pong balls. These ping-pong balls were all white. These balls were bouncing around in my mind, yet were not making me crazy. Right before I awoke from my coma, I saw four ping-pong balls line up next to each other. And then, a number appeared on each ball. Then I opened my eyes. My mom, dad and girlfriend were looking at me and started to cry tears of joy. To their surprise, I was coherent enough to speak. 'Paper, pen.' I whispered louder and repeated, 'paper, pen.' My mother handed me a notepad and a pen. I wrote down those numbers in order before I would forget.

"I already knew *where* to go, *what* to do and *when* to do it. *Exactly* a week later on a Thursday, April 4th, I played the lottery. Not only did I win the jackpot, but the numbers came up in the *exact* order as they did in my vision."

This was creepy. I couldn't resist asking him, "Do you mind sharing the amount of your winnings?"

"No, I don't mind at all," John replied. "$100,000." *How silly of me, I should have known.*

"Amazing," I said. "And you won the same amount on the craps table last night, too."

"True. And that's not a coincidence, either," John said.

"Same scenario. I had a dream a week ago about gambling in Las Vegas. I saw the Emerald City from the *Wizard of Oz* in the background and a crowd around a table. All were faceless except the woman to my right and the man to my left. I recognized them when I strolled into the casino. I started rolling the dice immediately after the woman. The point was nine. I rolled five total times *before* I rolled a seven. I placed each of my bets on the numbers I rolled each time: five, ten, ten and five, in that order. I cleaned house in a very short period of time. My investment of $500 turned into over $70,000, and then I knew I would roll a seven."

"That's when you asked to remove all of your bets," I said.

"Right," John continued. "In my dream I knew that the man would shoot an eleven. So I bet it all. That was it. I could not remove the $10,000 on the pass line, but I could handle that loss. Nothing else was recognizable; so the betting was over and I cashed out.

Truly remarkable. What do you expect, Craig? The freaks come out at night (and the daytime). And they're all attracted to me. This guy seems pretty normal, though. But the stories are, well, quite weird.

"I am in shock," I responded. "So how long do you think you'll be doing this? Will you be making a career out of your special talent?"

"No," John responded. "I just have one more journey to make, and then I'm sure it will be over, kind of like the genie and the three wishes. I really don't have an explanation why, but I'm fairly certain that my most recent vision will truly be the last."

"May I ask what it was?"

"Sure. It's a little more complex, but I think I remember everything. It will be worth the extra work," he laughed. "I am going to Aruba and gamble in June. I'll be playing six different games: Blackjack, Roulette, Craps, Baccarat, Caribbean Stud Poker and a $100 per spin slot machine. Six-hundred dollars is the bet on all table games, but the slots will just be $100. That's where I'll win the most. I anticipate winning another $100,000. Pretty good start for when I get married next year, huh?"

Not bad at all, John.

"I wish you well," I responded.

"Oh, it has nothing to do with luck," John said. "This is just a short term *gift* that I was given. A second chance at life, so to speak, and I'm not keeping all of the money, either. No, no. Half will go to charity. That's understood. That's the deal. And I have *noooo* problem with that, whatsoever," he clarified.

John reached into his jacket and pulled out a business card. "Give me a call at my office in July. I'll be back to work by then, and I'll let you know how everything turned out," he offered.

I took the card hesitantly. Questions swarmed my mind almost readying for an attack. "I will call, John. But I have to ask you a very important question," I stated.

He was so approachable and did have a free spirit about himself. Nothing seemed to alarm him. I suppose one would either be in an institution or just a fun-loving person after all of those visions and dreams. (He had chosen the latter, and I knew he would be more than willing to answer my question.)

Wanna Bet? (A Gift)

"Shoot," John said.

"OK, John, I just have to ask you why you would even share all this information with me. You don't know me from Adam, and although I think I believe your stories, you have to admit that they *do* seem pretty far out there. You are a fascinating man, and I feel very comfortable around you in the short time we have been talking; but why would you feel compelled to share all of this with *me?*"

He paused before he answered. "Because you were the *third face* in my Las Vegas dream. I saw you standing by the craps table on my way to the cage and you had a genuinely friendly face amid all of the strange occurrences that have happened to me. You are an exceptional person, Craig. You know that and I know that. For some reason, I know that you are a person who would actually understand all of this craziness. Do you really think I have decided to broadcast this to everyone I meet? Not a chance. I guess I've just accepted that this all happens for a reason, and it's not for me to question this *gift*. Plus, it's kinda turned out profitable. Could be worse, right?"

I laughed. "Sure could, John."

"Flight 456 to Pittsburgh now boarding first class, rows one through four," was heard across the hall.

"That's me," I said as I arose and offered a hand to John.

"It was a pleasure, Craig. God bless and give me a call in a few months."

"Will do."

I keep using this word, but I was totally floored again by someone truly *extraordinary*.

As I was sitting in the comfortable first class section of the plane in a window seat, a large man wrestled into the aisle seat next to me, severely limiting my personal space, I smiled, as it reminded me of the crush of the crowd around John's craps table. I thought about the numbers, the predictions. John will be $300,000 richer in just a few months because of a few images that came to his mind. Good for him.

I also thought about how symbolic each of the three scenarios was. For instance, all of the lotto numbers John envisioned seemed to have an affiliation with the number four. Four weeks in the hospital, four ping-pong balls, thirty-"four" years old, the fourth day of the fourth month of the year during the fourth day of the week....

And how about the Vegas deal? Five. Only five rolls, all numbers either five multiples or divisors of five (except the come out roll). All bets in denominations of five. Finally, "crazy sixes" in Aruba. Six different

149

games, $600 bets and probably six blocks from his new vacation home. Who knows?

Wait a minute. I looked down at my boarding pass. The man to the right was looking at my arm, I looked at my arm, too… It had goose bumps! Flight 4- 5- 6… Lotto… Vegas… Aruba. You've got to be kidding.

Do you really have to ask if the Aruba deal worked out for John? I think you know that answer. I would have flown down to meet him if I had actually been invited. But I have a feeling that's not really the way it works, though.

Enjoy the gift, John. I know I have.

CHAPTER FOURTEEN

The Specter of Il Duce

I was performing at the University of Texas in Austin on Halloween when Charlotte got the call that I had been drafted into the United States Navy. Well, not exactly. We did receive an offer to tour European NATO and U.S. Navy facilities in December, under the sponsorship of the Department of Defense and the U.S. Navy Personnel Command's Department of Morale, Welfare and Recreation. They were looking for something "family friendly" to send overseas during the holiday season. It had been a very long year, and while they offered to send Charlotte with me, I was a bit reluctant to take on the assignment as I wanted to spend some time at home. Finally, I agreed, but I discouraged Charlotte from coming along.

"It's going to be ten shows in eleven days, and all we'll do is stay on base. It will be boring," I said thinking back to my time in Saudi Arabia which, while it wasn't a military tour, was what I was expecting from this trip.

Charlotte insisted on going, and I am so glad she did! We had a wonderful time that included a lot of sightseeing squeezed in between the performances thanks to the wonderful hospitality of our hosts and our friendly NPC/MWR tour manager, Lou Kehrli.

The tour kicked off with an appearance in Naples, Italy, at the *Buona Festa Celebration* at Carney Park, a recreational facility situated in the crater of an extinct volcano. In Naples, we also got the chance to tour the ancient city of Pompeii which was destroyed by the volcanic eruption of Mount Vesuvius in 79 A.D. Our guide for the tour looked like a movie star. He was wearing pointy-toed Italian boots, large wraparound sunglasses and a black trench coat. His long, silver hair was neatly combed back. As we walked the streets of the ruins of Pompeii, he kept reminding us that the ancient city was a center of "Love and beez-nus, beez-nus and love." Pompeii was a great trading and commerce center in the ancient world, and if you were in the mood for a little love, there were tiles with phallus-shaped arrows on them pointing you toward one of the many houses of prostitution in the city!

In Naples, we met the one and only Charlie di Palma. He is a refrigerator of a man and reminded us of a shorter version of Bluto, Popeye's nemesis from the cartoon show. His forearms were as big as Charlotte's thigh! Charlie was born Balthazar di Palma in Hoboken, New Jersey, but went back to Napoli as a small child and currently enjoys dual citizenship. He was the best driver I have ever ridden with. Charlie was trained at the Alfa Romeo racing school, and he could weave in and out of Naples traffic like a magician. That is saying something because Naples traffic is unbelievably crazy. The only other city I've been in that rivals the level of Naples' out of control traffic is Cairo.

Once, we were getting back to base via some back roads and there were three dogs along the side of the road, just enjoying the sun.

"Charlie, look out, dogs!" I yelled from my seat on the passenger side.

"Don't worry, they're Napoli dogs, they stay put, they know. Well, the little one, he flinched a little, 'cause he's young," Charlie said as we zipped past the pooches.

I'm convinced we wouldn't have gotten to see and do as much as we did if it hadn't been for Charlie's skill behind the wheel. We even made it to the beautiful town of Sorrento, south of Naples on the Amalfi Coast. Driving with Charlie at high speed along the twisting, turning roads carved into the cliffs of the Amalfi Coast with the sparkling Mediterranean just off to our right, was something I'll never forget. It was hard to leave Charlie behind, but we had to continue the tour.

"Hey you guys, you're leaving early," Charlie said over the phone.

"How much earlier?" I asked.

"Just an hour. There's going to be a strike."

"How do you know?"

"The union, they announce it. Strike from ten o'clock until noon."

"They announced it?"

"Yeah, happens all the time."

"But aren't we flying in a navy plane?"

"Yeah, but we share the Naples airport with the Italians. We go by their rules, unless it's an emergency, and sorry, Craig, you ain't no emergency. Bah-ha-ha-ha," Charlie said with a huge laugh that is hard to put into words.

The Italian transportation system is prone to disruption. In fact, all of Italy is. Charlie knew this and took the chaos in stride.

"Hey Craig, you know what heaven is?" Charlie asked me on the way to the airport.

"No, Charlie, what's heaven?"

"Heaven is Italian food, Spanish dancing, French lovemaking and everything is run by the Germans."

I smiled.

"You know what hell is?" Charlie went on.

"No, Charlie, what's hell?"

"Hell is Spanish food, French dancing, German lovemaking and everything is run by the Italians! Bah-ha-ha-ha."

We waved goodbye to Charlie as we boarded the small, eight-passenger U.S. Navy airplane and departed for Spain.

The plane fell through the clouds, bouncing as we hit air pocket after air pocket. Between clouds you could see views of the Mediterranean in beautiful shades of blue and green. Suddenly, gorgeous, rocky mountains were in view along with a rock-covered coastline. It was absolutely breathtaking.

We thumped onto the tarmac, and the plane rolled to a stop as the engines shut down and the propellers began to slow.

"Where are we—Spain—already?" I asked. The cabin had been too noisy for any conversation during the flight. The co-pilot looked back.

"No, sir, change of plans. You're going to change planes here and fly on to Madrid."

"Where's here?" I asked.

"You're in Olbia, on the island of Sardinia."

I disembarked and looked around. It was just as beautiful from the ground as it was from the air. Layers of mountains of rock, as far as the eye could see, everything surrounded by the blues and greens of the Mediterranean.

"This is one of the most beautiful places I've ever seen," I stammered.

"It's like a fairy tale land," added Charlotte.

"We'll be coming back," Lou Kehrli, my tour manager, spoke up. "Our last stop is La Maddalena, a small island off the Sardinian coast. Wait 'til you see it, you'll love it."

We were met by an airport official and hustled through the Olbia airport to board another navy plane waiting to take us to Madrid. After touching Sardinian soil, I couldn't get my mind off this extraordinary place and for the rest of the tour, I dreamt of coming back.

I have to admit, Madrid did distract me a bit from my goal of getting back to Sardinia. We had a thirteen hour nonstop tour of this beautiful city that included touring the Royal Palace of Madrid, enjoying Flamenco dancers on the streets, a whirlwind tour of the Prado Museum and a late night dinner at Botin, the Guinness-certified oldest restaurant in the world. It opened its doors in 1725 and has been in business ever since. It was a favorite stop for Ernest Hemingway and he writes of it in *The Sun Also Rises*. The painter, Goya, worked as a dishwasher at Botin. Prior to dinner, we went to some tapas bars just around the corner from the restaurant, each serving only one specialty. My favorite was the mushroom house. You felt as if you were in a giant toadstool! From Madrid, we traveled to Naval Station Rota in the south of Spain for another performance. There, Manuel, the lusty Spanish sailor, quickly developed an attraction to Charlotte. He wanted her to leave me! He would look at her, look at me and look back at her and proclaim in a loud voice, "Dee-vorce!" I'm certain it was all good-natured fun, but I was looking forward to leaving Spain and returning to Sardinia.

We landed once again at Olbia and were met by Pietro, who was to drive us to the base. It was a forty-minute ride to the northern tip of the island. Charlotte, Lou and I craned our necks in an attempt not to miss any of the beautiful scenery.

We were scheduled to take a ferry over to La Maddalena, but a parade got in our way. As luck would have it, today was the annual Ancient Sardinian Society of Masks parade. This was an unexpected treat. It was the most bizarre parade I have ever seen. As you can imagine, most of the participants wore masks. There were men in horned animal masks resembling bulls who would charge into the audience at an unexpected moment terrifying and delighting the parade watchers. Others climbed the building facades that lined the streets. There were masked men with golden lariats who would lasso unsuspecting women along the parade route. Charlotte soon found a lasso around her waist and the masked man pulled her towards him. She tossed off the rope with a laugh.

"You should be honored," Pietro said with a smile. "They only lasso the prettiest girls."

On one parade float there were dummies hung, burned and buried, which, Pietro explained, were various Italian political figures. A drum corps of men in animal skins left a strong impression on my memory. The parade ended with a beautiful, young Sard woman riding an equally beautiful white horse. Both she and the horse were adorned with garlands of flowers. As I stared, Charlotte whispered in my ear, "You always were a sucker for a beautiful Italian on a horse!"

The parade ended. The crowd dispersed, and we headed to the ferry. A short and choppy twenty-minute ferry ride brought us to La Maddalena. As we sailed into the harbor, we were greeted by a picture book Mediterranean village. Pleasure boats, fishing boats and ferries dotted the harbor.

La Maddalena, like Sardinia, is technically Italian, but the residents have strong independent feelings just as they do on Sardinia. La Madd, as it is affectionately known, lies between Sardinia and the French island of Corsica.

We strolled through town, lunched at a café and in general, played the role of American tourist abroad. A Russian storm front was moving in and people were closing up shop for the daily period of rest common to all of Italy. As Pietro walked us up the hill to where we would be staying, we passed two stone columns. A skull and crossbones had been spray painted on each of the columns, and an ancient, rusty chain hung between the two. Looking beyond the columns, you could see a gravel road leading to a dilapidated villa. As it turned out, our inn was just across the road from this intriguing, yet spooky, structure.

We ducked inside the hotel just as the weather began to turn nasty. The wind picked up and sleet began to pelt the windows of the hotel. Pietro told us he'd return to the village to get the van and bring our gear to the hotel. We asked him to stay a while until the weather let up, but he insisted that he go.

"This is nothing," he said with a grin as he pulled his black knit cap farther down on his head, turned up the collar of his navy pea coat and darted out the front door.

The innkeeper welcomed us with espresso. Charlotte went up to the room to relax and I stared out the window at the old villa across the road.

"What's the story behind that place and why the skull and crossbones?" I asked.

"For a while, it was the home of Il Duce. Some say he's still there."

The look on my face must have betrayed my ignorance.

"Il Duce, the leader, Benito Mussolini," the innkeeper explained. This was a bit odd in itself. The week before, I had been on the island of Sicily and had had a wonderful dinner at a private golf club. The clubhouse was actually an old villa that was reputed to have been one of Mussolini's outposts on Sicily. Shortly before this, his name had popped up often as we toured Naples. Synchronicity seemed to be everywhere when it came to Italy and "Il Duce."

I, of course, knew of Mussolini, the fascist dictator who ruled Italy during World War II. "How does one become a dictator?" I asked. Little did I know that I was about to find out just how little I knew about Mussolini as the innkeeper began to spin a tale that was part history, part philosophy and part ghost story.

"Mussolini was a young bully, but smart—*very smart.* He was born in Italy but made a name for himself in Switzerland as a writer, a speaker and a political agitator. He got into a lot of trouble in Switzerland. He was jailed many times.

"He finally returned to his native land, served in the army for two years as required by the government, and then he began his writing and political agitating anew, this time in Italy. He got in good with the leading socialists and began to edit the official socialist newspaper. He was very successful with it. He stayed with it for years and then World War I began.

"At first, like all socialists, Mussolini was against the war, but then he saw it as an opportunity—an opportunity to get rid of capitalism and to bring about social reform. Mussolini was now pro-War and wrote about it, and that got him into a lot of trouble with the Socialist Party. He was forced to resign his editorship of the newspaper and to leave the party.

"He joined the war effort himself and was even wounded, but I believe it was in a training accident, not in battle.

"Italy emerged from World War I on the side of the Allies. It retained its African colonies and made out pretty well, on the surface. However, there are big problems. The economy was bust, unemployment was everywhere and there was a major political struggle going on for control of the country.

"After the war, Mussolini was now a confirmed anti-socialist. He believed Italy needed a strong, authoritarian government headed by a man with ruthless energy, who could overcome the political and economic problems Italy faced. He, of course, saw himself as that man.

The Specter of Il Duce

"Mussolini organized the Fascist Party here in Italy. The word fascism comes from the Italian word *fascio* and means union or league. It refers to the Roman symbol of authority, the *fasces*, the rods and ax carried by all Roman officials.

"Mussolini's party became very powerful. They wore black shirts and would roam the countryside attacking socialists and unionists. They would break up strikes and even burn down opposing parties' offices. They were bullies, just like Benito Mussolini. But it worked. Mussolini gained support. He preached that his way was the right way to fight the growing communist threat, and in 1921, Mussolini and 34 other party members were elected to parliament.

"The next year, the socialists called for a big strike to protest the fascists. Mussolini told the government to stop it, and then sent his own squads to break it up. The bully was getting braver at this point. He told the king to give control of the government to the Fascist Party or he would march on Rome and take control. Mussolini's militia was dispatched to Rome, but like all cowardly dictators, he stayed behind in Napoli to see what happened. The king gave in and turned the government over to Mussolini, who was made prime minister. Mussolini now began his work to convert Italy into a fascist regime."

The innkeeper looked directly at me as he took a sip of his espresso and explained, "In a fascist regime, you belong to the government."

As he lit a cigarette, he added, "And that, my American friend, is how one becomes a dictator. It takes a country in turmoil, where people are not happy, and there seems to be no happiness in the future. Then, a strong-minded bully comes along, and poof—a dictator is born. Il Duce would rule Italy for twenty-one years and rule it with an iron fist."

"I can't imagine people would be happy under his rule. Could they vote him out of office?" I asked innocently.

"Within two years they tried. A fake election gave the Fascist Party the majority of the vote. Some socialist was brave enough to challenge the election. Guess what? He was kidnapped and murdered. That is what a dictator does, whatever he must do to stay in power.

"Italy became a police state. You could not speak out. You could not speak against Il Duce—no unions, no free press, no freedom of speech and no opposition parties. The leaders of all the opposition parties were sent into exile.

"But some good comes from an iron fisted rule. In 1929, during the Great Depression, much of the world was in collapse, including the great and powerful United States. However, Italy was spared because of Il Duce's policies. This really cemented his popularity as doubters became believers.

"Il Duce had Italy, but he wanted more. He helped Croatian fascist Ante Pavelic with weapons and financial support. Pavelic unleashed a series of terror bombings in Yugoslavia and went on to lead the Independent State of Croatia during World War II. Pavelic was another evil, evil man. His regime was one of the bloodiest of the war and resulted in more than half a million deaths. These are truly evil men with much blood on their hands.

"Il Duce then turned his attention to Africa. He invaded Ethiopia and took over the country after a long and bloody war that Italy won due to superior air power and the use of chemical weapons. You asked how a dictator stays in power. Well, two years after Italy took control of Ethiopia there was an assassination attempt on the Italian colonial governor. As a result of that attempt, Il Duce ordered 30,000 Ethiopians executed!

"Il Duce then made a pact with Adolf Hitler's Germany and Japan to fight the spread of communism. Italy began to pass anti-Semitic laws discriminating against Jews. Eventually, 7,000 Italian Jews would be sent to German death camps. Of these, 5,910 were killed. More blood on the hands of Il Duce.

"Il Duce and Hitler had their 'Pact of Steel' as it was known. Germany invaded Poland. Britain and France declared war on Germany, and in 1939, World War II began. However, Il Duce did not join Hitler until a year later after it appeared that Hitler would conquer Europe on his own. Like all bullies, Il Duce was a bit of a coward as well. I don't think this set well with Hitler. He kept Il Duce out of the loop, and that infuriated the Italian dictator. So, Il Duce decided to invade Greece on his own, without telling Hitler first. It was a disaster. The Germans had to intervene. Il Duce then sent support to Hitler when he invaded the Soviet Union, another failure. The Allies invaded North Africa and took control of Italy's African Empire. Where Italy was concerned, it was loss after loss. Joseph Goebbels, the propaganda minister for Nazi Germany said, 'We have the worst allies that could possibly be imagined!'

"The Allies invaded Sicily. Il Duce was facing more losses and his popularity was sinking. His own party deposed him and he was arrested once again. He was placed in prison on the island of Ponza, just off Napoli. Then, the powers that be decided to move him to a more remote island, and that is where our story comes full circle. Mussolini is imprisoned here, on La Maddalena, in that villa across the road," the innkeeper gestured with his cigarette toward the sleet soaked window at the large mansion behind the stone gates.

"Wow," was all I could think to say. "Did you say something earlier about his still being there?" I asked.

"Oh yes, many believe his spirit roams the house."

"Did he die there?"

"Oh no, he was only here a brief time before he was moved to a supposedly more secure location. He was taken from La Maddalena and placed in a hotel high in the Abruzzi mountains, east of Rome. The German SS commandos raided the hotel and took Mussolini with them. It was a spectacular escape. Hitler tried to use him as a figurehead of sorts. He moved him to German occupied Northern Italy and set him up as the leader of the Italian Social Republic, but this was not to last. The real Italian government signed a truce with the Allies, and then Italy declared war on Germany. Friend became foe. It took another two years, but as you know, Germany was defeated."

"What of Mussolini?" I asked.

"Oh, the coward tried to escape to Switzerland dressed as a German soldier. He was recognized by some Italians, arrested and shot the next day near Lake Como. His body was sent to Milan. They strung him up by the feet with piano wire in the public square where crowds could jeer him and cheer his death. Benito Mussolini, Il Duce, the father of fascism—*dead.* You know, some hold him personally responsible for over half-a-million deaths. As I've said, a lot of blood on his hands, a lot of blood. No wonder his spirit is so restless."

"Yeah, what about that. What about his spirit roaming the villa next door?"

"It is said you can see Il Duce throughout Italy, if you only look. His iron fist left its mark. Personally, I've not seen him across the way, but I know of those who swear they have seen him imprisoned behind those walls, and I believe them."

Just then, there was a large crack of lightening and a boom of thunder as Pietro came through the door, straining under a mound of luggage. I ran to meet him.

"Let me help you. Just drop them here in the lobby we'll get them up to the room." I went outside to the van to help Pietro unload the remaining pieces of baggage and looked across the road at the old villa.

When we came back into the lobby, the innkeeper had vanished. I wanted to show off my newfound knowledge of Italian history and asked Pietro if he knew that Mussolini had been imprisoned on La Madd.

"Of course. He's still here. I've seen him," Pietro said. "You know, Mussolini haunts all of Italy. He was the worst leader Italy ever had. He was a puppet of Hitler and a coward at heart. He himself said, 'I am only the first actor in a vast comedy that we all recite together. I work and I try, yet I know that all is a farce.' Maybe that's how he lived with himself through all the killings and the eventual loss of power. But he was a fascinating man, just a very dark shadow on the Italian history books. You better get ready. Show time is in a little over two hours and the Box Office Theatre is sold out. I'll be back in about half an hour to take you, Charlotte and Lou over to the base." With a smile, Pietro was gone.

For the first time, I noticed a pair of field binoculars resting on the check-in desk. I picked them up and trained them on the villa across the road. The rain and sleet mixture was still coming down hard as I strained my eyes and examined the old house. I moved from window to window. A flash of lightening, a shadow exposed in the window. Was it my imagination? I rubbed my eyes and looked through the binoculars again. Something or someone seemed to be there. Another flash of lightening and a face was exposed, hard and mean with a set jaw and a ruthless look. Another flash, and it was gone. Did I see Il Duce or was my imagination running wild in this fairy tale land I found myself in? I wish I knew.

The tour ended on La Madd, and as we were flying from Olbia to Rome, I looked out the plane's window and reflected on all my experiences. Each stop had been unique and special. Everyone had done an extraordinary job when it came to hospitality and I could not have felt any more welcomed. I only hoped that the servicemembers and their families had received half the enjoyment from my performances as I had received from the experience of entertaining our troops overseas. It was an honor and a joy for me during this holiday season to bring a little bit of "home" to the U.S. troops who are so very far away from their homes and doing so much for our country. This was my first military tour, but it was far from my last.

CHAPTER FIFTEEN

Japanese Ghost Story

Tokyo is an extraordinary city. This metropolis, home to more than 12 million people, can seem like the set for a futuristic science fiction movie. There are high speed, elevated toll ways which zip you through the city. When you come to your exit, you drop down the ramp to the streets below and begin to pick your way through traffic to your final destination.

It is a study in contrasts as well. Most of the time it is preternaturally quiet. Charlotte and I were shopping in the Ginza district. There were thousands of people about but very little noise. The Ginza shopping area is similar to New York's Fifth Avenue. Tokyo is extremely expensive and is often referred to as the "most expensive city in the world." Despite the fact that Japan is about three years ahead of the rest of the world when it comes to electronics, very few were using their cell phones and those who were, were primarily text messaging.

We wandered into Mitsukoshi, a large department store. While we were on one of the many women's wear floors, Charlotte turned to me and commented that I looked "lost."

"Well, honey, look around," I said. "We're in a foreign country and I'm on the floor of a department store with 300 other people, all of them women! I'm the only man here and you're the only non-Japanese woman. I do feel a little out of place."

I'm certainly no expert when it comes to Japanese culture, but it does seem as if the women and men lead very different lives. The men tend to work long, long hours and the women serve in more traditional roles of raising the family and taking care of the home. Husbands and wives may only see each other a couple of times a week. Many Tokyo businessmen will keep an apartment in the city, work those long grueling hours and only come home on the weekends. Shopping with your wife is a luxury of time few can afford in this fast-paced city.

After spending an hour or two browsing all of Mitsukoshi's wares, Charlotte and I left the huge store and went back to the street.

"Char," I said while holding her hand (public displays of affection are not that common in Tokyo either). "Close your eyes and listen." We both stood motionless on the sidewalk, hand in hand, listening. The lack of noise was absolutely extraordinary. There were no car horns and no talking, we could have been in a park. When we opened our eyes, we were greeted by the site of thousands of Japanese walking in the streets. It was eerie!

Charlotte spotted a Starbucks (yes, they are everywhere) and we ducked inside. We placed our order and then took our cups to the street. As we sipped and walked, we noticed that no one else was eating or drinking on the street. We window shopped and drank our lattes. Charlotte finished hers and ducked into a store devoted completely to paper. I stood outside, finishing my drink. Pretty soon, I had two empty grande Starbucks cups in my hands. I looked around for a garbage can and couldn't find one. I started to walk looking for somewhere to ditch the cups, but there were no trash cans anywhere. What was most interesting was the fact that there was also no trash anywhere. Tokyo is extremely clean. I ended up walking the two blocks back to Starbucks to throw the cups away in the store.

When the Japanese wish to eat or drink, they do so properly. They sit down, have their meal and then go about their business.

It was time to head back to the New Sanno Hotel. We were staying there for two nights. On the first night, I was scheduled to give a performance.

The New Sanno is located in the heart of Tokyo's embassy district. It is owned by the Japanese government but really caters to U.S. military personnel and government officials who are either on business or vacation in this dynamic city.

It was the start of my first military tour to the Far East, following the success of my first military tour which had been to Europe about six months earlier. We were on the island of Honshu for a series of shows. After this stop, we were to fly on to Okinawa and then back to mainland Japan and the island of Kyushu before heading to Korea for three more performances.

The New Sanno's Embarcadero Lounge was filled for the show, and afterwards I found myself talking with a group of men who were all expatriates, United States citizens living abroad. One man, an elderly gentleman with thick eyeglasses and a quick, hearty laugh, had lived in Japan for forty years. Each of these men was married to a Japanese woman. I commented on the fact that it seemed like almost all of the expats we meet are married to Japanese.

"Oh, there is a special magic about Japanese women, as you'll find out," said a young, recently married U.S. Embassy employee.

"The hell he will!" said Charlotte who was seated by my side and we all laughed.

"I love it here," said the old man with the thick glasses over a glass of Kirin beer which is my favorite Japanese brew. "Have you had much of a chance to look around the city?"

"Just a bit," I answered. "We are on a jam-packed schedule. In fact, tomorrow is our only official day off on the tour."

"Well, let me see what I can do to make your stay in Tokyo a little more interesting."

After one or two more Kirins, Charlotte and I headed to our room as the expats stayed behind, no doubt closing the bar.

The next morning we awoke, and the message light on our phone was blinking. I picked up the receiver and punched "0."

"Front desk," answered the receptionist.

"Hi, this is Craig Karges in room 309. Our message light was on but I'm sure it wasn't on when we went to bed last night and I'm certain the phone hasn't rung since."

"Oh, yes, Mr. Karges. We have an envelope for you at the desk. You can pick it up at your leisure."

I was dressed and ready to go in ten minutes. As Charlotte took over the bathroom, I headed down to the lobby.

"Good morning Mr. Karges. We heard wonderful things about the show last night," beamed the receptionist as I approached the front desk. "Here's your envelope."

"Thanks and good morning to you too," I countered.

I took the envelope to a sitting area off the main lobby and opened it. Inside was a series of directions to the nearest subway entrance and a note telling me to get off at a particular stop, Shibuya, and ask for Hachiko. That

163

was it. No name, no signature, absolutely nothing else. I thought back to my bespectacled friend from the night before. Perhaps this was his doing. Charlotte and I had no concrete plans for the day; so I rushed back to the room and burst in on her as she was putting the finishing touches on her make-up.

"Come on honey, we're going on a treasure hunt!"

A few blocks away from the hotel we found our subway entrance. I'm not a big fan of subways. I rarely take one in New York. And when in London, I rarely venture on the tubes. I just find it intimidating for some reason. You would think the idea of a Japanese subway would intimidate me as well. For some reason it didn't. Maybe it was the excitement of the quasi-mysterious message, or the fact that the system is incredibly easy to use. But for whatever reason, Charlotte and I found ourselves zipping beneath the streets of Tokyo to our appointed stop. Needless to say, the Tokyo subway was spotless and extremely quiet despite the large number of people crammed into the various cars.

We exited at Shibuya station and began asking for Hachinko. We were directed to a bronze statue of a dog—an *Akita*—in fact. As we walked up to the statue a diminutive Japanese lady of indeterminate age approached us.

"Mr. and Mrs. Karges?" she asked.

"Yes," we replied, amazed that she recognized us and curious as to what lay ahead.

"Hello, I am Narumi-san. I will be your guide today." The woman bowed deeply.

It was apparent that our new found friend from the night before had set this up. We were to have our own personal tour of Tokyo.

"This is Hachinko, man's best friend," Narumi said, gesturing towards the bronze canine statue.

"Oh, we love dogs," Charlotte chimed in, "all dogs are man's best friend. What makes Hachinko special?"

"This statue has become Tokyo's most famous meeting place, and there is a story behind its creation. Hachinko was born in 1923 in Akita Prefecture. His master was a professor at Tokyo Imperial University. Each day, Hachinko would accompany his master to the train station. In the afternoon, the dog would return to greet his master when he came back from teaching. When Hachinko was two, his master passed away while teaching a class at the university. Hachinko was adopted by a gardener who lived in the Asakusa district of Tokyo. However, everyday, until his death some eleven years later, Hachinko would make his way across Tokyo and wait at Shibuya station for his master to return. Everyone—all the commuters—knew Hachinko and were amazed at the animal's loyalty. Hachinko died at thirteen years of age. Every year, on April 8th, we hold a commemorative festival here at the statue to honor the memory of Hachinko. We Japanese appreciate loyalty.

"Now come, there is much to see and do in Tokyo!"

We followed Narumi about the city, through the subway system. We made stops at the Imperial Palace and Gardens as well as Buddhist temples and Shinto shrines. It was a whirlwind trip. At a Shinto shrine, we "piggybacked" onto a tour group. Apparently Narumi knew the tour guide. We heard some Americans talking and we engaged them in conversation. When you travel abroad, it seems special if you are in the minority—one of the few Americans. However, a part of you always feels a bit homesick, and when you hear an American accent (and it's not an "ugly" one), your curiosity is piqued.

"Hi, we're Craig and Charlotte Karges, from West Virginia," Charlotte, by far the more sociable of the two of us, introduced us to the small group of Americans.

"West Virginia, I used to live in West Virginia," a short, ponytailed and bearded man spoke up.

"Really, where?" Charlotte asked.

"Bethany, ever heard of it?"

"Of course, it's right up the hill from our house. We live in Wheeling. In fact, we have a good friend who is an art professor at Bethany College, Ken Morgan."

"Kenny Morgan? You're kidding. I know Ken well. I used to teach philosophy at Bethany."

We exchanged a few more pleasantries before Narumi hurried us along. It is amazing that no matter where you go in the world you can find some kind of connection to your life back home.

We ended up back in the Ginza at twilight not far from where we had been the day before. We were standing in front of a beautiful building that appeared to be a theater.

"Narumi-san, is that a theater?" I asked.

"Not just a theater, it is one of the two most important Kabuki theaters in Tokyo. This is the Kabuki-za Theater. Only the National Theater in Nagatacho rivals it for its productions of Kabuki drama. It was built in 1925, and it owes part of its beauty to the architect's blending of Western and Japanese shrine influences. Look at the display boards, they have photos of the actors in tonight's production. Do not leer at the women, Karges-san, they are men. Men play all the roles in Kabuki."

"What's this production about?" I asked.

"Oh, this is one of Japan's most famous ghost stories. We have many ghost stories and we love them all. I believe it is because of Shintoism which is still our primary religion. We believe that when we die, our spirit is destined for an eternal world. However, there is also an in between world where unhappy spirits can return to menace the living. The Shinto religion is filled with ceremonies to appease the spirits of the dead. You want them on your side! This particular play tells the story of the maid at the well."

"Are you familiar with this story?" I asked trying to coax more information from our affable tour guide.

"Certainly! In the 1700s during samurai time, there was a warrior samurai named Aoyama Tesson. Tesson lusted after one of his servants, the beautiful Okiku. The passion that Tesson felt for Okiku was not shared by the lovely maiden. This infuriated the powerful samurai and he plotted a way to make Okiku his.

"Tesson owned a valuable collection of Dutch plates—ten in total. He put Okiku in charge of caring for the plates. One night, Tesson stole one of the plates away and hid it. Later, Tesson asked that Okiku bring all ten plates to him, but, of course, she could find only nine. She counted again and again, but it was always just the nine. Okiku couldn't understand what happened to the tenth plate. Tesson said he was willing to forgive Okiku if she would become his mistress. Okiku refused. Tesson was enraged. He killed the young maid and threw her body down a well.

"From the day of her death onward, Okiku's ghost rose from the well each night. The ghost would count to nine and then let out a pitiful yet horrifying cry and disappear back into the well.

"The samurai was tortured by his guilt and he asked a friend what he could possibly do to exorcise the ghost. Tesson's friend had an idea. One evening, he hid next to the well. As usual, Okiku's ghost appeared. When the ghost counted nine, the samurai's friend yelled 'ten' and the ghost disappeared, never to return."

"When will the play start?" Charlotte asked.

"Very soon. You can stay and watch it if you like. It will run about three hours and I believe the only seats available will be far up in the balcony. You may need binoculars to really appreciate the production," Narumi said.

Charlotte and I looked at each other.

"Any other suggestions to finish off our tour?" I asked Narumi.

"Yes, a trip to Roppongi, follow me."

We went back underground to the subway system. When we emerged at Roppongi station night had fallen, but Roppongi was lit up like a Christmas tree. Forget what I said about Tokyo being quiet. Roppongi is where the party is! There are so many bars and the party spills out on to the street. If Ginza is the equivalent of New York's Fifth Avenue for shopping, then Roppongi is the equivalent of New Orleans' Bourbon Street for partying. Narumi bid us a fond farewell and refused to take any money for her time.

"Don't worry," she said with a smile, "I have been well compensated. Now go and enjoy yourselves. You will find many friendly people here!" With a final bow, she went off into the night.

Friendly people were plentiful in Roppongi! After many Kirin's, some rice wine and sake we headed back to the New Sanno, our heads filled with stories of ghosts, dogs, palaces, temples and shrines. Tokyo certainly has much to offer and many stories to tell.

CHAPTER SIXTEEN

Atlantis Found

In February of 2004, I embarked on my second European tour under the sponsorship of the Department of Defense and the Morale, Welfare and Recreation Division of the United States Navy, hereafter referred to as MWR. This was to be a carbon copy of my first tour in 2002. It was an exciting trip and my first official military tour. These tours cover a lot of miles in a short period of time, but we also manage to have fun, especially with Charlotte on board as road manager.

To give you an idea of the travel a typical tour entails, here is the 2004 itinerary. The first stop was in Madrid, Spain, for the NATO Joint Command Headquarters Southwest where I performed for a crowd of families and service members representing 12 countries. From Madrid, it was on to the southern tip of the Iberian Peninsula and an appearance at a joint Spanish/U.S. naval facility called Rota. It is a beautiful spot, and on a clear day you can see the northern coast of Africa across the Straits of Gibraltar. From Spain, we flew to Naples, Italy, for a performance at the base there. We then drove north to the lovely town of Gaeta for another show. A short flight from Naples took us to the island of Sicily for an appearance at the naval air station there. While on Sicily, we were able to climb around on Mount Etna, an active volcano. This was the first of any sightseeing we had on this particular tour. I have two distinct memories of the Etna adventure: exploring abandoned, mountainside homes that had been half buried by the volcanic lava flow, and watching a beautiful, blonde, Italian fashionista attempting to navigate the craters of Etna in a tight, black dress and stiletto heels! From Sicily, we headed to Greece for two stops. The first stop was at the Souda Bay navy base on the island of Crete. We then went on to the NATO facility, Joint Command South Central, in Larissa. Upon leaving Greece, we returned to Italy and the beautiful island of La Maddalena. Then, we headed home. This tour covered 15,000 miles in thirteen days. It included nine performances, plus seven American Forces Network television and radio interviews. When you consider the travel time from continent to continent and back again, you can see that there wasn't a lot of time for anything but work, but I truly enjoy my work and a very interesting thing happened to us on Crete.

We landed with a thud on the tarmac at NSA Souda Bay. The pilot and co-pilot hurried us off the plane, and we were rushed into the small terminal building. A bit later, our luggage appeared. This was unusual as we typically off load our own baggage, but these two flyboys were determined to get us into the terminal as quickly as possible.

"We had a bit of a problem during our approach, lost an engine," the pilot said matter-of-factly.

I thought I had heard a loud noise and I had felt a sudden drop in altitude during the descent, but that was nothing unusual. On these Department of Defense tours, we would fly to Europe on commercial airlines, but once on the Continent, we traveled from base to base in very small, U.S. Navy passenger planes. We were always issued earplugs to wear due to the noise levels in the planes, and the flights were frequently bumpy as we were flying at low altitudes over the Mediterranean.

"Is everything OK now?" I asked.

"Well, no," the co-pilot responded. "We're going to get a mechanic to take a look. We're supposed to leave for Naples, but I think we'll be staying here a while. What time is your show tonight?"

"I'm not sure. It's always early, usually around six o'clock. Hope to see you there."

"Well, no you don't," the pilot responded. "If we're there, that means the plane is still out of commission. We don't want that."

Souda Bay was always one of my favorite stops in Europe. It was the only unaccompanied base I visited. It was just sailors. There were no families and they definitely needed a distraction from time to time.

That evening the show went great. The audience began to arrive an hour-and-a-half prior to the performance, and by the time I took the stage the place was packed with sailors. They filled every available seat, stood against the walls and watched from open doorways. Among the sea of faces, I spotted our pilot and co-pilot from earlier in the day.

I'm convinced that my popularity on Crete was due to two factors. The first was that these women and men had very little to do on base. The second was the promotional skills of the Kriti Girls, a trio of vivacious young women who worked for MWR and promoted the heck out of my show and any MWR sponsored event.

After the performance, we had an early dinner. While we were eating, the pilot and co-pilot appeared at our table.

"Great show man, I'm sure glad I got to see it," the pilot said.

"Thanks so much. How's the plane coming?" I asked.

"Not so good. We're working with a team of mechanics to get her up and running again, but no luck so far."

"What happens if she's down for good?" Charlotte asked.

"You don't go to Larissa," the co-pilot answered.

"What? You're taking us to Larissa?" I asked.

"Well, we weren't supposed to, but they changed the schedule. Our orders are to stay here with you and fly you to the next stop on your tour. If we get the plane fixed in time it will be Larissa. If not, it will be Olbia on Sardinia for your show at La Madd."

Early the next morning we headed over to the terminal for what we hoped would be our flight to Larissa. The pilot and co-pilot were seated in the terminal, glum looks on their faces.

"Good morning, I don't have to be a mind reader to know we won't be taking off anytime soon," I greeted them.

"Good guess. I don't have any update for you other than the fact that we're still grounded. They asked that you two go over to the MWR office," the pilot said.

As we walked through the office door, we were greeted by Soula, one of the three Kriti Girls.

"Hey you two, thanks so much for coming back. It was the best event we've done since the last time you were here," Soula said.

"Thanks Soula, we love coming here. Souda Bay is one of our favorite stops. Do you know what's up with Larissa? Can we get a flight there if our plane is permanently grounded?" I asked.

"We're working on it. I don't think there's any way you can make the original show time, but they are making announcements on the base that you will be there for a nine o'clock show instead of the four o'clock start time."

"Will anybody be there?" I asked, knowing that most of the people at the NATO base lived off base, and the show had been scheduled for four o'clock to accommodate people getting off work and children leaving the base school.

"The question is, will *you* be there?" Soula answered. "Hey, the show is moved back until nine, and you're not leaving here anytime soon. Would you like to take a quick tour of Chania?"

"Sure!" Charlotte said. She was anxious for some entertainment after a week of bouncing around the Mediterranean in small planes and seeing nothing but military bases.

"I don't know," I said. "Shouldn't we stay here just in case the plane gets fixed?"

"Nah, we have time. Come on, we'll get a driver and go into town," Soula said as both she and Charlotte broke into big smiles.

Chania was a twenty-minute drive away. It is a picturesque Greek harbor town. We strolled through the public market where grocers, fish mongers and butchers still sell their wares. At the risk of insulting the merchants, Soula cautioned us not to stare at the decapitated animals and other novelties lining the stalls. It was hard not to stare at a pig's head staring at you from a tabletop.

From the public market, we took a walk through the adjacent public garden where the air smelled so much better. Then we headed down to the harbor. What a beautiful sight. At the entrance to the harbor there is a renovated fort, and opposite the fort is a magnificent, centuries-old lighthouse. The harbor is protected by a breakwater consisting of massive stones, and in the middle of the stones lies the ruins of another fortress. The brightly painted houses and shops clustered in a semi-circle around the bay were a joy to look at, and it was great fun navigating some of the tiny, narrow streets which cut through the buildings like a maze. Everywhere you looked, men were sitting outside enjoying a cup of Greek coffee, a strong concoction with foam on the top and the grounds in the bottom of the cup. Charlotte and I took it all in as the sun sparkled off the bright blue waters of the bay. It was actually enough to make me quit looking at my watch and wondering if we were ever going to make it to Larissa.

"Do we have time for some shopping, Soula?" Charlotte asked.

Soula looked at her watch, made a short phone call, did some quick mental calculations and then answered, "Not much. It looks like you're going to get out of here. They're flying in the part they need from Naples; so I need to have you back on base in about ninety minutes to be safe. Tell you what, I know the man who owns that shop," she said as she pointed to one of the colorful buildings lining the harbor.

"He has good quality merchandise and he'll give you a fair price, plus he speaks excellent English."

"Let's go," Charlotte exclaimed as she headed straight for the shopkeeper's storefront window displaying a number of Cretan souvenirs.

Soula and I caught up with Charlotte inside the shop. She had already introduced herself to Ted, the owner. Ted was a short, barrel-chested man with a head full of long, curly, gray hair and a bushy mustache. He had a twinkle in his eye as he helped Charlotte try on a necklace.

"Isn't it beautiful?" she asked as Soula and I joined her at the jewelry counter.

"That's a very good choice, Charlotte," Soula said. "It's a Greek Key necklace."

"Yes, the Greek Key," Ted chimed in. "We call it that because the square pieces in the pattern resemble a key."

"It is pretty," I said, admiring the simple elegance of the design.

"This Greek Key pattern has a rich and long history. The ancient Greeks used it as ornamentation on their temples and pottery. The ancient Romans adopted it as well. But it is not found in just this part of the world. A similar pattern is found in the Dong Son culture of Vietnam and even the Hopi Indian culture in your own country," Ted explained.

"Is there a connection?" I asked.

"Everything is connected to Greece," Ted replied with a smile, "Greece is the cradle of all civilization. However, some people believe the Greek Key design to be Atlantean in nature. Others say it is like a maze, a labyrinth. Remember the story of Theseus killing the Minotaur?"

Charlotte and I nodded our heads, as we tried to reclaim our forgotten knowledge of Greek mythology.

"I am not certain you do remember," Ted said picking up on our confusion. "The Minotaur was a monster with the head of a bull and the body of a man, and it lived here on Crete, in a labyrinth. The Minotaur was born from an unnatural union between Queen Pasiphae and a magnificent white bull."

"You don't mean," I interrupted Ted's story.

"Oh yes, that is exactly what I mean. Queen Pasiphae was the wife of King Minos, a great warrior king said to be the son of Zeus and the mortal Europa. Minos had threatened to attack Athens. The Athenians wanted none of it, and they offered to send seven young men and seven young women each year to Crete if the Cretans promised not to attack. These youngsters were to be food for the Minotaur! King Aegeus of Athens agreed to this. Theseus, the king's son, volunteered to be one of the seven young men. When he arrived on Crete, he met Princess Ariadne, King Minos' daughter, and she fell in love with him at first sight. This Princess of Crete did not wish to see her love killed; so she conspired with him and was able to sneak a ball of twine and a sword into the opening of the labyrinth."

"Oh yes, I remember the story, Theseus unwound the ball of twine as he went through the labyrinth so he could find his way out of the maze. He fought and killed the Minotaur with the sword and rescued the Athenians," I said.

"Exactly right. Theseus, Princess Ariadne and the Athenians sailed away in secrecy. On their way back to Athens, they landed on the island of Dia. It was there that the beautiful but vain Ariadne was left. She fell asleep as the Athenians sailed back home. Some say the god Dionysus claimed her for his own, but I don't know."

Charlotte and I looked at each other. It was as if Ted was reciting history, not myth.

"That was a cruel thing to do, just to leave her alone on an island," Charlotte said.

"Yes and Theseus paid for it in a manner of speaking. He had arranged with his father, King Aegeus, to fly a white flag on their return home if he survived the Minotaur. He forgot, or was cursed by Dionysus or Minos, and the black flag they had flown when they left Athens was still flying when they arrived in port. King Aegeus saw this black flag, believed his son to be dead and in his grief flung himself into the sea where he drowned. This is why the area is known as the Aegean Sea to this day," Ted explained as he folded his hands together and rested them on the jewelry countertop.

"So, this is meant to be a labyrinth?" Charlotte asked, turning Ted's attention back to the necklace.

"You can look at it any way you wish," Ted said. "A labyrinth, the waves of the sea, eternal life, eternal love, the four seasons, or the key to the secrets of the world."

As Ted was talking and Charlotte was admiring her new piece of jewelry, my eyes were scanning Ted's shop. He had a number of interesting items tastefully arranged throughout the small space. My eyes fell upon a bone-handled knife in a silver scabbard. I walked over to it, picked it up and hefted the piece in my hand. As I brought it back to the counter, I asked Ted about it.

"Oh, that is a Cretan Dagger," Ted explained.

I knew I wanted it the moment I picked it up but I also wanted to know a little bit more about it. Ted was happy to fill me in.

"It is beautiful, is it not? Handmade by a local artisan. This specific design goes back a long way. We Cretans are known for our skill in warfare. Edged weapons like your dagger (Ted already knew he had made another sale) and war helmets were first made here. It is said that Crete was the home of Zeus' attendants and they carried out his wishes, making an art form out of battle. Our archers were renowned throughout the known world. They fought off the Romans. Their accuracy was almost supernatural.

"Crete has a long and bloody history. In the Middle Ages, Crete was occupied by the Saracenes from Spain. It went back to Byzantine rule until the Byzantine Empire was destroyed by the Fourth Crusade. In dividing up the Byzantine lands, the Venetians became our occupiers. The Venetians dominated Crete for more than four-hundred years. Then the Turks came. As I said, a long and bloody history. And throughout it all, you could always find a Cretan Dagger attached to any warrior, indeed, attached to any Cretan male. It was there and put to good use during the struggle over Macedonia and the Balkan Wars. It was even carried into The Second World War by Greek soldiers.

"You have no doubt noticed the V shape to the hilt of the knife, this notch here," Ted said as he placed his thumb into the notch at the top of the hilt and withdrew the weapon from its sheath.

"Resting your thumb in the notch gives you maximum power as you strike down upon your enemy," he explained as he quickly raised and lowered his arm in a series of midair strikes.

"The dagger is also quite magical," Ted continued. "Sorcerers would use newly made black hilted daggers, never a white hilted one and never a previously used black hilted one, to draw a magic circle in the ground. They would then pierce the center of the circle with the dagger. They could then stay within the circle and summon demons to do their bidding. As long as they stayed within the circle, no harm could come to them."

"Sold!" I said.

"Thank you for your patronage," Ted said. "Now you can each leave Crete with a treasure, a story and an Atlantean connection."

"What do you mean, Atlantean?" I asked.

"Some believe that the Greek Key pattern goes back to Atlantis and some believe that the Cretan Dagger is from there as well."

"Atlantean, Atlantis—you mean the fabled lost continent?" I quizzed the shopkeeper.

"Oh, it is not a *fable* and it is not *lost* either. In fact, it is quite close by," Ted said as he inclined his head toward the storefront window and the sea beyond.

"Crete *is*, or *was* Atlantis?" I asked.

"No, not Crete, not precisely," Ted answered.

"You undoubtedly know the story of Atlantis," it was more a statement than a question and the three of us nodded yes.

"As you are no doubt aware, it was Plato who gave us our first record of Atlantis. He said the story was handed down from generation to generation. The origin of the story goes back to 700 B.C., three hundred years before Plato, and an Athenian statesman who heard the history of Atlantis directly from Egyptian priests.

"Plato described the city of Atlantis as a magnificent circular city on a large island. At the center of the city was elevated ground, a huge hill with precipitous sides. Upon this acropolis the finest of palaces were built. These nobles could look down upon Atlantis and behold a series of encircling canals and harbors. An image from on high which would closely resemble the pattern of the Greek Key," Ted said as he tapped the necklace Charlotte still wore.

"The Atlanteans were artistic, intelligent and civilized. They were great seafarers and humanitarians. They governed themselves in a peaceful and sensible fashion. The entire citizenry would assemble once a year to settle any disputes. They were an envied race. So far advanced and mysterious to the people they traded with, people such as the Egyptians. The story goes that they became victims of their own success and their pride was their downfall. They angered the gods as the Atlanteans thought they were equal to the residents of Mount Olympus. The gods took their vengeance on Atlantis. They destroyed it by sending earthquakes, floods and rainstorms. The once great city was destroyed, slipping into the sea," Ted finished his brief history of Plato's Atlantis.

"You don't strike me as the kind of person who still believes in Zeus and the gods of Mount Olympus," I said, "but when you speak of Greek mythology, it seems as if you're speaking of actual history," I voiced what

Charlotte and I had thought as Ted was telling the story of Theseus and the Minotaur.

"It is history of a different kind. The Greek gods and myths are part of the reason we are who we are today. I simply honor the old traditions. However, I do believe in Atlantis, and I am not the only one.

"Remember, the story of Atlantis is said to have originated with Egyptian priests. During the Egyptian Fourth Dynasty, approximately 2500 B.C., there was a civilization which dominated trade throughout the Mediterranean region. They were here on Crete, and they built lavish palaces and created beautiful artwork, very much like the description of the Atlanteans. This was, naturally, a long, long time ago, millennia before Plato, and long before Plato's time this civilization ceased to exist. There were rumors and legends, among them the story of Theseus and the Minotaur which we spoke of earlier, but no dominate civilization resembling Atlantis.

"It was here on Crete in 1900 when Sir Arthur Evans discovered the remains of the city of Cnossus, the capital of Minoan culture and Europe's first civilization. It was Evans, by the way, who dubbed the culture Minoan after the legendary King Minos. Another scholar saw a connection with the Minoan civilization and Atlantis, especially as seen through the eyes of the ancient Egyptians. This great seafaring culture would be like nothing the Egyptians had ever encountered before. Ancient Egyptians, as advanced as they were, did not venture far from their homeland. However, at the height of Minoan power and influence, this mysterious race vanished, never to be seen again. You can easily see how the truth of Minoan Crete could be turned into the legend of Atlantis," Ted concluded.

"So was Crete Atlantis, or wasn't it?" I was intrigued with this history lesson.

"It would be more accurate to say Crete is a fragment of what was once considered to be Atlantis," Ted answered.

"In 1932, a Greek named Spyridon Marinatos was investigating the mysterious disappearance of the Minoan culture. He was trying to discover the lost harbor city of Amnisos which King Minos had built as the harbor entrance to his capital city, Cnossus. Young Marinatos was not having much luck finding Amnisos. Then, on the last day of his expedition, when he had all but run out of funds, he unearthed a Minoan fresco. He later returned to the site and excavated an entire harbor town complete with a royal palace.

"Marinatos made a further discovery. During his excavation, he found large building stones far away from their foundations as if they were thrown toward the sea. He also discovered in the lower level of a building vast amounts of pumice. All of this indicated that perhaps a volcanic eruption had taken place.

"Seventy miles north of Crete lies the island of Thera and two other smaller islands. Scientists believe these separate islands were created with one massive volcanic blast around 1500 B.C., which is just about the time that the Minoan culture vanished.

"Marinatos theorized that this blast could have created the island we know as Crete today, as well as Thera and the other two islands, and destroyed the entire Minoan civilization in the process. He studied the eruption of Krakatoa near Java. That was a catastrophic event which happened in 1883, do you know it?"

"I've heard of Krakatoa," I responded.

"It changed the world," Ted stated. "Thirty-six thousand people killed, tsunami waves more than 30 meters high crashing into Java and Sumatra at more than 80 kilometers per hour. You see it don't you? The earthquakes, rains and floods of the gods!"

"It does make sense," I said.

"And that is not all. Later on, a Greek and a Hungarian teamed together and excavated parts of Thera, discovering Minoan ruins which were obviously destroyed by a volcanic eruption. Further study indicated that this eruption on Thera was four times as powerful as Krakatoa! Can you imagine the destruction?" he said excitedly as he banged both his fists on the countertop.

All three of us stared at Ted, wide eyed.

"So the legend of Atlantis was created out of Egyptian storytelling based on the Minoan civilization, and Plato served as Atlantis' press agent." I summed up what I thought Ted had told us in an attempt to calm him down.

"I believe so, yes," Ted said calmly.

"C'mon guys, we have to go," Soula interrupted. "We're going to be late."

We quickly paid for our purchases and headed out the door and up a steep, narrow, winding staircase to meet our driver who raced back to the base. As we approached the terminal our flight crew greeted us.

"Are we all gassed up and ready to go?" I asked.

"You are, we're not," the co-pilot replied.

"Another change of plan," the pilot added. "They flew our part in from Naples and we have another hour or so of work ahead of us, but you're going on to Larissa in style. The part came in on the Admiral's LearJet.

That's your ride over there," he said as he jerked his thumb toward a gleaming jet sitting on the tarmac.

We quickly boarded the jet and were airborne in minutes. It was quite a ride. There were no bumps, no unusual noises and no earplugs. It seemed as soon as we were up, we were beginning our descent. We landed in darkness at a Greek air force base one hour before the new show time. The NATO team from Larissa was there to meet us, gyro sandwiches in hand.

We were on base thirty minutes before the show was to start, and despite the fact that there was a day-of-show time change and the fact that most people live off the base, the room was packed. Extra chairs had to be added, and I was greeted by a full house of families from nine countries. The show was salvaged, we had a wonderful afternoon on Crete, and we solved the mystery of Atlantis!

On the way back to the Greek air force base in the morning, the driver pointed out Mount Olympus in the distance. It was odd. I just never thought there really was a Mount Olympus, but there it was. I thought about the ancient Greek gods and how Ted would tell the stories as if he were reciting history not myth, and I considered how history, myth and legend combine to create a culture. No place is that more evident than Greece.

CHAPTER SEVENTEEN

The Fortunes of Singapore

You know you have a long flight when you leave the continental U.S. and your layover stop is Hawaii! I was just starting my second tour of U.S. Navy facilities in Asia. The schedule was the same as the summer before; however, we added Guam at the start of the tour and Singapore as our last stop with visits to Japan and Korea in between.

The tour was scheduled to kick-off where "America's Day Begins," on Guam, the westernmost U.S. territory in the Pacific. After 4,500 miles and ten hours of flight time, we touched down in Honolulu where we disembarked, refueled and re-boarded for the next 3,900-mile leg of the journey. It was another seven hours in the air; but eventually Charlotte, our tour manager, Bob, and I found ourselves on the island of Guam in Micronesia. Guam is located roughly halfway between Japan to the north and Australia to the south, and it is a long way to Guam!

As we stepped off the plane, the humidity hit us like a freight train and my glasses fogged over. A friendly U.S. Navy Morale, Welfare and Recreation guide greeted us. She was a native of Guam and welcomed us with the customary "Hafa Adai" (sounds like half-a-day) or "Hello" in Chamorro. Chamorros are Guam's original inhabitants. When you hear the name "Guam" it doesn't conjure up the image of the beautiful tropical island this place is. Guam's sister island, Saipan, sounds much more exotic, and both islands compete for the hordes of Japanese tourists who head to Micronesia for vacationing and shopping. I think they should change the name from Guam to Chamorro to honor the indigenous people and to increase tourism! Some say Guam stands for Guaranteed Under American Military. There is a large U.S. military presence on the island and, of course, that's why I was there.

Guam was to be a brief stop, but we did get to tour the island a bit before the show. Bizarre wildlife abounds on Guam. There are frogs the size of softballs! As you walk the island roads you can't help but notice the hundreds, and I mean hundreds, of flattened giant frogs, the victims of vehicle tires. You also can't help but notice the popping sound when you're in a vehicle and you run over one of the unfortunate ones. On the other end of the spectrum is the tiny coqui frog. The male coqui sings all night long from sundown until sunrise in a mating ritual. Its song sounds just like ko–kee; hence its name. While this may sound pleasant, you have to realize that the ko–kee sound emitted by these little amphibians can sometimes reach as high as 100 decibels, about the same noise level as a snowmobile or motorcycle! And then there is the brown tree snake. This reptile is nasty and is responsible for annihilating the majority of the native bird population on Guam. The brown tree snake has very few predators on Guam and can grow much larger than normal size on the island. An average brown tree snake is about three to six feet in length; however, the longest brown tree snake ever recorded was found on Guam and it was nine-and-a-half feet long! The species slipped into Guam around 1950, probably as a stowaway in ship cargo from its native habitat of Australia or Papua New Guinea, and it has wreaked havoc ever since. The snake can be very aggressive when confronted. It strikes a strange "S" shaped pose, virtually standing on its tail. These snakes are also responsible for thousands of power outages all over the island as they climb and hang on the power lines. Throughout Guam, you will see brown tree snake traps. These are cages, attached to the power lines in hopes of trapping the reptile.

Now, I don't want you to have nightmares about Guam! It is actually a lovely place, bizarre wildlife aside. The show on the island was at the Top 'o the Mar restaurant on Nimitz Hill overlooking Asan Bay—a beautiful spot. And after we enjoyed a spectacular Micronesian sunset, I worked my magic to a standing ovation and our Asian tour was officially underway.

From Guam, it was on to Korea—sort of. One week before our departure on this particular tour, Charlotte received a travel advisory for

The Fortunes of Singapore

Korea from the U.S. State Department. Due to North Korean leader Kim Jong Il's saber rattling, we were informed that the Korean peninsula was in "Force Protection Bravo." That meant a curfew and the buddy system were mandatory for all military personnel. We were given the option to cancel the tour (or at least the Korean leg of it), but "the show must go on" and we were given a special clearance for the Korean leg of the tour. Now, it seemed as if a typhoon was going to do what Kim Jong Il couldn't, put a halt to our travel to Korea. We were scheduled to fly from Guam to Busan, Korea, for an appearance at U.S. Fleet Activities Chinhae. However, Super Typhoon Dianmu grounded us in Osaka. Dianmu means "Mother of Lightning" in Mandarin Chinese, and it was quite a storm. We rode out the storm at Kansai International Airport in Osaka, Japan.

Kansai is an extraordinary place. It is built on an artificial island in the middle of Osaka Bay and is an engineering marvel. There was no room to expand the Osaka Airport so they took it out to sea. Watching the effects of Dianmu while stranded at this floating airport is something I will never forget. Waves were crashing against the runways, and you could see the wings of grounded airplanes move up and down at the will of the winds.

As we waited out the typhoon, we tried to reroute to Seoul and salvage the Chinhae show. Eventually, we followed Dianmu out of Osaka and made it to Seoul. The Chinhae show was lost for the time being, but we picked up the tour the following day with a full house at the Navy Club on the huge Combined Forces Command military base in Seoul.

From Korea, we headed to the "Land of the Rising Sun" and barnstormed our way across the island of Honshu, Japan, for a series of three shows in and around Tokyo. It was a short flight from Tokyo to the island of Kyushu for an appearance at U.S. Fleet Activities Sasebo.

Our tour manager, Bob, had not been feeling well the entire trip and was hospitalized in Sasebo for a suspected blood clot in his right leg. The show went over great in Sasebo, but Bob didn't fare quite so well. Fortunately, it wasn't a blood clot, but he was diagnosed with an infection serious enough to send him back to the United States for further medical treatment.

We received word that the U.S. Navy had rerouted me back to Korea so I could play the Dianmu-canceled Chinhae show. While I was glad to be able to get the show in, I was giving up my only day off on this particular tour. Charlotte and I had planned to tour the 99 islands around Sasebo. It's actually a chain of more than 200 islands, the densest concentration of islands in all of Japan. The islands are various sizes and each possesses a distinctive, intricate shoreline. Officially, this island oasis is known as the Kujuku Islands and makes up the Saikai National Park. Charlotte was able to cruise the islands on a sightseeing powerboat. She said they were awe-inspiring! So, it was in Sasebo, that we all parted company. I was off to Korea, Bob would be going back to the United States and Charlotte would head to Okinawa, the next scheduled stop on the tour.

It took five flights on three airlines in two countries to make the Chinhae show happen, but it *did* happen. Unfortunately, my arrival in Korea coincided with the first day of monsoon season! The staff at Chinhae was very appreciative that I had made the effort to return to the Korean peninsula. They showed their thanks by taking me on a tour of the neighboring Korean Naval Academy and the Republic of Korea navy base, Korea's largest naval base.

At the base, there was a strange looking ship docked in the harbor. At first glance, it reminded me of a Viking ship, but on closer inspection it was much more Asian in design.

"That, Mr. Karges, is the Korean turtle ship," my guide, a young, American navy petty officer explained.

"It was the first ironclad warship in the world," our Korean navy driver said with pride.

"It was invented and built by Admiral Yi Soon Shin, the most famous admiral in Korean history. You may have seen a statue of him in town," the Korean went on.

"Yes, I believe we circled it before coming onto the base," I said remembering seeing a life size statue of a military man of some type through the sheets of rain that accompanied my visit to Chinhae.

"Admiral Yi conquered the seas with this turtle ship during the Korean and Japanese war of 1592 through 1598, and this exact replica of the ship was created in his honor," the Korean explained.

"Can we board her?" I asked.

"So sorry, not today; however, I can tell you a bit more about her," the Korean said as he turned off the ignition and we sat in a parking lot overlooking the ship as rain beat down upon the vehicle and sliced into the water below.

"The deck is made firm with boards from two inches to a foot thick, and it is roofed with iron plates on the boards. Numerous spikes on the plates prevent the enemy from boarding. The crew could look at the enemy from the ship, but the enemy could not see into the ship from the outside. As you can see, the bow is shaped like the head of a dragon and the stern is the tail of a turtle. A gun port is installed at each side of the dragonhead, and there are six more on the sides of the ship. The shape of the ship gives her its name, 'turtle ship.' It is easy to see why, yes?" the young Korean asked me.

"Oh yes, she's really beautiful and very unusual looking. It's amazing that Admiral Yi created this in the 16th century," I commented.

"Yes, a fearsome sight for his Japanese foes. She sailed beautifully with eight oars on each side and two sails for maneuvering. The masts were designed to stand up or lay down as needed.

"The turtle ship had a total of 24 cabins. Two were used as storage for iron and metal works, and three were designated for guns, bows, arrows, spears, swords and other weapons. The rest of the cabins were quarters for the crew. In the upper part of the ship there are two more cabins, one for the captain and the other for the officers."

"Sixteenth century warfare," my American guide said with a grin.

"The study of world naval history reveals that Admiral Yi Soon Shin's turtle ship was the most unique and epic achievement of its time," the Korean sailor concluded with more than a hint of pride.

"We best be headed back to base," the American petty officer said as he put his hand on the Korean's shoulder from the back seat.

That evening, despite the rain which had not let up since my arrival, the appropriately named Turtle Cove Club was packed, and I had the honor of performing for Vice Admiral Sur, commander of the Republic of Korea fleet and the second highest ranking officer in the ROK navy.

About 1,000 miles south of Korea is the Japanese island of Okinawa, the next stop on the tour. My travel orders had me returning to Japan via a very convoluted, circuitous route. I thought that the natural routing would take me directly from Busan to Seoul, Osaka or Tokyo and then nonstop to Okinawa. I entered Japan through some small airport, and I had a great deal of difficulty clearing customs despite the fact that I was on military travel orders. I couldn't find anyone who spoke English well enough to explain what the problem was. Eventually, they threw up their hands in disgust and let me in.

Upon landing in Okinawa, I was reunited with Charlotte. Kurt, our host for our time on the island, explained that I wouldn't be allowed back in Japan if I left, went to Korea and tried to reenter the country.

"We did it on the last tour," I said.

"No, you didn't. You either played Korea first or Japan first. You didn't bounce back and forth between the two countries," Kurt insisted.

"Yeah, I guess you're right," I said thinking back to the previous year's tour.

"What if they wouldn't let me back in?" I asked.

"We would work something out. I think there was a contingency plan to send you on to Singapore and then back here," Kurt informed me.

"I wish someone had told me," I said a bit surprised.

"Relax, it worked, didn't it?" Kurt asked, and I had to admit that it had.

"Wait a minute. They would have let me come in from Singapore but not Korea?" I asked trying to understand the situation.

"Yeah. Craig, there's still some animosity between the Koreans and the Japanese," Kurt tried to explain. "Personally, I'm American and Okinawan. Dad was an American Marine and Mom was Okinawan. While Okinawa is a prefecture of Japan, we like to think we're pretty independent. Actually, our culture is more Chinese than Japanese, and the American presence here because of the military is overwhelming."

Animosity between the Koreans and the Japanese? I thought back to Admiral Yi and the Korean-Japanese war of 1592-1598. I remembered from the year before when we had toured the Changdeokgung Palace in Seoul that our guide kept mentioning the fact that parts of the palace had to be rebuilt every decade or so due to fires. Our tour manager, Lou, innocently asked why there were so many fires. Our tour guide looked around, lowered her voice and said, "The Japanese, they came many times." There was also that confusion I had when flying Korean Air or Japan Airlines. On the Korean Air route system map, the body of water between Japan and Korea was identified as the Korea Strait while JAL identified it as the Sea of Japan.

But I was on Okinawa now. It was always one of my favorite stops on this Far East Tour, and this year was no exception. The doors to the Crows Nest Club ballroom opened two hours early, and a queue had already formed. Thirty minutes before show time the house was full, but people kept coming. Every chair was moved out of the adjoining nightclub to help accommodate the crowd, and as I took the stage it was standing room only, the ballroom packed wall-to-wall with sailors, Marines, civilian workers and their families. It is a great memory of this particular tour.

The end of tour was almost in sight. Charlotte and I flew from Okinawa to Taipei, Taiwan, to connect to a China Airlines flight for the four-hour journey over the South China Sea to reach our final destination, Singapore.

The Fortunes of Singapore

As if brown tree snakes, typhoons, missing tour managers, state department warnings and monsoons weren't enough, I should point out that we were traveling in the middle of a SARS scare. SARS is an acronym for Severe Acute Respiratory Syndrome, a respiratory disease. Throughout this tour, the airports were filled with travelers whose faces were covered with masks. We considered wearing one but opted not to, although Charlotte felt that some of the plaid Burberry designer facemasks worn by the more affluent Japanese women were quite stylish. In Taiwan, we had to walk through heat sensors. If a passenger were giving off too much heat, he would be pulled from the queue and examined. We were in line with one such woman. She caught up to us later and let us know that she was OK. She had been wearing too many layers of clothing. Once she removed some of them, her body temperature cooled down and she was permitted to continue her journey. While we were boarding our flight to Singapore, a young lady standing behind us fainted. She was helped to her feet and insisted on boarding the plane. She was denied boarding and taken off to a room for examination. We never saw her again.

Word had reached us on Okinawa that we would be staying off base in the luxurious Raffles Hotel in Singapore as a way of rewarding us for this rather tiring tour. We were really looking forward to this first time visit to the small island city-state.

Singapore is located off the southern tip of Malaysia, just 84 miles north of the equator. Despite the fact that I've traveled over four million miles in 17 countries on four continents, I've never been in the Southern Hemisphere. Singapore is the closest I've ever gotten. Singapore is a real melting pot with a multicultural population of nearly five million people and is considered the jewel of Southeast Asia. Almost everyone in Singapore speaks decent English, except for the Indian driver who picked us up at the airport.

We were anxious to check into our hotel and have a grand dinner. We'd been talking about it all day. However, it seemed as if our driver was taking us away from the bright lights of Singapore. I tried to ask him about the hotel.

"Raffles Hotel?"

"No."

"We're supposed to go to the hotel."

"No."

We were getting further and further away from where I believed the city center of Singapore to be.

185

"MWR?" I asked.

"Yes," he replied.

"Logistic Group, Western Pacific, U.S. Navy Contracting Center," I said mentioning the groups I would be performing for the next day.

"Yes."

I just sat back in the seat with my head next to Charlotte's and said, "I guess we're going to the base."

"I just hope they have a restaurant," she said.

After a thirty minute drive, we pulled on to the base. It was very dark. It wasn't an active military base but rather a former British military base dating back to the early 1900s when Singapore was a British Crown Colony.

Our driver pulled up to a barricaded roadway and got out of the car. He walked back to the trunk, opened it and began to remove our luggage. Charlotte and I joined him wondering what was coming next. He set all the bags on the ground and then pointed over the barricade to a building about 100 yards distant as he handed us a set of keys.

We played charades with the Indian and came to the realization that the building was our next destination. He jumped in the car and disappeared as we began dragging our two weeks worth of clothes and show props toward the four-story structure. As we approached the building, we halted. There were armed guards, Singapore military, at the front of the building. I tried to engage them in conversation but all we got was an indication that we were to go to the fourth floor of this building and presumably make ourselves at home. It took two trips each for us to get all the bags up to the fourth floor while climbing a darkened stairway. The light bulbs were either extinguished or burned out. We entered a loft-like apartment, complete with multiple bedrooms, and we wondered aloud if we were sharing it with anyone else. We had a key to the floor and an additional key to one of the bedrooms.

"Hello? Anyone here?" We called out.

No response.

"Well, I guess it's all ours," I said.

"I'm really hungry," Charlotte said.

"Me too, but I don't know what to do. I didn't see a restaurant or a place to get food of any kind, did you?"

"Nope."

"I'm going to call Mike on his cell and see why we aren't in the hotel," I said getting irritated that we had no idea what was going on.

When I finally got Mike on the phone, he sounded a bit tipsy.

"Mike, I thought we were going to be off base, in the Raffles."

"Sorry about that."

"Is there anyplace we can get something to eat on base? We haven't eaten all day."

"Not at this hour. Again, I'm sorry."

"Well, do you mind if we call a taxi and go back downtown and check into a hotel? We'll be back on base tomorrow say around four o'clock for the six o'clock show."

"Do as you like," he said with no concern in his voice as he hung up his phone.

I started looking for an information booklet that would have a taxi service's number in it.

"Honey, just forget it. We don't even know where we are. Let's just go to bed. We can see Singapore tomorrow," Charlotte advised.

I agreed with her, and we showered and went to bed without knowing if we were sharing the apartment with anyone else.

At 1:00 a.m., an alarm went off in an adjoining bedroom.

"What? There must be someone else here," I said groggily.

The alarm kept buzzing and buzzing. I walked the halls in an attempt to find the bedroom containing the buzzing alarm clock. I located the proper door and banged on it.

"Can you turn that thing off? We're trying to get some sleep!"

No answer. It soon became apparent that no one was in the room.

"Oh great," Charlotte said, "I can't sleep with that thing going off."

I leafed through a small phone directory and punched in the number for what I believed to be base security. A woman answered and I explained our predicament.

"I'm sorry sir. I'm the only one in the office and I can't leave. You can come over and get a key to that room if you'd like."

"I just got here and I don't even know where I am."

"There's a map in the directory, just follow it to building J."

"It's 1:15 in the morning and there are armed guards outside."

"They won't bother you. It's less than a mile walk, just make sure you have your passport and travel orders on you."

I got dressed and headed out into the night.

"Good luck honey," Charlotte said as I headed down the darkened stairwell.

I eventually found the security office, got the key and headed back. The desk worker explained that I could get a taxi the next morning. She told me where to go in Singapore and where to be dropped off on the base when we returned for the show. It was my first official welcome, and I did feel a bit more comfortable.

Charlotte was glad to see me when I got back to the apartment. We entered the bedroom with the offensive alarm clock and silenced the machine. Then we set our own alarm and went back to sleep.

The next morning, a taxi dropped us off on Orchard Road. Our first order of business was breakfast at a nice bistro, and then we were off to explore Singapore. Orchard Road is jam-packed with shopping possibilities, from high end, international department stores, to designer shops, to tiny boutiques. We wandered in and out of stores taking in some of the wonders of Singapore.

Singapore is a multi-religious country where everyone seems to get along. In fact, the government promotes religious tolerance. Racial and religious harmony is always a top priority. You'll find Buddhist and Hindu temples as well as Shinto shrines, Muslim mosques and Christian churches throughout the city.

On the fringe of Orchard Road lies the Tanglin Shopping Center, and this is where we spent the late morning as well as early afternoon. It is the oldest shopping complex in Singapore. We befriended a tailor at the Tanglin Silk Store, and he created a beautiful chocolate brown three-piece suit for me as well as two silk jackets for Charlotte. Our time in Singapore was short to be sure, and he had to send our clothing to the U.S. He said if we had an extra day in the country he could have completed the work and we could have taken it home with us. That is fast!

We spent so much time in the Tanglin Shopping Center because of Charlotte's love for antiques. It was filled with dealers in Asian antiquities, antiquarian books, 19th century photographs, Japanese woodblock prints and Qing Dynasty porcelain along with carpet merchants, jewelry and curio shops. It was the modern equivalent of a bazaar from an Indiana Jones film, and Charlotte just fell in love with it. She was determined to find the perfect souvenir of this trip and kept running back and forth between antique dealers comparing antique Buddha heads.

As Charlotte shopped for antiques, I wandered into a curious looking store not far from the shopping center. It appeared to be a fortunetelling shop of some type.

"Welcome friend," said the bald Asian man, wearing a long black robe.

"Hello," I responded, meeting his gaze and then looking around the unique shop.

"How is your day?" he asked.

"Oh, I'm really enjoying myself but I have to admit, I'm very, very tired."

"Have a seat," he said as he pulled out one of two chairs situated around a small, round table.

I was in a daze from lack of sleep and an overload of sights and sounds in Singapore. I immediately slumped into the chair.

"Would you care for some tea?" My host asked.

"That would be great," I said as the small Asian man disappeared through a beaded curtain and returned half a minute later carrying two small teacups. He sat opposite me at the table.

"What are you, some kind of fortuneteller?" I asked.

"In a manner of speaking, yes. However, I do not really read the future, I guess at the future based on the omens in the present. Life is an ever-changing set of conditions. If you pay attention to the present, you can improve upon it. Improve upon your present, and your future is improved as well," he said with a grin before adding, "Would you like a consultation?"

The tea was good and I felt very relaxed; so the word "sure" slipped from between my lips, and my host opened his hand to magically reveal three Chinese coins.

"I shall do a casting with you based on the I-Ching, *The Book of Changes*. You are familiar with it?"

"I've heard the term," I admitted, "but I don't know much about it, and I don't remember coins being involved."

"Well, the traditional I-Ching casting is done with rods made from bamboo or yarrow stalks, but it takes some time and many of my Western visitors do not seem to have much time; so they find the process tedious. This will be much faster."

"I do have to catch back up with my wife," I said.

"Very well, but before we begin, let me introduce myself, I am Master Ju."

"And my name is Craig, Craig Karges," I said a bit embarrassed by my lack of social grace in this situation.

"Well, Mr. Craig Karges, let me tell you before we begin that the I-Ching is the oldest system of fortune reading in the world. It dates back over seven-thousand years to the very first emperor of China, Fu-Hsi. The system was divinely revealed to him in a vision when he saw a three-lined pattern on the side of a hippogriff."

"A hippogriff, what's a hippogriff?"

"A winged creature with the body of a horse and the head of a dragon," Master Ju said seriously while looking me straight in the eye.

"Oh, maybe I should be getting back to my wife," I said.

"No, no. I am only telling you the story of the I-Ching. You do not have to believe it to benefit from it. You would not be the only one who does not believe in hippogriffs. There are those who think Emperor Fu-Hsi is a mythical creature too," he said with that grin of his.

"OK, I'll bite. What do I have to do in order to get my reading?"

"You are very impatient," Master Ju stated.

"My apologies, but my time is limited."

"This will be worth your time, I promise."

"This first three-lined-pattern, or trigram, envisioned by the emperor was expanded over the years to 64 hexagrams, or two of these three-lined-patterns on top of one another creating a six-line pattern." As Ju said this, he drew a series of six parallel lines, one above the other, some broken, some not.

"These 64 hexagrams represent the answers to all possible questions you have about your life. They reflect the natural patterns in nature. The hexagrams are based on the Yin and Yang of the universe. You know Yin and Yang?"

My mind flashed to the black and white swirling symbol I had often seen in the past. I looked about Ju's shop and pointed to just such a symbol on a pendant hanging in the corner of the shop, "That's the symbol for Yin and Yang isn't it?" I asked.

"Yes, yes, very good," Ju said, "but, of course, it is more than just a symbol. The universe is composed of opposites; however, these opposites complement each other. The nature of Yang is firm and active while Yin is passive and yielding. This is why the Yang line is unbroken and the Yin line is broken. The concept of Yin and Yang is reflected in all areas of life, and all areas of life are reflected in the 64 hexagrams of the I-Ching. Changes to these hexagrams, additions and subtractions, were made over thousands of years. Do you know Kung-Fu-Tse?" Master Ju suddenly asked.

"Do I know Kung Fu? You mean the martial art?"

"No, Kung-Fu Tse is better known as Confucius," Ju stated.

"Oh sure, the great Chinese philosopher," I said with recognition.

The Fortunes of Singapore

"Twenty-five-hundred years ago, Confucius said he wished he could live fifty years longer solely to devote those fifty years to the study of the I-Ching," Master Ju said.

"The I-Ching reached Japan about one-thousand-four-hundred years ago. Marco Polo brought it to Europe in 1298, when he returned from China. It continues to spread, and today it comes to you, Craig Karges," Ju went on as he handed me the three Chinese coins.

"This side of the coin shows its value," Master Ju said as he tapped one of the coins in my hand, "while this side does not," he added, flipping the same coin over in my hand.

"The value side is Yin, the opposite side is Yang. Please take the coins in your cupped hands, shake them and drop them on the table," Ju instructed.

As the coins fell to the table, I noticed that two landed value side up and one did not.

"Two Yin and one Yang which would result in a broken line being drawn. We do this a total of six times to achieve a hexagram. If the majority of the coins are Yin, a broken line is drawn. If the majority shows Yang, a solid line is created. However, before casting, you must consider a question about your life," Ju explained.

"Do I have to tell you the question?"

"No, I would rather you did not," Ju said, somewhat to my surprise.

I have to admit I was bone-tired. It had been a very long two weeks with so many travel difficulties, the topper being the previous night in Singapore. I had many emotions fighting for the control of my behavior. I was a little angry, a little disappointed and a lot tired! However, I was enjoying the performances and I loved Singapore. I only wished I could stay a few days longer, but I couldn't as I had to be back in the States for yet another presentation. There were so many extraordinary things to see and do here. I wanted to catch a production at the state-of-the-art performing arts center, the Esplande; go on a nighttime safari at the award winning Singapore Zoo; cruise out to Sentosa Island and enjoy its beaches, nature park and restaurants; see the botanical gardens; and explore the Raffles Hotel.

As I considered my question, my mind kept coming back to my current situation and if I would ever return to Singapore. I shook the coins vigorously in my hands as I thought, *Will I arrive home without difficulty, and will I ever return?*

The coins clattered on the table and the first line was drawn. I repeated this five times to create a six-line hexagram that Master Ju began to study. To me it looked like (from the bottom up), a solid line, a broken line, another broken line and then three solid lines in a row. Master Ju was apparently seeing much more.

"This is the Wu-Wang, hexagram number 25 of the 64 I-Ching hexagrams," he explained.

"What does it mean?"

"Innocence."

"Innocence?"

"Yes, to me anyway. I would counsel you this way: you are in the middle of a chain of events that you cannot control; you are innocent; the results of this chain of events may not be what you expect; or your desired outcome may not come to fruition; but things will end favorably if you allow yourself to go with the flow of what is happening around you," Ju said as he folded his arms and rested them on the small table.

I just sat there considering the possibilities.

"Ponder this Craig Karges. Think of my statement's relevance in the light of the question you asked," Master Ju said.

"Well, I can see a number of connections," I said.

"Let's try something deeper," Ju said as he grabbed my wrists and asked me to grip his.

"Think about your question," he instructed.

And I did. *Will I arrive home without difficulty, and will I ever return?*

"Ah, you asked more than one question, yes?" Ju said to my surprise.

"Yeah, I guess I did."

"It has to do with travel, travel you are experiencing now."

I didn't say anything and I tried to restrain from giving him any feedback with my body language. I wanted to see if he could somehow mystically divine my question.

Ju went on, unfazed by my lack of response, "You are traveling for business, not pleasure. You have had a very long and difficult trip with many obstructions along your path, many surprises and most of them unpleasant. You will have at least one more unpleasant surprise before you return home, perhaps two. However you will overcome them both. Ah, you will be able to do at least one of the many things you wish to do. And a short while after your trip is finished, you will receive a pleasant surprise to help you remember this particular journey, and you will cherish it. This gift coupled with your experiences this evening will be the Yin to the Yang you have experienced throughout your current travels. And I hope that one day your future travels bring you back to Singapore and back to see me, Master Ju."

"Thank you Master Ju," I said while shaking my head in disbelief over the accuracy of the reading.

I glanced at my watch and saw that I had spent over an hour with the geomancer. I quickly paid him and rushed out the door to find Charlotte, all the while marveling that I had stumbled on such an extraordinary experience.

Charlotte was leaving one of the antique shops with a find of her own, a two-hundred-year-old alabaster Shan Buddha head.

Is this the pleasant surprise Master Ju spoke of? I thought, but then remembered he said it would come a short time after my trip was finished; so I dismissed the idea.

We were running late and had to get back to the base for the show. We hailed a taxi and arrived at the venue. It was about an hour before I was to start the performance at a very unique tented and ceiling fan equipped clubhouse patio with a stage and full PA system.

Our contact, Mike, greeted us immediately.

"Craig, Charlotte, I am so sorry about last night," he said. "I heard about all the problems you had, and I'm sorry about the hotel. You were definitely supposed to be at the Raffles. I just dropped the ball. I was in town for a lunch meeting which turned into a three martini lunch. Then I met some friends for dinner and wine—a little too much wine—and one thing led to another," he trailed off and looked down at his shoes.

"No worries, we made out OK," I said.

"I was going to be with Raj at the airport to pick you up, but I just didn't make it. Raj was a bit out of his element, as well," Mike explained.

"We could tell. Doesn't speak much English, does he?" Charlotte asked.

"No, but he's a good, good man, and he really bailed me out last night. After the show, I'm taking you to the Raffles, and Raj will be there in the morning to get you to the airport."

"We'll definitely take you up on the offer of the Raffles, but we'll taxi to the airport. I think we'll have to leave the hotel before four o'clock in the morning," I said.

"I know, I know, but it's the least we could do, and Raj doesn't mind," Mike said with finality.

While I was performing, Charlotte went back to our guest apartment and packed up our suitcases. Before we knew it, we were back in the center of town and checking into the Raffles Hotel.

There were so many other, extraordinary things to see and do in Singapore—explore the Raffles Hotel — " you will be able to do at least one of the many things you wish to do. " Master Ju's statement ran through my mind.

The Raffles' colonial-style architecture dates from 1887, and it's named after Sir Stamford Raffles who founded Singapore (The Lion City) in 1819 as a settlement and trading post for the British East India Company.

The Japanese occupied Singapore during World War II. When the occupation began on February 15th, it is said that the Japanese soldiers entered the hotel only to be greeted by all the guests dancing one final waltz in the ballroom. Three years later, during the liberation of Singapore, more than 300 Japanese soldiers committed suicide in the hotel using hand grenades.

We strolled the arcade with boutique stores the likes of Louis Vuitton, Tiffany & Company, and an Armani home store as well as art, antique and furniture galleries. Then, we had dinner at Doc Cheng's.

Legend has it that Doc Cheng was actually Cheng Soon Wen, the number one son of a wealthy rubber family dynasty in Penang. Wen's father died in a wild, drunken driving accident when he crashed his car into one of his favorite rubber trees on his plantation. The widow Cheng moved her family to Singapore where they purchased a mansion and hosted parties... a lot of *very wild* parties. Soon Wen loved the party life a bit too much; so his mother packed him off to Bangkok to live with a cousin. Bangkok proved to be a better playground for Soon Wen than Singapore! He was then sent to England in an effort to tame the young man. To everyone's surprise this did the trick! He graduated from Oxford with honors and went on to the Royal College of Surgeons, all the while experiencing the very best of London's epicurean delights. A scandalous affair with a well-known London socialite had Soon Wen packing his bags again, but he was sidetracked on his way home to Singapore and remained in Hamburg, Germany for some time. In Germany, he came under the tutelage of a Dr. Martini. After several years in Germany, he made it back to Singapore where he opened a medical practice not far from the Raffles Hotel. However, the Raffles exerted quite a pull on Doc Cheng (as everyone in Singapore referred to him), and he spent more time at the hotel than he did at his practice. Eventually, he moved his entire practice to the hotel's billiard room. It is said that the sick and injured coming to the Raffles became such a common sight that one day a man with a broken arm was simply checking into the hotel, and he was whisked to the billiard room where Doc Cheng reset the arm over a gin and tonic and a bowl of nuts! Doc Cheng continued to practice medicine from the Raffles up until the early part of World War II, when it is said he removed shrapnel from one of the hotel's gardeners after an air raid by using the billiards table as his operating table. Doc Cheng was a firm believer in the curative powers of good food and drink, often prescribing a strong Scotch instead of a pill. He was often heard to say: "The art of medicine consists of amusing the patient whilst nature cures the disease." Doc Cheng survived the war and passed on later. The restaurant is the hotel's tribute to the man, the myth and the legend, or so the story goes.

Regardless of the "truth" behind the legend of Doc Cheng, we had a wonderful meal in this eatery specializing in Western cuisine with an Asian twist. I shall always remember Doc Cheng's and the curried crab cakes with pineapple salsa along with the curried crab bisque. We dined in a tented booth as a very large Indian man, complete with turban and wearing a military style uniform, waited on us.

You can probably tell from this chapter that this was a very long and tiring trip. During the meal, Charlotte excused herself to go to the restroom, and I lay my head back on the cushioned booth and proceeded to doze off. I awoke staring into the eyes of our tall, Indian waiter who was towering over me!

After dinner, it was time to experience Singapore nightlife. We were determined to make Doc Cheng proud! We started in the hotel at the Long Bar. It's a two-story establishment designed to resemble a Malaysian plantation from the 1920s and it is home to the Singapore Sling invented by bartender Ngiam Tong Boon. The original recipe calls for equal parts gin, cherry brandy and Benedictine. The concoction is shaken and then strained into a glass and filled to taste with club soda. Current versions of the drink (including the Raffles' current version) add fruit juices and other ingredients not found in the original. Charlotte and I enjoyed our Singapore Slings, and then we were off to an evening of bar hopping and sight seeing, ending the evening at the Chijmes (pronounced chimes) complex. This is a magical, enclosed village of restaurants, bars, clubs, boutiques and galleries created from a former cloistered convent called the Convent of the Holy Infant Jesus. The actual 1904 gothic-style chapel has been restored and is a National Heritage Site. The courtyard trees are lighted at night, and Charlotte and I stared down, watching the revelers among the lighted trees before joining them behind cloistered walls.

At two o'clock, we decided we better head back to the Raffles. We never slept that night, but we did have time to pack and shower before meeting Raj and heading to Changi International Airport to start the first leg of our trip home.

We arrived at the airport at 4:00 a.m. only to be told that our flight had been canceled. *You will have at least one more unpleasant surprise before you return home.* We were able to reroute onto another airline for a seven-hour flight from Singapore to Tokyo's Narita International Airport. That flight was followed by a twelve-hour flight to Chicago. We experienced an extraordinary phenomenon as we actually arrived in the U.S. on the same day and at the same time that we departed Tokyo. This was thanks to the magic of the International Date Line. We collected our bags in Chicago and rechecked them to our "home" airport, Pittsburgh, Pennsylvania which is about an hour from our actual home in the West Virginia mountains. We arrived in Pittsburgh, but our bags didn't! How can they make it from Singapore to Tokyo and from Tokyo to Chicago and then get lost on the fifty-minute flight from Chicago to Pittsburgh?

You will have at least one more unpleasant surprise before you return home, perhaps two. However, you will overcome them both.

My bags caught up with me late that night at the Pittsburgh Hilton where I stayed as Charlotte traveled back home. You see, my government work still wasn't finished. I had to deliver the closing keynote presentation for the U.S. Department of Energy's Human Resource Symposium the following morning. After the presentation, it was finally time to head home and get some rest. This tour encompassed nine performances and over 27,000 miles of air travel during 17 flight segments on eight different airlines. What a trip it was!

I thought about Master Ju after returning home. The unpleasant surprises were obvious, and we did overcome them. However, I was still awaiting the unexpected, pleasant surprise.

And a short while after your trip is finished you will receive a pleasant surprise to help you remember this particular journey, and you will cherish it.

A few days later, a large package from Korea arrived in the mail. As I ripped it open, I *was* surprised and very touched when I found a beautiful replica of legendary Korean Admiral Yi Soon Shin's 16th century turtle ship. It has a place of honor in my office library, and I do cherish it as I cherish the memory of our short time in Singapore.

CHAPTER EIGHTEEN

Vampires in the Balkans

In May of 2005, I was "drafted" by the United States Army for a series of performances in the Balkans. I knew this tour was going to be a bit different from my previous military outings, because I was technically headed into a war zone. That reality hit home when I signed an "Assumption of Risk" agreement with the production company releasing them of any liability in case of injury—including death! There was also that nagging contract clause which reminded me that I was responsible for returning all military issued equipment including helmet, chin strap and body armor!

I arrived in Europe via Frankfurt, Germany, where I picked up a connecting flight to Vienna, Austria. In Vienna, I met my tour manager, Jeff Davidson. Jeff is a military tour veteran. In fact, he had just finished working sound and lights for the Iraq portion of Jessica Simpson and Nick Lachey's *Nick and Jessica's Tour of Duty* television special.

From Vienna, it was on to Pristina, in Kosovo. Kosovo is kind of a "No Man's Land" surrounded by Albania, Macedonia, Serbia and Montenegro.

Upon arrival in Kosovo, all the sound equipment was confiscated by customs! We were notified that the equipment would be impounded until the proper paperwork was generated. That was the bad news. The good news was that we were greeted by an armed military escort. With a cutvee (SUV) up front and a Humvee bringing up the rear, we headed off to Camp Bondsteel which would serve as the base of operations for the Kosovo Forces (KFOR) portion of the tour.

The following day, the sound equipment was bailed out and we met up with another armed convoy and headed off for Camp Monteith where I performed for Task Force Sidewinder to a very enthusiastic reception. It was the same the following day when I performed for my host base, Camp Bondsteel.

As we convoyed around Kosovo, I noticed a number of road signs with images of animals on them. I asked our KFOR contact about this and she told me that due to the confluence of cultures and languages in Kosovo and the fact that the region is not really a country, the roads are named after animals to make navigation easier to understand. For example, "Go to the intersection of Rat and Stag and make a left on Rat!"

Next stop, Sarajevo, Bosnia-Herzegovina, for the second half of the tour. An armed convoy escorted us back to Pristina International Airport. On the way, we passed a UN Police drugs and/or weapons bust. A trio of Mercedes sedans and a van were pulled to the side of the road. The vehicles were being searched as the drivers and passengers were being frisked and handcuffed. This was the only hint of any trouble I experienced while in Kosovo.

Flying back through Vienna, we were greeted by "Mac" McNeill and "Road Rage Rudy" upon the arrival of our Austrian Airlines flight in Sarajevo. Mac's most important piece of advice was to stay on the hard (paved) surfaces at all times. There are an estimated one million undetonated land mines in and around Sarajevo!

It was an overnight at Camp Butmir and then a "meet and greet" and impromptu show for the HQ Commandant, Colonel Peterson, before we boarded Rudy's deluxe (no kidding!) tour bus and headed off on a two plus hour trek through the mountains to Eagle Base.

Both Camp Butmir and Eagle Base were once part of SFOR (Sarajevo Forces) Task Force North, an American led force. However, with the Iraq War taking precedence, the bases transitioned into EUFOR (European Union Forces) bases with NATO and EUFOR peacekeepers from 16 nations present, along with a small contingent of Americans. This multinational environment was fascinating, even if the language barriers made the performances somewhat more challenging!

The Eagle Base appearance was held in the Fest Tent where the show went over extremely well for the multinational Brigade North.

It was back down the mountains, with Road Rage Rudy, the best bus driver in the world, behind the wheel for a return to Sarajevo.

Before the Camp Butmir performance, I was treated to the "Mac Express" tour of Sarajevo. This was a real highlight of the trip. It was conducted by the one and only Mac McNeill, the fastest and most entertaining tour guide ever! We zipped around the city visiting the Olympic stadium

Vampires in the Balkans

(Sarajevo hosted the 1984 Winter Olympics) and viewing the city from the surrounding mountains.

Madness reigned here for nearly five years in the 1990s as the Serbians held the city under siege with daily shelling from these very same mountains. More than 10,000 citizens were killed and much of the city was destroyed. Sarajevo was dubbed "The Most Dangerous City on Earth."

Sipping espresso in the heart of the old city section of Sarajevo, it was hard to equate this beautiful European city with that bloody time period. However, you didn't have to look far to notice the mortar fire pockmarks in the buildings and the occasional building or home that was battered and beaten to near oblivion and beyond salvation. And then there were the cemeteries—there are many graves in Sarajevo.

This entire area was once part of the Austro-Hungarian Empire. In fact, Sarajevo was the site of the assassination of the Austrian Archduke, Franz Ferdinand, which started World War I. Serbs who were worried about being persecuted under Austrian rule killed Ferdinand and his wife Sophie. The country of Yugoslavia was created at the end of World War II. In 1991, Yugoslavia began to fall apart and various sections began to claim their independence. The remnants of the Yugoslavian army, in a pretense to hold Yugoslavia together, attacked two of the newly created republics, Slovenia and Croatia.

In an attempt to gain international protection, Bosnia declared its independence; but many Bosnian-Serbs rejected this. Coincidentally, the Yugoslavian army was made up primarily of Serbians. This is when the shelling began, and it didn't let up for nearly five years, the longest military siege in modern times.

Walking around Sarajevo, I noticed some mortar fire marks in the ground. They appeared to be painted red, and I asked Mac about them.

"That's the Red Rose of Sarajevo," he said. I must have looked at him in puzzlement because he added, "The mortar fire spreads out on impact and takes on the resemblance of a rose. When the mortar fire marks are painted red, that indicates someone died here because of that shell. It's a tribute to their memory and the memories of all who died during that time period."

It is very hard to get your head around the entire Bosnian-Serbian situation. Sarajevo is definitely on the fast track to recovery. The Sarajevo region is now part of Bosnia and Herzegovina (BiH). Shortly before I began my tour, there was a ceremony that was supposed to be historic. The purpose of the ceremony was to induct several hundred new soldiers into the Army of Bosnia and Herzegovina from the Serbian dominated Republic of Srpska. When the BiH national anthem played, there was booing and catcalls from the crowd. When it came time for the new soldiers to swear allegiance to BiH, they refused as a group and declared their loyalty to Srpska. It was a very embarrassing afternoon, and a further example of the fragmentation that is taking place in this part of the world.

As my tour of the old city section of Sarajevo continued, we stopped at another outdoor café for yet another espresso. Some gypsy children came up to us, and Mac engaged them in conversation and a smile along with the occasional euro. In addition to the children, we were also approached by older men and women dressed in layer upon layer of outdated clothing on this mild June day. These citizens mingled with the beautiful people who pranced around the old city in Europe's finest fashions. It was a study in contrasts to say the least. Mac and Jeff decided to follow a couple of the more *beautiful of the beautiful* people down the street. I declined and decided to have another espresso.

As I was drinking and thinking, a distinguished looking man approached the table. He was dressed in a black suit complete with vest and tie. He needed a shave but his eyes were bright and I was curious as to what he might want.

"Hello my friend, are you American?" He asked.

"It's that obvious?" I said.

"Well, yes. Does that embarrass you?"

"Not at all. Sometimes I'd like to pass for Canadian, but I'm proud of where I'm from."

He laughed and asked, "Are you enjoying Sarajevo?" His English was excellent.

"Very much so. Unfortunately, it's a short visit, just business really with this afternoon off for some sightseeing."

"You should come back when you have more time. The region is filled with beauty and history."

"I've been getting a bit of a history lesson as well as a geography lesson."

The man was incredibly polite and well spoken, but I was tiring of the conversation. I was thinking about reaching into my pocket and giving him a euro or two. Then I felt as if that might insult him, and I still wasn't sure what he wanted; so I asked, "Do you live in Sarajevo?"

"No, just visiting. My name is Dimitri and I am from Romania. You have been there?"

"No, not this trip. I'd like to go though. I enjoy traveling anywhere new."

"Actually, I live in the Transylvania region, you have heard of Transylvania?"

"Oh yes," I said, "Dracula, Vlad the Impaler, the most famous vampire ever."

"Yes, yes, a terrible, savage and ruthless ruler but not a vampire. I have an affinity for the old stories. That is part of the reason I am here. Did you know that the best documented case of a vampire happened in Yugoslavia?"

"No," I said trying to finish up our conversation before he asked for a pint of blood. But before I knew it, the old man was seated across from me, motioning to the waiter for an espresso for himself and another for me.

"The vampire was named Arnold Paole. But I am getting ahead of myself. You have to understand what this area of the world was like in the early and middle 1700s. It was under Hapsburg rule. The Hapsburgs' enemies were the Turks. The Hapsburgs were Catholic, and they thought the Orthodox Serbs in the area were helping the Turks," he explained.

"One way the Catholic Hapsburgs convinced the citizenry of their spiritual superiority was to hunt down and kill vampires. Unfortunately, they were actually playing on the people's superstitious nature, and many of the so-called vampires were actually the same Orthodox Serbs the Hapsburgs believed to be collaborating with the Turks. Convenient, eh?"

I nodded my head yes and asked, "So these weren't real vampires? They were just people accused of being vampires, innocent people killed like the innocents killed in Scotland and Salem, Massachusetts in my country where we had the Salem Witch Trials," I said, as I attempted to answer my own question.

"Oh yes, many innocent people died. But that doesn't mean there weren't real vampires as well," he said.

"Like that Arnold guy you mentioned earlier."

"Yes, Arnold Paole."

"Well, you have me hooked, tell me more," I said.

"Delighted. I love practicing my English. It is a most difficult language to master. Arnold Paole returned to his village near Belgrade as a young ex-military man. This was in 1727. According to all outward appearances, he seemed normal. He became engaged to the daughter of a rich man and appeared to settle down.

"However, as his betrothed, Nina, spent more time with Arnold, it became clear that there was something troubling him. Others who tried to get close to him felt the same way. Something was not right about the man.

"One day, Nina confronted him. Arnold admitted to her that he was bothered by the idea of a premature burial. This seemed quite odd to her, and she felt that there was something more to the story; so she pressed on in her questioning. Arnold revealed that he had been visited by the undead while he was in Greece, serving in the military. Arnold went on to tell her that he found the vampire's grave and destroyed the body hoping it would rid him of any evil his encounter with the undead may have caused."

"And she believed him?" I asked.

"Yes, and with good reason. These were different times my young American friend. And, as you will soon find out, she had every reason to believe him and every reason to fear him."

Despite the warm, sunny day, a shiver ran down my spine. Not so much from his words, but from the look in his eyes and the intensity with which he spoke.

"During harvest time, Arnold fell from a wagon and died. Within a month villagers reported seeing Arnold Paole roaming the village at night. Some people said he visited them, and four of those people died shortly after reporting the visit of the vampire. After months of these sightings, the decision was made to disinter his body.

"Two soldiers from Belgrade along with two army surgeons, a drummer boy and a sexton of the church formed the committee that was to open the casket. When Arnold Paole's casket was opened what they found was not the body of a man who had been dead for months, but instead, the body of a man who could have died the day before. Not only that, but there was fresh blood about his mouth. Upon closer examination, they found the old skin peeling off and a layer of new skin appearing beneath the old—like a snake!" He shouted as he jabbed his hand at me, his index and middle finger pointing at me like the fangs of a serpent. I jumped in my chair.

"And his nails," he went on, " a new set of fingernails was growing beneath his old nails." Dimitri shuddered as he said this.

"The committee was horrified and the decision was made then and there to destroy the body. Garlic was spread over the body and a stake was driven through Arnold Paole's undead corpse. Blood gushed from the body and a terrible shriek was heard. Make no mistake about it; Arnold Paole was indeed a creature of the night.

"Then, the committee dug up the graves of the four who had died after being visited by the vampire. Stakes were driven through their bodies and then all five bodies were burned, their ashes buried in consecrated ground."

"And so ends the tale of Arnold Paole, vampire?" I asked.

"No," Dimitri curtly replied as he fixed me with a stern stare. I felt myself sink further back in my chair.

"Five years later there were more deaths in the village, three in total. The commonality was that each of these people had lost an extraordinary amount of blood. As in the case of Arnold Paole, the bodies were exhumed. What they found were fresh, well fed bodies which looked like they were resting. When they compared the bodies of the suspected vampires to those of people who died at the same time, there was no sign of decomposition with the vampires, and yet, the other bodies were in advanced stages of decay.

"To be safe, the poor souls believed to be vampires had stakes driven through them, were decapitated, and once again these bodies were burned and the ashes buried in consecrated ground. And so ends the story of Arnold Paole and his children of the night," Dimitri intoned as he swirled the last of his espresso in his cup and downed it quickly.

"Fascinating," I said, "but do you believe the story?"

"Yes. It is very well documented. There was an official inquiry by the Austrian government, and all that I told you was what was reported and signed off on by three army surgeons, a lieutenant colonel and a sub-lieutenant. It is a matter of history; it is a matter of record. Now, if you will excuse me, I must go," he said quickly as he rose from his chair and placed a ten euro note on the table.

This gesture shocked me as I was assuming I would be on the hook for the espresso at least.

"No, let me pay," I said, "your story was well worth a cup of espresso."

"No, my pleasure. You helped me practice my English, I am grateful." And with that, he was off just as my tour manager and entertainment contact were returning to the café.

"C'mon man, we better go," Jeff said. "We've got about ninety minutes to show time."

Back on base, I filled the very American Sam's Bar with an enthusiastic crowd for the final show of the Balkans Tour. Following an autograph signing session, I joined the rest of the base for the Italian National Celebration (Italy's equivalent to the Fourth of July) that lasted into the wee hours of the morning. For me, the highlight of the celebration had to be the "a cappella" rendition of *Take Me Home Country Roads* (West Virginia's unofficial anthem), sung by Jeff, three Brits, an Austrian, a Fijian, a Bulgarian and me! Only on a NATO base in the Balkans!

As I headed back to my room for the night, I couldn't help but think about the monsters of old, the vampires, and the real monsters that inhabit the world today. The monsters that caused so much death and destruction in this beautiful city of Sarajevo.

CHAPTER NINETEEN

Virgin Islands Twilight Zone

Have you ever felt as if you'd stepped into *The Twilight Zone?* Sometimes I feel as if I live half my life there! However, a three-day period a half-dozen years ago really stands out in my mind.

It all began with a great booking. I was hired to go to St. Thomas in the U.S. Virgin Islands for a return appearance for a leasing company. This was their annual sales meeting, and I had worked it a few years before. The event was held at an all-inclusive resort (all the food you can eat, all the alcohol you can consume), and my client wanted me to arrive a day early to guarantee that there would be no travel problems; so he kindly offered two days at this beautiful resort.

At the time, US Airways was still flying direct to St. Thomas from my home airport, Pittsburgh, Pennsylvania. I booked a flight and was fortunate enough to get an automatic upgrade to first class due to my frequent flyer status with the airline. It looked great on paper—two days at an all-inclusive resort in the Virgin Islands along with a nice fee and first class air. Ah, the best laid plans....

Two weeks before my scheduled departure, I received a call from a speakers bureau wanting to know if I could "bail them out of an awkward situation." It seemed that an after-dinner speaker they had booked for a financial services event in South Florida had to cancel. The client's second choice was me and now they wanted to contract the event.

"They should have picked me in the first place," I laughed.

I didn't really want to do the date, as it would ruin any leisure time I had to spend in St. Thomas. However, when you're self-employed and you've lived through some very difficult times financially, you learn to take work when you can get it because you never know when the phone will stop ringing.

I had to check with my other client first to make sure he was OK with the fact that I would be coming in on the day of the event instead of the day before. He was, especially since he knew I was going to be coming from South Florida, and I was scheduled to arrive in the Virgin Islands around noon.

I took the financial services date and changed my flight plans. Now, instead of first class travel direct from Pittsburgh to St. Thomas, I was on an early morning American flight out of Miami in coach, in a middle seat headed to San Juan, Puerto Rico, where I would connect with a "puddle jumper" prop plane to take me to St. Thomas.

The financial services date was at the PGA National Resort, and that night, as the show began, so did my "Twilight Zone" episode.

I was about twenty minutes into my performance, and I noticed a man in the audience getting a bit agitated. One of the principals from the company was onstage taking part in a demonstration and this audience member seemed to be heckling him. All of a sudden, two security guards swept into the room and hustled the audience member out of the ballroom. I returned to the show, and we proceeded without incident to my final bow.

Afterwards, all the principals of the company approached me and explained that the gentleman in the audience had an "unhealthy obsession" with the man on stage. In fact, he wasn't even supposed to be at the meeting. The hotel made him check out of his room, threw him off the premises, and the local police issued a restraining order. Apparently, he already had a restraining order in effect in New Jersey, the headquarters of the company and the home of both men, the stalker and the stalker's target.

I left around 3:00 a.m. to drive to Miami International so I could be on the earliest flight to San Juan. I arrived in St. Thomas without incident and rented a car to drive to the resort. I had intended to take the shuttle. I had another early morning flight the next day requiring me to leave at 3:00 a.m. again, and I remembered how unreliable the shuttle service at this resort was from a previous visit. I wasn't even sure the shuttle would be running at that hour.

The cruise ships were in port, and traffic was extremely heavy as I crawled through the mountainous, winding roads toward the resort. I really had to concentrate on the road as it is "British style" driving in the Virgin Islands. You drive on the left hand side of the road. I checked-in and found a note requesting a two o'clock meeting with the client. It was almost two o'clock; so I quickly ditched my luggage in the room and headed to the hotel ballroom. No one was there to meet me. I tried the various cell phone numbers I had for my contacts and just got voice mail. I was hoping to make this a quick meeting so I could grab a couple hours sleep. I had been on the road for nearly eleven hours at this point.

Around 2:30 p.m., I decided to head back to my room, about a ten minute walk. Upon entering, I noticed that my message light on the phone was blinking. I dialed into hotel voice mail, and found it was my client who had called. He apologized for not being there and asked if I could please meet him at three o'clock? There went my power nap.

I went back to the room at three o'clock, and no one was in sight. I called the cell numbers again, but no one answered. I hung around for another thirty minutes and then headed back to my room. I walked in and the message light was blinking again. It was another apology from the client and a request to meet at four o'clock.

This time I showered and dressed for the performance since the event was to kick off at five o'clock with cocktails. I was back in the ballroom a little after four o'clock and only the hotel staff was visible. I began to set up my props and check out the stage area. At around five o'clock, my client came in, apologizing profusely for keeping me running back and forth. We had a quick discussion so I could further customize the presentation a bit and then the client mentioned the fact that I would be going on after some "island entertainment."

During dinner, my head started to throb. I rarely get headaches, but the weird experience from the night before, coupled with very little sleep, an early morning flight and the game of tag my client and I had played all afternoon resulted in a great pounding in my temples.

I made it through dinner, and it was time for the island entertainment. Four men on stilts walked into the room beating tin drums and yelling. My head was getting so heavy! A glass walker and fire-eater entered the room, each performing her specialty. The glass walker even ate some glass and held the microphone up to her mouth so we could all hear her crunching down on the shards. Lovely! My headache was getting worse as I heard my introduction. I thought, *I have to follow all that?* But I did and the show was extremely well received although afterward I could barely remember performing.

It was time to get some sleep. I had to be up and on the road again at three o'clock in the morning to clear customs and catch my five o'clock flight. I got a bit of sleep, but my head was still pounding as I started driving back down the mountain road to the airport.

No one was on the road that early; although I did pass a few roosters wandering along the side of the road and a couple of men who did the international sign for do you want/do you have any pot, by miming the smoking of a joint.

When I got into town, a Mercedes Benz convertible pulled up next to me. It was a four seater. The unusual thing was that there were four DVD screens within the car. There were two mounted in the headrests of the front seats, one above the glove box and one on the steering wheel! Four big men were stuffed into the car. The top was down and they were laughing and loudly enjoying a porno movie which I could hear, as well as see!

Things just kept getting stranger and I was glad to see the airport come into view. As I approached the check-in counter, I noticed a man who looked exactly like Jean Claude Van Damme except that he had very long hair tied into a ponytail which went halfway down his back. "Jean Claude" was talking to the ticket agent. He was accompanied by a beautiful blonde woman, and both of them looked as if they were on a movie set. I even thought I might have stumbled onto a movie shoot.

I came up behind them and heard some snippets of what seemed to be an agitated conversation. "Jean Claude" was mad about something. The problem seemed to resolve itself; the blonde kissed "Jean Claude" goodbye and left. I proceeded to check in and then join "Jean Claude" and the rest of the passengers in the customs queue. When it was my turn to enter customs, I noticed that customs agents were grilling "Jean Claude." I went through without mishap and joined the other passengers in the boarding area.

There was a problem with our five o'clock departure. Apparently, the door could not safely latch, and there were no mechanics around to fix it. We had to wait for the first plane to come in from San Juan. This situation resulted in a nearly two-hour delay. I would definitely miss my connecting flight to Cincinnati and was re-booked San Juan to Miami to Cincinnati before the plane ever took off.

We finally boarded the plane and it was packed with as many passengers as possible, because this was to be the second flight to San Juan that day; and we had passengers from both flights onboard. Before we took off, a flight attendant walked through the plane doing a head count. She stopped at "Jean Claude" who was seated one row behind me and asked for identification. He complied and asked, "What's the problem?"

"Nothing sir, we just wanted to make sure you were on the plane."

With that we took off. "Jean Claude's" seatmate mentioned that he had seen the customs people grill him.

"I think it's your hair," the man said. "My son has long hair too, and he's always getting hassled."

"No, I don't think so," "Jean Claude" replied. "I paid for my ticket with cash this morning and it's a one-way airfare. I think security flagged me for that reason."

As the propellers started to turn and we headed down the runway, I turned my attention to my seatmate. She was a very large island woman who barely fit in the seat. In fact, she took up some of my real estate, but I didn't mind, I was just glad we were taking off.

"Hi, my name's Maria," she offered "and I'm terrified of flying."

We took off and it was a short but very bumpy flight. Maria was all over me, grabbing me constantly every time we hit a bump while yelling "Sweet Jesus save me!"

I did feel sorry for her and wondered why she had chosen to fly at all. It turned out that she was going to San Juan for a wedding. We talked a bit about the wedding and her family and she calmed somewhat. Maria offered a big "Hallelujah" when our plane bumped down onto the tarmac in San Juan.

As we rolled to a stop, the captain's voice came over the intercom. "I'm sorry folks but something unusual has happened. We don't normally do this, but we're going to have to ask all of you to clear customs once more here in San Juan." A collective groan emerged from the passenger seats. "We're parking at a secured area and you'll be taken by bus to customs."

My new flight itinerary was now in jeopardy. We had to reclaim all our checked luggage and be screened all over again. As I approached the customs area, I saw "Jean Claude" being taken away in handcuffs. When it was my turn to be screened, the customs agent just waved me through. "We found what we were looking for," he said by way of explanation.

I guess "Jean Claude" was up to no good. By the time I got to the ticket counter, my plane was leaving in twenty minutes. Since I had to recheck my bags, there was not enough time for them or me to make the flight; so I was re-booked once again, same itinerary, San Juan to Miami to Cincinnati just two hours later. Fortunately, my show (outside Cincinnati on the University of Dayton campus) was a late night event, and I was still going to make it.

By the time we boarded our Miami flight, I was wiped out. My headache had finally disappeared but I was exhausted. With all the flight changes and surrounding weirdness at the PGA Resort, in the Virgin Islands and here at the San Juan airport, I just wanted to try to catch some sleep as I had only had about seven hours worth in the last two days.

I had a window seat and I tried to cozy up as much as possible to get some rest on the flight to Miami. My seatmate showed up. He was an elderly man, handsomely dressed in a brown suit, complete with tie. He was bald and had an unusually large mole on the side of his head. I just hoped he wasn't one of those talkative flyers.

I was asleep before we even took off. I don't know how long we'd been airborne, but I got the strange feeling that someone was watching me. I inched open my eyes and awoke with a start when I saw a big, brown eye staring right at me! "Whoa," I shouted as I practically jumped out of my seat. Just at that time, I realized it wasn't a big, brown eye but my seatmate's big, brown mole!

He looked over at me, "What's the matter?"

"I'm sorry," I stammered, "just having a bad dream, I've not had much sleep lately."

"You *should* be a little restless, you picked a bad day to fly."

"You're telling me," I said, wondering if he had had problems similar to mine on this day.

"It's December 5th you know."

Actually, I had forgotten it was the fifth of December, which also happens to be my birthday.

"I didn't realize, but thanks for reminding me," *what a way to celebrate a birthday!*

"Yes sir," the old man went on, "it's December 5th, and we're flying through the Bermuda Triangle!"

I had, of course, heard of the infamous Bermuda Triangle where planes and boats are said to have disappeared under mysterious circumstances, but I wasn't sure that I believed in a malevolent force emanating from these waters.

"I'm assuming you're a believer," I said.

"You would be too, if you knew what I knew. Let me tell you a little story.

"It was late afternoon on December 5th, 1945, exactly sixty years ago, when a group of five Avenger torpedo bombers took off from Fort Lauderdale Naval Air Station on a routine navigation exercise.

"The group leader was Lieutenant Charles Taylor, an experienced flight instructor. About ninety minutes into the exercise, a message was picked up by another plane flying nearby. It seemed that Taylor had lost both his onboard compasses and was trying to orient himself and his flight team. Taylor was trying to get back to Fort Lauderdale and was apparently lost.

"The other pilot picking up the message, Lieutenant Robert Cox, tried to help Taylor by orienting him toward the sun. But even though it was a clear day, Taylor was flying in some type of fog and couldn't find the sun. Suddenly, Taylor's transmission just stopped, and shortly after that Cox's radio ceased to work. Cox made it back to Fort Lauderdale."

"But what about Taylor and the other planes?" I asked.

"Not so fortunate," Mole Man said ominously.

"Around 5:15 p.m., just over three hours into the exercise, the ground crew picked up another message from Taylor saying, 'We'll fly west until we hit the beach or run out of gas.' That was the last anyone heard of Lieutenant Taylor and the 13 crewmen of Flight 19.

"A Mariner flying boat with another 13 crewmen was sent up to find Flight 19. The Mariner and all aboard were never heard from again," he said as he poked a finger into my forearm, and a shiver ran down my spine.

"For the next five days, a total of 930 sorties were flown over the area but not a trace of the five Avengers or the Mariner was to be found. No wreckage, no crew, no nothing."

"Wow!" I exclaimed, "And this happened sixty years ago?"

"To the *day* and that's not all," the Mole said. "On December 4th, 1970, notice the similarity in dates?" he asked. "A fella named Bruce Gernon took off from the Bahamas with his father acting as co-pilot aboard his Beechcraft Bonanza. Gernon was headed to Palm Beach."

"Did he make it?" I asked.

"Oh he made it, but he had one helluva experience! Upon takeoff he saw a weird, cigar-shaped cloud. He tried to avoid flying into the cloud, but every time he altered his course the cloud seemed to move with him. At last, he saw what appeared to be a tunnel running through the cloud with clear skies on the other side, and he flew into it hoping to escape this strange phenomenon. That didn't happen. Once inside the cloud tunnel, he noticed that the walls seemed to be glowing white, and there were many other smaller clouds rotating clockwise around the tunnel's wall. His plane also seemed to pick up incredible speed as both he and his father experienced weightlessness.

"Emerging on the other side of the cloud, he wasn't in clear skies at all; but in a greenish white haze. He tried to find his location, and to his horror discovered that his compass was now rotating counterclockwise, and his navigational systems were down; he couldn't make contact with radar control."

The Mole was really warming up to his tale and I was starting to find it a bit unsettling. It's not the kind of story you want to hear when you're flying at 35,000 feet within the confines of the Bermuda Triangle!

"Gernon could finally spot land through the freakish haze. He calculated the elapsed time since he left the Bahamas and figured that he was near one of the Bimini Islands. As he flew closer, he recognized the land mass. It was Miami Beach!" He exclaimed, poking me in the arm again.

"Why is that significant?" I asked.

"It would have been impossible for him to have flown to Miami Beach in the short amount of time he had been airborne. It was at least *twice* the distance his plane could have flown.

"Anyway, Gernon got his bearings back and landed in Palm Beach. He survived the Bermuda Triangle and lived to tell the tale."

"You certainly have a lot of knowledge on this subject," I stated.

"Oh, it's a passion of mine, has been ever since December 5th, 1945. You see, I was one of the men on the ground then, and I lived through the confusion and the mystery. I was just eighteen-years-old and still wet behind the ears, but it affected me deeply," he explained.

"And you're not afraid to fly through the Triangle?" I asked.

"Nope, not now. I've lived my life. I'm seventy-eight years old. I'm headed to a funeral now—an old and dear friend—the *last* one. I married a Puerto Rican woman and we moved to San Juan years ago so I could be close to the mystery, and she could be close to her family. She died a few years back. We have no children. I have no living relatives, and I can't help but think that if I'm truly to uncover the mystery of the Bermuda Triangle wouldn't the greatest thing be to become a victim of it? To disappear like the men of Flight 19 and to finally know what really happens?"

"Maybe for you," I said, "but I still have some living to do!"

He laughed and then I asked him what theories he had developed about this infamous phenomenon.

"First off, know that it's *real*. Too much has happened over the years. I just told you two stories, there are dozens more.

"The Bermuda Triangle is a vile vortex which roughly runs from the Bahamas to Puerto Rico to Florida. There are positive and negative vortexes located around the world. Stonehenge and the Bermuda Triangle are negative ones. The Hawaiian island of Kauai has the largest collection of positive vortexes followed by the Red Rock Country of Sedona, Arizona, all examples of positive vortexes, they emit a positive energy that you can feel and benefit from. The negative vortexes affect you in negative ways; they can suck you in and destroy you. I'm not sure if it's electromagnetic fields run amok or if there is some kind of evil intelligence behind them. My best guess is that it's just the spirit of the earth, both the good and the bad, manifesting itself at different points on the globe. Did you know that on the exact opposite side of the world there is an area known as the Devil's Sea where the same type of Bermuda Triangle-like phenomena occurs?"

I admitted that I had heard of the Devil's Sea and started to ask another question, but my new friend was staring up at the air vents trying to put his vortex theory into words that I would understand if not completely accept.

"It's like this," he went on, "the earth is encircled with strong, powerful lines of energy. These lines intersect at different points on the globe and that's when strange things happen. You can sensitize yourself to these power grids. I know I can sense them. This earthen power grid has been present forever, and as we keep monkeying around with the land and the atmosphere, we change the balance and location of the power points. And, like I said, there are good areas and bad areas always seeking some kind of balance. The light and the dark, the good and the evil." As the Mole said these words, he held his hands out palms up and kept adjusting them, the action resembling a balancing scale.

At this point in the conversation, we hit a big pocket of turbulence and I jumped, feeling like my former seatmate, Maria.

My Bermuda Triangle expert just laughed, "Getting a little jumpy, eh?" he asked.

"It's an interesting story and a fascinating theory," I said.

"We're just beginning our descent to Miami, breaking through the clouds. We made it—the Triangle's not going to get us," he chuckled.

We did indeed make it, and we parted ways in Miami. The Mole (I never did learn his name) off to bury an old friend, and me off to Ohio to entertain a crowd of college students.

CHAPTER TWENTY

Arizona Snow Vortex

Despite the fact that I've appeared in 17 countries on four continents as well as all 50 states, I rarely get a chance to see anything. It's usually the airport to the rental car facility to the hotel to the venue and then back to the hotel to get some sleep before I'm up early the next morning to catch another of the seemingly never ending flights I find myself on. If I do have a day off on the road, I usually head back home to West Virginia to spend time at my house with Charlotte and the dogs. Why have a house if you're never there?

One March weekend I found myself with a Saturday and Sunday wide open. The open weekend was sandwiched between two performances in Arizona. It seemed kind of foolish to fly across the country to go home for two days and then fly right back on Monday. Plus, the following week was extremely light, and I was going to be home for most of it; so I opted to stay and explore the Grand Canyon state.

I first thought that I might go skiing north of Flagstaff, but a quick Internet search uncovered the fact that Arizona was in the middle of a drought, and none of the ski resorts had opened at all this particular season.

I enjoy hiking, and I love the Red Rock Country of Sedona; so I thought that would be my next best option. Judy Lawhead, my trusted travel agent for more than twenty years, recommended the Enchantment Resort as a wonderful place to stay. We booked the room and I was off.

Friday night's show was at Embry Riddle Aeronautical University in Prescott. I flew into Phoenix, and two hours later I was nearing my destination. As I drove up the mountains and into Prescott Valley, I noticed the outside temperature dropping dramatically on my dashboard thermometer. By the time I reached Prescott, it was 32 degrees and snowing! That's right, snowing in Arizona in March during a drought year when none of the Arizona ski resorts had even opened due to the lack of snow. I phoned Charlotte to let her know I was in town, and she reported that it was 60 degrees and sunny back home in West Virginia.

Charlotte and I have a fondness for Prescott, Arizona. We first visited there in the mid '80s and fell in love with the place. At that time, we thought about retiring there (we occasionally still think about it) and we discussed buying property. My intuition told me it was the right thing to do, but our bank account said it wasn't to be. I wish I had trusted my intuition! A few years later, Prescott was named the "Most Livable City in America," and it exploded. What was once a quaint village has become a bustling town. While no longer the "Mayberry of the West" as many locals referred to it, it still has a lot of charm if you can afford the real estate!

I couldn't cancel my Enchantment reservation; so I thought I might as well head to Sedona the next day. Maybe the snow would lighten up. The show at Embry Riddle went exceptionally well despite the snowstorm. The auditorium was filled to overflowing, and the students gave me a standing ovation. At least I wouldn't need the weekend to lift my spirits as a result of a less than successful show.

As I went to sleep Friday night, I thought I would wake up to the Arizona sun and no more snow. I was wrong. It was still snowing, but at least the roads appeared to be clear. I headed over to a nearby mall to pick up a Starbucks latte and a pair of gloves. As I walked into Sears, I saw that naturally all the spring merchandise was on display.

"Any gloves left?" I asked a young clerk.

He laughed and pointed toward a sales rack and said that there might be something over there. There was only one pair left, a pair of Dockers®' leather gloves with Thinsulate™ lining for $10 (regular price $40). I had already saved $30 and things were looking up.

An hour later, I was in Oak Creek, Sedona's neighboring town, and I saw a sign that indicated that I was at the trailhead for the Bell Rock Trail. Bell Rock happened to be one of the Sedona vortexes I wanted to check out on this trip.

Arizona Snow Vortex

Sedona became very popular in the '80s along with the New Age movement when word got out that Sedona was situated in the middle of four powerful vortex points. These vortexes are thought to be energy points which send out positive energy that can affect people in any number of ways. When meditating within the field of a Sedona vortex, people have reported spontaneous healings and the channeling of departed spirits and even alien beings to name but a few of the weird and wonderful effects these special areas bestow upon those seeking their special power.

There is Cathedral Rock that is known to have magnetic energy that is said to affect one's psychic functioning. Bell Rock and Airport Mesa send off electrical energy that stimulates the mind and elevates consciousness. The most powerful vortex of all is Boynton Canyon. Its forces are electromagnetic in nature and combine the very best of both types of positive energy flow created by the other three spots.

I pulled into the national forest visitor center and did a quick consultation with a posted trail map, and then I was off to visit my first Arizona vortex. The snow had tapered off, and the hike was refreshing due to the 35 degree weather which kept me cool under several layers of clothing.

A mile later and I was at Bell Rock. I took a detour up onto the rock formation, and I surveyed the valley below. Stunning! The collection of buttes, mesas, pinnacles and canyons was a sight to behold. It took millions of years to create this special place. The Red Rock formations (Cathedral Rock was in plain site to my left) were snowcapped, as was the desert floor. This, I thought, was one of the advantages of taking a hike in the snow. Rarely do you get to see these beautiful natural structures and the surrounding desert covered in a blanket of snow. I was immediately glad I had come to Sedona, despite the snow. Because of the snow, I was having a special experience. The trails are usually extremely busy, populated with hikers, mountain bikers and even horseback riders. I ended up hiking eight miles that day and only encountered a half-dozen people.

From my vantage point atop Bell Rock, I decided to focus and meditate a bit, welcoming any positive energy that might come my way. I have to admit I felt nothing special—only the exhilaration I always feel when I am in a setting as beautiful as this.

Looking down from Bell Rock to the trail below, I noticed a large, black dog (at least I hoped it was a dog) and wondered if I would encounter the animal as I made my way further along the trail.

I hiked down Bell Rock and continued on the trail. This particular trail runs from Oak Creek to Sedona and covers about four miles one way. A half mile back on the trail the big, black dog came into view. It seemed to be by itself. The canine spotted me and then looked to its right. I spotted what must have been its owner—a woman dressed in a down jacket with a bright red scarf tied around her neck and a matching woolen hat atop her head.

Just then the dog started running toward me.

"Stand down Raven!" I heard the woman's voice command.

Great, I thought, *attacked by a killer hound from hell at my very first vortex!*

As Raven ran up to me I said, "Hey Raven, how you doin' pup?" This is my typical dog greeting, and it usually seems to work. Raven sniffed my gloved hand and then I petted her large head.

Raven's owner came up to me. She appeared ancient, her skin deeply wrinkled and covered in a permanent Arizona tan.

"I just didn't want her jumping up on you. Her paws are a mess," the woman said.

"She's a good girl," I replied. "Beautiful too."

"Don't be getting any ideas about my Raven sonny, she's all I have!"

I was taken aback and just looked at her.

"Nice day," she cackled and then she and Raven were off and I pushed on.

Three miles later, I was at the end of the line and turned to head the four miles back to complete the hike. At that point, the snow and the wind kicked up. Snow was pelting my face. My constant view of Bell Rock was now obliterated, but I pushed on thinking it was only four miles back to the car.

I'm definitely a day hiker (in reality more of a half day hiker). I like trips of seven miles or so, and then I like to head back to a nice hotel for a good night's rest. While on the actual hike, my mind wanders. Exercise increases the blood circulation to your brain, and you can have some amazing ideas while hiking. I contemplate everything from the meaning of life to what I'm going to have for dinner. Halfway back, trudging through the now muddy trail and the snow while fighting the wind, all I could think about was a big glass of red wine and some jacuzzi time!

As I approached Bell Rock, I noticed another benefit of the snowfall. The landscape I had passed a couple hours before had now changed. There were streams and waterfalls running off Bell Rock making the magnificent natural formation even more beautiful.

Snow covered, I made it back to my car and made a special note to buy a hat for tomorrow's hike!

Arizona Snow Vortex

From the rental car, I phoned Enchantment to get driving directions to the resort. As the receptionist instructed me on the route, everything sounded vaguely familiar. Perhaps Bell Rock had kicked up my psychic functioning a bit... I began driving toward Sedona proper, and I glanced down on the seat next to me and noticed my scribbled driving directions for the Boynton Canyon vortex. That's why the resort directions sounded so familiar. Enchantment is located directly in Boynton Canyon.

The snow in the canyon seemed even heavier as I drove up to the guarded gate. I was waved through and told to go to the clubhouse for registration. Enchantment sits on 70 acres within Boynton Canyon and is truly an extraordinary property. The guest rooms are all adobe casitas, individual out buildings seemingly cut into the canyon. You feel as if you are a cliff dweller like the Native Americans who inhabited this area for centuries. There is even a destination spa which in addition to top-of-the-line treatments offers everything from past life regressions to psychic readings. Only in Sedona!

The Red Rock Secret Wilderness surrounds Boynton Canyon and the resort is watched over by "Kachina Woman" a wind-carved rock formation that seemingly guards the entrance to the canyon. The Yavapai Apache consider this canyon their "Garden of Eden" where the human race was born. The area was inhabited by many different tribes. In addition to the Yavapai Apache, the Navajo, Hopi and Zuni all spent time here. Nine hundred years ago, the Sinagua Indians mysteriously left behind many cliff dwellings in the canyon. In the 1400s the Sinaguan people completely disappeared. No one knows why.

As soon as I arrived at Enchantment, I was, indeed, enchanted, and I knew I would be coming back. I registered at the clubhouse—there's nothing I like better than checking into a $500 a night resort wearing muddy hiking boots and torn jeans—and then followed the golf cart driving bellman in my rental car to my casita. He indicated that I should park between a Porsche Carrera and a BMW 7 series. This is a swanky joint! After a good room service meal that included half a bottle of red wine I had a long bath and I was off to bed. I was tired, happy and dreaming of exploring Boynton Canyon in the morning.

At 7:00 a.m., I peeked through the casita window blinds to find it was still snowing. In fact, you couldn't see the red rock formations at all. If the electromagnetic vortex emanating from the canyon had the ability to cause strange weather patterns, I was a believer already! There was a very real chance that I would be snowed in. On the news the night before I had seen

217

where some areas of northern Arizona had reported over three feet of snow. Roads in certain areas of the state were closed. The road to the Arizona Snowbowl ski resort was closed and they were going to send a crew up on Monday to assess whether or not they should open and salvage a bit of what was left of the thus far nonexistent ski season. Arizona definitely needed the precipitation. It hadn't rained or snowed for a record one-hundred-forty-three days.

I rolled over and went back to sleep to be awakened by birds singing at 9:00 a.m. I pulled aside the curtains covering the sliding glass doors leading to the balcony, and my view was back. The snow had tapered off to flurries, and I was gazing at a winter wonderland. Today's hike was certainly going to be interesting. I tried to decide when to go, but my decision was made for me when I found an invitation to a champagne brunch with my complimentary newspaper and orange juice just outside my casita door. I made a reservation for 2:00 p.m. It was the only time still available, and figured I would take my hike after brunch to work off what I was sure would be an overindulgent meal. I was also hoping that by the time I went on the hike others would have gone before me so that I could follow their footprints in the snow.

I did some morning writing. One of my goals for the weekend was to finish at least two chapters of the book you're reading now! I'm proud to say I met my goal and had a lot of fun doing it.

I headed off to brunch just prior to 2:00 p.m. As I expected, it was excellent and I overate. The Yavapai restaurant offers a panoramic view of the canyon and like the rest of the resort and canyon area, it was just beautiful. A couple of mimosas, some southwestern style free range chicken, fresh fruit, cheese and grilled mahi-mahi completed the meal. I topped it off with a piece of key lime pie and a strong cup of coffee.

Before leaving the clubhouse, I stopped by the gift shop and picked up a $30 Enchantment logo baseball cap to protect my head from the snowfall. There went that $30 I saved on the gloves!

It was now time to head to the Boynton Canyon trail. I didn't have to worry about finding footprints in the snow. The trail was covered in red mud and was quite easy to follow. This was a five-mile round trip, deep into the canyon and then back out. About halfway back the mud disappeared, and the trail became snow-covered; but there were still some footprints to follow. As I kept pushing on, the elevation continued to increase and the footprints became less and less. I guess more than a few hikers abandoned the trail a mile or so in. That was definitely their loss. The trail became more beautiful the further back I went. I had to keep reminding myself to watch where I was walking as my eyes kept drifting skyward toward the beautiful canyon walls.

I noticed I was lingering much longer on this trail than I had on the Bell Rock pathway the day before. It was sensory overload to try to take it all in. And, it was preternaturally quiet. During the entire five-mile hike, I encountered not more than a half dozen people and no dogs!

On my way back out of the canyon, the sun finally peeked through the gray clouds, illuminating the canyon walls, and yes, making them even more wondrous. As I hiked back, it was so quiet. I heard an occasional loud thump behind me as a large mound of snow fell from tree branches and landed near the trail, sounding like the footfalls of a giant. It was as if "Kachina Woman" had come alive and stepped down from the canyon wall and was escorting me out of "her" canyon.

By the time I finished the five-mile hike, that famous Arizona sky was in evidence as more and more of the clouds drifted away.

But did I experience anything? You bet I did! I definitely communed with nature and with God. I believe that God is everywhere, but I know that God is in Boynton Canyon! Regardless of your spiritual beliefs, you can't come to a place like this and not be affected by it. Even if you only have a scientific appreciation of nature, you will be awed.

What a wonderful trip! I wouldn't trade my snow covered Arizona weekend for anything. And I still had to visit the spa.

The Mii amo Spa (Mii amo is a Native American word in the Yuman dialect meaning "journey") is quite the place. I had an 8:00 p.m. appointment for my favorite treatment, a ninety minute deep tissue massage. I went down about 7:00 p.m. to spend some time in the facility before my treatment.

My first stop was the Crystal Grotto, a Kiva inspired room that has as its centerpiece a large illuminated crystal. The idea is to enter the chamber, stand on the earthen floor and get in touch with the earth. Then, walk clockwise around the room and take the furthest available seat. Before sitting, you do some deep breathing and then sit down and meditate on the crystal and focus on any special intention you may have in your life. This is exactly what I did, and then I donned my bathing suit and headed to the heated outdoor pool to swim some laps.

There's something about swimming under a full moon in a sacred canyon that gives you goose bumps. I had the pool to myself as well as the hot tub, and then I headed in for my treatment. A very thorough deep tissue massage had me primed to fall asleep quickly and deeply.

I awoke the next morning to find the snow still there and the temperature back down to 30 degrees. I had to dig my rental car out of the snow since I hadn't driven it once I arrived at Enchantment. My new gloves came in handy as I clawed the ice and snow from the windshield—the Phoenix Hertz office doesn't typically provide snow scrapers with their March rentals.

The next stop on my Arizona working vacation was Yuma. There are two ways to get from Sedona to Yuma, the easy way and the fun way. I always take the fun way. The easy way is mostly interstate driving, and you travel back through Phoenix. The fun way starts on Highway 89A. Coming out of Sedona, you pass through the old copper mining town of Jerome. Jerome is akin to a living ghost town with great galleries, boutiques and restaurants as well as spectacular views. Jerome was built high atop Cleopatra Hill, and from Sedona on a clear night you can see the lights of the town shining brightly, indistinguishable from the stars in the sky. Through Jerome, you continue your ascent into the Prescott National Forest. The road tops out at an elevation of over 7,000 feet (and on this particular day, a temperature of 25 degrees). This scenic serpentine road takes you into downtown Prescott and then back into the Prescott National Forest for a series of switchbacks which will have you feeling as if you're a dog chasing its own tail.

Finally, you come to Yarnell as you prepare for one of the best parts of the drive. It's a steep, mountainous road that runs down to the valley below the Weaver Mountains. The view from the top of the mountain is picture postcard perfect and the drive down can be a white knuckle event.

When I hit the floor of the valley, all the snow was gone except for a small clump of ice desperately clinging to the bottom of my windshield, and the temperature was now 50 degrees.

A little over five hours after leaving Boynton Canyon, I was in Yuma in the southwest corner of the state on the border of both Mexico and California, and it was 70 degrees. The clump of ice had disappeared 90 miles back.

The show in Yuma was for Arizona Western College. The campus is located west of town and pops up like an oasis in the desert. It's surrounded by palm trees and sits atop a small hill. Once again, we had an overflow audience and a great show that energized me for my three-hour drive to Phoenix.

I was scheduled to appear on Good Morning Arizona (Phoenix's number one morning television show) at 6:45 a.m. I checked into my Phoenix hotel just before 2:00 a.m. and was asleep in a few minutes. A few hours later, I was up again. Show business is such a glamorous life! I did some early morning mind reading on the television show and shared in studio guest duties with Dr. Ruth Westheimer, the famous sex expert, and a miniature cow! Before I knew it, I found myself on a flight back home.

On the trip home, my mind kept returning to Boynton Canyon, and I realized I was truly under its spell. Everything else paled in comparison—the shows, the excitement of doing live television, even Bell Rock and the fun drive from Sedona to Yuma. I knew I would be back, and I knew I would revisit the area again and again in my dreams.

"Sometimes dreams are wiser than waking."—Black Elk, Ogala Sioux (1863-1950)

CHAPTER TWENTY-ONE

The Biggest Fan

How can anyone live in the Wheeling, West Virginia, area (we refer to it as the Ohio Valley) and not be a Pittsburgh Steelers fan? Well, I'm sure some of the residents right across the Ohio River to the *west* of us might not agree with me. Their loyalties may lie just *north* with that other team called the *Browns*....

Anyway, we live, breathe and adore the "Black and Gold" in these parts; so I was excited to be offered the opportunity to create a television special around the legendary franchise.

Take one "Terrible Towel," a yellow towel used by Pittsburgh Steelers fans to celebrate victories and rally the team, hide it somewhere in Heinz Field (a 65,450 seat NFL stadium), blindfold me and then send me out to find it! This extraordinary event was billed as the "Super Bowl of Hide and Seek" and became the focus of the television special.

The special began to take shape over the summer of 2003. I was touring in Japan in June and picked up an e-mail out of the blue from Mark Barash, VP of Programming for the tri-state NBC affiliate Cox station group. Mark was interested in rebroadcasting in prime time my special from 2000 called *Experience the Extraordinary* which we had done together. As we discussed possibilities via e-mail from Asia and later by phone after I returned to the States, a new vision began to emerge. We talked about doing a new special consisting of unaired footage from the first program along with highlights from the original broadcast and about 25% brand new material.

Mark is a sports nut, and as I've said, Pittsburgh (the largest market served by the stations he represents) loves the Steelers. Mark asked if the new material could focus on the "Black and Gold." I'm pretty comfortable with creating special theme material because of my corporate work; so I pitched a half-dozen ideas to Mark including the stadium hunt. He loved it and wanted to have the project taped, edited and aired by October. The problem was finding the time to do it.

After I got back from Asia, I did a two-week run in Canada at Casino Windsor. The original idea was to tape the material at the Steelers' training camp in August when I came back from Canada. When I returned, we had yet to get approval; so, I headed to Florida for some corporate work. I came back from Florida—still no approval. I was home for a few more days before I set out on a 29 shows in twenty-nine days back to school college tour. Time was running out.

Mark arranged for some former Steelers to agree to appear on the special. I flew home in mid-September, and the next day we were at the Le Mont restaurant in Pittsburgh where we shot the special material with former Steelers Randy Grossman, Louis Lipps, Robin Cole and Todd Kalis. The Le Mont is a beautiful spot; it overlooks Heinz Field as well as all of downtown Pittsburgh. The material was all done in one take, and it was the first time I had done many of the routines—a nerve wracking experience to say the least! I hoped that some of it would look good enough to make the final cut.

One example of this special material had Randy Grossman dealing through a large stack of NFL trading cards which bore the likenesses of past and present Steelers. Grossman dealt through the cards as Louis Lipps and Robin Cole passed a football back and forth behind Grossman's back. I asked Grossman to stop at any point in the stack. He happened to stop on Jerome Bettis. I then asked Lipps to toss Grossman the football, which had been in play the entire time. You guessed it, the ball was signed by Jerome Bettis!

I left town the following day for another week of on the road performances. When I returned home, it was time to shoot the *Terrible Towel Telepathy Test*. I met the crew and Todd Kalis at Heinz Field on a cold September afternoon. It was the first time I had ever been in the new stadium. If you've never been in an NFL size stadium, it is awe-inspiring, especially when it is totally empty. 65,450 seats!

I was kept in seclusion while Todd hid the towel. Once the towel was hidden, a stadium security guard securely blindfolded me. He placed a steel plate over my eyes, wrapped yards of athletic bandage around the plate and then placed an opaque, black hood completely over my head and tied it off around my neck. It was then my job to find one towel somewhere in the stadium. While it was edited down for television, the hunt took only twenty minutes, and I was successful. What an experience! As the announcer for the special said, it was like trying to find a needle in a haystack in hyper drive!

It was then time for the final edit. Cox liked all the special Steelers material and ended up creating an entirely new special entitled *Bedazzled Boys of Black and Gold*. I had nothing to do with the title! It was definitely an on-the-fly production but it turned out well, looked good and got good ratings as well for the three NBC affiliates in the Tri-State area of Pennsylvania, Ohio and West Virginia.

How did I find the towel? Call it mind reading, intuition or just plain magic, whatever you're comfortable with. I'm not going to shed any light on the subject. I frequently say, "My job is to entertain through the creation of mystery while opening minds to unlimited possibilities." I like to think I created a special mystery that afternoon at Heinz Field. Telling you how it was done would destroy some of the mystery and part of the entertainment.

Two years later, I was in downtown Pittsburgh with some free time, and I was reliving the hunt for the "Terrible Towel" as I was admiring the stadiums built along the Monongahela River. PNC Park was built exclusively for the Pirates baseball franchise, and Heinz Field was constructed to hold 65,450 borderline insane fans who love the Steelers and the Pittsburgh Panthers college football team. What magnificent structures! Out of town broadcasters calling baseball and football games have christened both facilities as the very best for watching professional sporting events, respective to each venue.

It's actually humbling to walk past these two structures. The talent, time and yes, *cash* that it took not only to tear down the old Three Rivers Stadium; but to start from scratch and construct two *brand new* facilities, is truly a wonder. And the view! What an awesome view of Mount Washington across the rivers with the incline lift and the skyscrapers towering over the enormous water fountain at Point State Park where the three rivers meet. By the way, the other two rivers are the Ohio and Allegheny—my fifth grade geography teacher at St. Vincent School would be proud!

I was just admiring the view when I passed a gentleman who was working outside Heinz Field. Anyone reading this book should know by now that I have a knack for picking certain types of people out of the crowd.

The Biggest Fan

I introduced myself, but the old gentleman didn't offer his name in return; so I named him myself, "Fred." My mind is also kind of weird. I silently named this guy Fred because of his uncanny resemblance to Fred G. Sanford on the *Sanford and Son* television show. There was something unique about him. He was rough around the edges, but he also had an exceptionally eloquent presence, a deep-rooted, total conviction and outright peacefulness seemed to fill this person. Involuntarily, I stopped just to observe this possibly "extraordinary" man.

Fred was polishing with extreme pride the statue of former Steelers' owner, Art Rooney, which is located right outside Gate B. Every detail was addressed as if Fred was creating this work of art himself. Mr. Sanford turned to look my way.

"He was a good man, Chief was," he said with a gravelly, deep voice. *Yes, this was Fred Sanford!*

"What?" I responded.

"The Chief. He done good not just for the team, but for those who need it the most," Fred continued.

"I don't know what you mean. Who's The Chief?" I inquired. Well, I should have just asked someone who the Pope was in Vatican City, or who Michael Jordan was in Chicago, or who Harry Potter was at Hogwarts! OK, you get the point, *stupid question, Craig!*

"Where you from, boy?" Fred bit back.

"Wheeling," I said.

"Well if you don't know who The Chief is, then you might as well be from Cleveland," Fred answered wittily.

The Chief, I found out was, of course, Mr. Art Rooney. Beloved, cigar chomping, caring owner of the Pittsburgh Steelers and philanthropist extraordinaire. The man who created a dynasty in the 1970s and who positively impacted thousands of lives during his time on earth. His complete biography was verbally presented to me by Fred, since I obviously insulted him by not knowing who The Chief was.

"OK, I'll never forget the legacy again," I said.

Fred stepped down from the statue and headed toward me. "Pleasure to meet you, son. Don't mean no disrespect to you, but you should know little 'bout history here if you be walkin' on Steelers' sacred ground," he explained.

"Point taken. And I do now. Thanks for the background on Mr. Rooney," I said.

"So how often do you take care of this statue," I asked to be polite and change the focus from my not knowing who this legend was.

"Do more than that. I work all around the grounds outside this field. Shine the statues, tend to the grounds, and then some. Been doin' it for over thirty years now," he explained.

"Wow. You work for the organization?" I asked.

"No, just a contracted company that takes care of the maintenance and what not, but I love the Black and Gold. Never missed a game since I've been here. 'Course I spent many a year workin' outside Three Rivers Stadium. Kinda miss that fishbowl in a way," Fred added.

"So, you've been to every home game?" I asked.

"Not inside," Fred answered.

"You watch from the clubhouse or a standing room only spot?" I pried.

"Nope. Never been inside either place, new one or old one," Fred responded.

"You mean to tell me that you've worked outside the grounds of both Three Rivers Stadium and Heinz Field for more than three decades and you've never even been inside *either stadium?*" I chirped.

"You got it. Woulda liked to, but no need. Myron keep me company and I see the game in my mind."

Who's Myron? Should I even ask? What will he think of me? How should I know who Myron is? I can't ask. "Who's Myron?" I asked.

Three-two-one… Explosion! "What planet you from, boy?" Fred blasted me. "Myron Cope's been the voice of the Steelers for as long as I can remember. He's a legend as much as any of the greats that ever played here. Myron is the man, and don't you forget it!"

Mental note #2: Myron Cope is "good." "I won't," I replied.

"OK, then," he answered. Fred calmed down just a *little*.

"So you have been working outside the former Three Rivers Stadium and the new Heinz Field and have never seen a live game?" I asked for confirmation anyway.

"Told you, no need to. Just by listenin' I see things in my mind that wouldn't even come close to the real thing and sure as sugar is much better than watchin' the T.V. Really no need, besides couldn't afford a ticket anyhow.

"I ain't braggin'. It's not my way you know, but I've known who the Steelers were gonna pick in each draft since 1969," Fred told me. "Players and symbols come to me in my dreams," he explained.

Here we go again. How do I run into these folks? "Is that right?" I asked.

The Biggest Fan

"You think I'm makin' it up?" Fred shot back at me.

"Not on your life," I wisely responded. *If he only knew my extraordinary background. A fluke running into this peculiar fellow? I think not.*

"'Cause I ain't lyin'," Fred continued to try to convince me although I truly believed him even before he spoke a word.

"In 1969, when the Steelers were in need of defensive players, I had a 'nature dream.' I was in a forest and was surrounded by hundreds, maybe even *thousands* of enormous trees. They almost touched the sky, but something was different about 'em. They didn't have no leaves or nothin' and these trees were a funny color, too. The whole forest looked like a haze was hoverin' over me, and the bark on the trees was not brown but had a green color to 'em. And there was a homemade wooden sign on the nature trail that said Laurel Caverns. Laurel Caverns is just down the road from Pittsburgh near Uniontown; so I thought I might have just picked up on a conversation or saw or read somethin' to make me dream about it. No matter, that clue alone helped me figure out what I was seein' not *before*, but *after* the draft was over that year. I'm tellin' you, I had this dream six times if I had it once, and I was bound 'n determined to figure out what it meant. There's no way I can explain why I knew this recurrin' dream meant something. I just *felt it*. But what? And *why me?* I didn't think too much about it until the 10th round in the draft that year. Then it all came together for me, and I figured out that that dream *did* mean something, and I wasn't crazy. The Steelers picked a huge young man out of Alabama A & M that year who would contribute more to the 'Steel Curtain' defense during his career than anyone in franchise history. No, the dream about the trees was not because this guy was a towering 6' 6" tall. And the Laurel Caverns sign was not out of place, either. The first two letters of each word on that sign in my dream solved the mystery. And those trees weren't *trees*, they were wood, *green* wood. That's right, my man—L. C. Greenwood was a member of the Black and Gold for the next twelve years, and I knew they were gonna choose him *before* they said his name. But it didn't stop there. You wanna hear another good one?" Fred asked excitedly.

Stunned and surprised upon hearing this fascinating story, I hesitated, but answered, "Yes, of course."

"This is a funny one and wasn't too tough to figure out, neither. Before the 1971 draft—about the same two weeks or so before they selected their top players—I started with the dreams again. Every night the same situation for no reason at all, but I knew that it was gonna help me find out one of the players they were choosin' that year. The dream had me standin' at the door of a blue barn on a farm lookin' at a blue fence with a bunch of hogs rollin' around in the blue mud. Not so much a dream this time, but more of a flash of this scene every night. I love the game and know about the pros and the young college kids, too. It's my life. So I just had to figure out what this dream was about. There's no way this was a fluke. It happened before with the Laurel Caverns and green tree dream, and I knew I had the player the Steelers were gonna choose this time. Blue represented the college that this defensive player came from—Penn State—right down the road from us. And I knew that the Steelers were interested in this guy before the draft, too. That's what made the pigs confirm the pick before they used the second overall selection to pick linebacker Jack Ham. Get it? Hogs, pigs, ham? I liked that one. Another future Hall of Famer, too! Ready for another one?"

No chance to respond and I wasn't leaving anyway. These stories were too good!

"I'll give you a hint on this one, too. I picked two future defensive players who were eventually on their way to Canton, Ohio enshrined as legends. This next one was a little tougher, but I figured it out before the draft, anyway. Years ago, I knew the Steelers were maybe lookin' at goin' after a wide receiver in the draft. A few weeks before they were gonna pick their rookie players I kept havin' the same dream over and over again. Like the others, this dream wasn't scary or weird, but I didn't know why it kept poppin' in my head every night. I don't travel much and have never seen much outside of the city, but in the dream I was in the country. Don't know where, but man was it beautiful. Just me standin' by a lake... could almost feel the peaceful breeze and smell the fresh air, too! And each time in the dream, a beautiful bird would appear swimmin' toward the shore all graceful and white as snow. It swam slow, almost like it was glidin' on the water. Although I never saw one in real life, I knew what kind of gorgeous bird that was. Remember the story the *Ugly Duckling?* Well, this wasn't ugly, it was a swan. Lo and behold, two weeks later in 1974, the Steelers took a young man out of the University of Southern California in the first round and the rest is history. Lynn Swann was as graceful on the football field throughout his career as that bird in my dream, and I knew later that was the reason I had that vision," Fred said.

This man had a passion about his football team and the sport itself. And I firmly believed that there was no coincidence in the metaphorical dreams he had enabling him to predict the Steelers' draft picks. As I mentioned earlier, I just knew this was a special man, and our paths did not cross by accident.

"Absolutely fascinating," I said. Once again I was dumbfounded to have run across such a fascinating person "by chance." *Yeah, right.* "I honestly believe that you truly had these premonitions and I enjoyed listening to your stories."

"Thanks. I know you do. For some reason, I just wanted to share those stories with you. You're a good man. I can just tell. I don't know why, but I felt that you would understand and believe what I told you to be the truth. Kinda far out there, but I had a feelin' that you wouldn't find the dreams too hard to believe. Thanks for listening," he added.

I shook his hand and started walking away. Fred approached me. "Hey, one more quickie that just happened about a year ago. Same thing. Two weeks before the draft I kept dreamin' of London, England. You know about that clock they got over there?" he asked.

"Yes. I'm familiar with Big Ben," I responded.

"That's the dream, and they picked up a future Rookie of the Year from Miami of Ohio named Ben Roethlisberger. That one was easy. Knew that was comin' the first night it appeared in my mind," Fred said.

As I was walking away, it occurred to me that one of my friends had given Charlotte and me his season ticket seats for the Steelers versus Baltimore Ravens game in two weeks. I told him I wasn't sure if we could attend, but he insisted I take them "just in case" since he wouldn't be in town. Earlier that week, Charlotte informed me that we had been invited to go out of town by another couple and that she would be making arrangements. *Brainstorm.* Believe it or not, I had the two tickets in my car and started to break into a jog and then a full sprint back to the parking lot. I couldn't wait to make the pick up and get back to the statue. Section 502—two seats together. This could work out perfectly. After sprinting most of the way back to the Art Rooney memorial, I slowed down so I wouldn't appear to be overanxious. A young boy was sitting on the bench near the statue while Fred shined away.

"I've got something for you," I said.

Startled, Fred turned around and smiled at me. "What's up?" he asked.

"My treat to you," I said as I handed him the two tickets. Tears welled up in his eyes, but he maintained enough composure to look at me and touch his heart with his fist showing his deep-rooted appreciation.

"What'd that man give you, grandpa?" the young child asked.

Fred choked up and answered, "A little slice of heaven, my boy. Me and you are gonna see just a little slice of heaven."

CHAPTER TWENTY–TWO

The White Witch of Jamaica

One of the great things about my work is that I get to travel all over the world. One of the disappointing things about my work is that I rarely get to spend any "quality time" in any of the exotic or interesting locations I travel to. There's always another engagement in another city.

One year, I was doing a series of appearances for a financial services firm. These dates had me traveling from Hawaii to Jamaica. Each meeting was held at a first class location: The Four Seasons on Maui; the LaCosta Spa & Resort in Southern California; the Fairmont Hotel in San Francisco; The Greenbrier Resort in West Virginia; and Orlando's Grand Floridian. I spent less than twelve hours in each location with the exception of Jamaica, the last stop on this corporate tour. Charlotte and I decided to block off some time and enjoy ourselves on the island prior to the Jamaican presentation.

We were staying at the Ritz-Carlton Rose Hall and had a beautiful suite overlooking the Caribbean Sea. This was to be a relaxing mini-vacation of fine food, good drinks, a spa day and sun, sun, sun! Charlotte never left the resort property; however, I did sneak away for a snorkel trip to a protected marine park where I had a nasty encounter with some fire coral, but that's another story. This was December and a time to reflect, relax and enjoy.

The Ritz is located in the Rose Hall section of St. James Parish near Montego Bay. Rose Hall is named for the Rose Hall Plantation, which dates from the 1700s and is the focal point for this tale of the extraordinary.

A shuttle from our gated hotel property (all the hotels in the Montego Bay area of Jamaica are gated!) took us across the main road and up a narrow, winding lane to the great house. Built between 1770 and 1780, the mansion is a beautiful construction of stone and timber. The commanding view of the Caribbean Sea from the house was breathtaking. I felt as if I had stepped back through time, or I was about to be in a scene from *Pirates of the Caribbean.*

The original plantation was purchased in 1746 by Henry Fanning. He soon married Rose Kelly, a parson's daughter. However, within six months of the marriage Fanning died.

Rose then married a local planter by the name of George Ash. Ash died two years later, leaving behind a sad and lonely but very wealthy widow.

The following year, Rose married her third husband, Norwood Witter, and this union lasted for thirteen years. It was said that Witter was a cruel man who married Rose for her money. However, Rose outlasted Witter as well and married yet again, this time to a widower, John Palmer.

It was her fourth husband, John Palmer, who built Rose Hall. At the time of its construction, it was the finest residence in Jamaica. Rose and John Palmer ruled over Rose Hall for the next twenty-three years hosting society events and watching their fortunes grow as their sugar cane plantation flourished.

Rose Kelly Fanning Ash Witter Palmer passed away in 1790, and the plantation and great house became the sole property of John Palmer. Palmer married for a third time. He took a young, twenty-year-old bride named Ann James. Palmer passed away five years later, and Rose Hall (along with all of Palmer's extensive Jamaican land holdings) was left to his two sons by his first marriage, both of whom lived in England. Palmer's young widow, Ann James, left the island and went to England to live as well. The two offspring died without ever setting foot in Jamaica, and Ann James never returned to the island.

During this time, the great house was neglected, and the actual business of running the plantation was in disarray until the arrival of John Rose Palmer, John Palmer's great-nephew. The house and land fell into the possession of John Rose Palmer and he relished his role as Jamaican plantation landowner, restoring the property and tidying up the business end of running a plantation.

The White Witch of Jamaica

Our timeline now has us in 1820, with John Rose Palmer in residence at Rose Hall and running a large plantation; however, times were changing. The price of sugar cane had dropped. The British Empire had abolished slavery, but the Jamaican plantation owners were still holding on to the old ways as they depended on slave labor to create their fortunes. Jamaica was becoming a dangerous place.

Enter Annie May Paterson. Annie was the daughter of an English mother and an Irish father who moved to Haiti to start a business under the auspices of Haiti's King Henry Christophe. While in Haiti, Annie became a favorite of a voodoo high priestess who was a confidante of King Christophe. This voodoo queen taught Annie spells and schooled her in the ways of voodoo magic. From all accounts, Annie was an excellent pupil.

Annie's parents and the voodoo priestess passed away. Annie didn't want to return to the British Isles; so at eighteen years of age, she headed to Jamaica and married John Rose Palmer in 1820. For the next thirteen years, Annie Palmer—the White Witch—brought death and destruction to Rose Hall.

When you tour the great house, you are given the option of hearing the story of Annie Palmer, the White Witch, sober, or you can choose to sip a cup of witch's brew while roaming the house and grounds. Charlotte and I chose to partake of the brew, a tasty concoction of rum and fruit juices—at least I think that's what it was!

Annie's story is as nasty as she was beautiful, a raven haired and dark eyed enchantress by all accounts. She claimed that John was a bad husband who drank and abused her. She began taking slave lovers, and after three years of marriage John Rose Palmer was no more. His body was never found. Rumor had it that Annie poisoned him and then brought her slave lover in to taunt him as he lay dying. The lover hastened Palmer's death by suffocating him with a pillow. Just to make sure her husband was dead, Annie poured boiling oil into his ears causing his brain to explode and reportedly splattering bits and pieces of the organ on the walls of the bedroom. It was said that every time the walls were painted, the blood would continue to show through. Special wall coverings were now in place over the stains our tour guide informed us with a mischievous grin.

For thirteen years Annie Palmer, the White Witch, ruled Rose Hall with an iron hand. She was fond of midnight rides on horseback. She would dress as a man and carry a whip. Any slave she encountered out and about after dark would be mercilessly whipped.

Per Annie's instructions, bear traps were placed around the plantation. Slaves trying to escape and caught in the traps would be returned to Annie who would have their legs amputated and their still much alive bodies thrown into a stone cellar to rot and die.

Any babies born from slaves and suffering from deformities were taken out into the hot sun and left to die.

A maid tried to poison Annie and was caught. She was convicted of attempted murder and executed. At Annie's insistence, the maid's head was brought back to Rose Hall and mounted on a long bamboo pole as a reminder to her slaves, white staff and lovers that you don't mess with the White Witch! To say that Annie was a cruel mistress is an understatement!

During her time at Rose Hall, Annie took many lovers and had two more husbands. The marriages all ended quickly with the husbands being stabbed and strangled by the White Witch. Annie claimed that each was taken ill by some tropical disease, and the bodies were quarantined for the protection of the locals. In reality, slaves buried the bodies on the property. Those slaves were then killed, oftentimes being beaten to death at the rear of the mansion as Annie stood on a small balcony and watched.

In 1833, a new bookkeeper came to Rose Hall and Annie was smitten with him. However, this new employee fell in love with his maid. Annie tried in vain to bed the bookkeeper, and when she was unsuccessful she had the maid killed out of jealousy. Now, it so happens that this maid was the niece of one of Annie's slave lovers. The uncle was so upset over the death of his niece that he found the courage to storm Annie's bedroom and kill her.

With Annie dead, the slaves took their final revenge, mutilating her body and destroying much of the interior of Rose Hall, paying particular attention to the destruction of any likeness of the White Witch.

The slaves refused to bury Annie Palmer, but some townsfolk finally did, leaving the body in an unmarked grave on the property.

Later, she was exhumed and given a proper burial in a sarcophagus-shaped grave in the east garden. Four crosses were etched onto the gravestone, one facing each direction. However, the cross facing to the north and the sea would disappear over time due to the high winds sweeping in from the Caribbean. It is believed that the lack of the fourth cross enabled Annie's spirit to escape the confines of her tomb and wander about the former plantation.

With the house partially destroyed and it's long, bloody history well known, Rose Hall could not attract another resident and sat still and silent as it slowly decayed. During this time, the mansion became known as "The Most

Haunted House in the Western Hemisphere" and there were many sightings of Annie's restless spirit roaming the grounds.

Famed psychic, Eileen Garrett, visited the property in the 1950s and reportedly communed with the spirit of Annie Palmer. Garrett fell to the ground and in voice not her own said, "Let no one think that this is the end of me. My shrieks will live, and those that would seek to inherit will find a curse upon them."

In 1978, a group of psychics visited Rose Hall. A séance was held and the spirit of Annie Palmer was contacted. During the session, Annie confessed to killing all three of her husbands as well as many lovers. She also said she would be the last mistress of Rose Hall and indeed she has been. No one has lived there since.

In recent years, Rose Hall has a much happier story associated with it. John W. Rollins, an American businessman and the former lieutenant governor of Delaware, purchased the great house and plantation. Rollins has restored much of Rose Hall with period furniture and hardware. It is a majestic property, which has become a tourist attraction. On the former plantation's acreage, you can also play the beautiful and challenging White Witch golf course!

The sightings continue. Many tourists report strange images appearing in photos taken on the property. Annie's image has also been seen in the mirror in her bedroom. I'm happy to report that our tour was Annie Palmer encounter free!

Rollins, the savior of Rose Hall, was a friend of country music legend Johnny Cash. Cash visited Jamaica frequently and owned property there. It seems as if Cash fell under the spell of the White Witch too. He wrote a song about Rose Hall, and if you're fortunate enough to find yourself in Jamaica on a tour of the great house you will end your tour graveside at Annie Palmer's final resting place and your tour guide will sing for you ....

On the island of Jamaica a long, long time ago
On the Rose Hall Plantation where the ocean breeze flow
Lived a girl named Annie Palmer
She was the mistress of the slaves
Slaves all lived in fear to see the frown on Annie's face
Where are your husbands Annie
One, two and three
Are they sleeping beneath the palm trees near the Caribbean Sea
At nights I hear you riding and

I can hear your lovers call
I can still feel your presence about the great house at Rose Hall

After this graveside concert, Charlotte and I boarded the shuttle and headed back to the Ritz-Carlton for a sunset drink and then a wonderful dinner, our last in Jamaica. The next morning I was in the spotlight, onstage at 8:00 a.m. entertaining, motivating and educating 200 financial advisors. A few hours later I was on an airplane leaving Jamaica. All the while, the White Witch was never far from my thoughts. I guess I came under her spell too!

CHAPTER TWENTY–THREE

America's Dairyland to the Lowest Spot on Earth to the Conch Republic

One of the things I love about my job is that each year I never know what my experiences will be: how the year will start, how it will end and what will happen in between. It's the uncertainty that is really exciting. The variety of venues I play each year also keeps things interesting. The start and finish of 2007 provide a perfect example of what I'm talking about.

My first appearance was early, January 3rd. It was an annual leadership conference for a utility contractor in Madison, Wisconsin. January in Wisconsin, it's always a lovely time of year there! Anyway, I was providing after-dinner entertainment for 400 men, most of whom were dressed in flannel shirts. My second-to-last performance in '07 was in mid-December for a private equity investment firm and multi-national holding company based in Kuwait. So I went from performing to a sea of flannel to performing to a sea of keffiyahs (the traditional Arab male headdress) in less than twelve months.

The Kuwait-based company had wanted me to come to Dubai the year before for this annual event. Unfortunately, I was heavily booked at the time and didn't have the days available to travel over and back. When they contacted me the following year, I was elated. I have always wanted to visit Dubai. As we were finalizing the details of the contract, I asked my contact via e-mail for the Dubai venue. His response to my e-mail informed me that the conference wasn't going to be held in Dubai this year. Instead, the meeting would take place in Jordan. Jordan? I never really thought about going to Jordan. I was assured that I would love it and if I had any extra time I should pop over to Syria for some great sightseeing as it was just next door!

I had been to the Middle East a few times, two tours in Saudi Arabia for Aramco Oil and one trip to Egypt. However, this was to be my first post 9/11 trip; so I was a little apprehensive.

As it turned out, I didn't have any time for sightseeing anyway. It was to be a quick trip sandwiched between two presentations for a financial services company. The first one was at the Ritz-Carlton Half Moon Bay just south of San Francisco. What a wonderful property. I had to be back in the States two days after my presentation in Jordan to work another date for the same financial services firm, this time on the East Coast at the Ritz-Carlton Key Biscayne near Miami.

I almost didn't make it out of Jordan!

The flight from San Francisco to London's Heathrow was perhaps the best service and best accommodations I've ever had aboard an aircraft. I was flying business class on British Airways (why is it that business class on foreign airlines typically outclasses first class on U.S. airlines?). From Heathrow, it was straight on to Amman, Jordan.

The event was held at the Kempinski Ishtar Resort on the Dead Sea. It was a fantastic location. My plane landed in the early evening and Joseph, my driver, met me at baggage claim. We jumped into his Mercedes sedan and we headed down to the Dead Sea.

As we drove the black ribbon of highway surrounded by desert landscape and dropped deeper into the valley that would eventually take us to the Dead Sea, my driver shared his love of Jordan and history with me.

"You know I am a Christian," he stated.

"Oh, I didn't know," I replied.

"I told you my name is Joseph. Joseph is a Christian name," he said. "Are you Christian?"

"Yes, Roman Catholic," I replied.

As we were having this religious discussion, we came to a military roadblock. The soldiers stopped the car, searched the trunk and looked underneath the vehicle with mirrors attached to long poles and then let us pass.

"Is that a common event?" I asked my driver.

"Oh yes, it's the Middle East. A very complex region as perhaps you've heard," he answered, and I noticed a smile play about his lips and a twinkle in his eye as I observed his features in the rearview mirror.

"Since you are a Christian, you should see where Jesus was baptized," Joseph suggested.

"Is that here?"

"Just ahead."

Sure enough we drove by a road sign proclaiming in multiple languages (including English) that just off the road was the site of John the Baptist's baptism of Jesus in the Jordan River.

"The River Jordan feeds into the Dead Sea. However, the river is being diverted more and more frequently for irrigation purposes. As a result, the Dead Sea continues to drop by an estimated three feet per year. In thirty years time, the Dead Sea may be completely dry. The shores of the Dead Sea are the lowest point on the earth not covered with water—about 400 meters or 1,300 feet below sea level. And, the lowest point continues to get lower. In order to save the Dead Sea, there is an effort to divert water from the Red Sea to the Dead Sea. The project is called, naturally enough, *From Red to Dead.*

"Besides the River Jordan and the Dead Sea, there are many religious sites in Jordan," Joseph went on, "Mount Sinai, where Moses received the Ten Commandments, for example. You could spend a month here and not see everything. We also have the ancient city of Petra that is not far from your hotel. It was made famous in the Indiana Jones film, *The Last Crusade.*"

My mind flashed to the image of Indiana Jones on horseback riding up to a secret city hidden in rock, and I immediately knew what Joseph was talking about.

"And, Syria is just a short trip away," Joseph suggested.

"Unfortunately, I don't have the time," I said. Truly regretting the fact that I would have to miss out on Mount Sinai, Petra and the various religious sites, not to mention that side trip to Syria!

"At least I'll get to swim in the Dead Sea," I said.

"I don't think you want to swim in it. Just float and stay on your back. The water is filled with all kinds of minerals and you don't want to accidentally ingest anything that could make you sick, especially when you are this far from home," Joseph cautioned.

"You realize, all five Cities of the Plain were located around the Dead Sea," he continued.

"Cities of the Plain?" I left the question hang in the air.

"The biblical Cities of the Plain. Sodom and Gomorrah were but two," Joseph clarified.

"Oh, I know those. Destroyed by God because of the wicked ways of their inhabitants," I said.

"Destroyed by brimstone and fire from the Lord out of heaven," Joseph's voice rose and deepened as he quoted *Genesis.*

"God told Abraham that he would destroy Sodom because of the evil there. Abraham pleaded with him to spare the city. A bargain was struck. If 50 righteous people could be found in Sodom, the city would be saved. Fifty could not be found. If 45 righteous men, women and children could be found, the city would be saved. Forty-five could not be found. If 30 or 20 or even ten righteous people could be found, Sodom would be saved. Not 30, not 20 and not even ten could be found. Only four. Abraham's nephew, Lot, his wife and their two youngest daughters," Joseph continued.

"God permitted Lot, his daughters and wife to escape the city by striking the rest of the inhabitants blind. As they were leaving Sodom, God's angels told them not to look back. Lot's wife could not resist. She looked back and was instantly turned into a pillar of salt. Look, you can see her there," Joseph pointed to another tourist sign, this one informing us that we could indeed see Lot's wife as she existed now—a pillar of salt!

As Joseph continued talking, I truly began to realize what an extraordinary place I had come to.

"One of your fellow countrymen tried to find the Cities of the Plain. His name was Ralph Baney and he was a minister from Kansas City. Mr. Baney received special permission from King Hussein to search the bottom of the Dead Sea for Sodom and Gomorrah. The diving was very dangerous. Parts of the Dead Sea are 200 feet deep, and under the surface it is as black as night. The Dead Sea has the highest saline content of any sea in the world, seven times greater than the waters of the ocean. Baney had to carry more than 200 pounds of equipment just to be able to sink below the surface. And, as I already warned you, if you ingest some of the Dead Sea, you yourself could be dead!

"Baney did eventually find what he thought was a roadway in a shallow, southern section of the Dead Sea. He believed he had found, if not Sodom or Gomorrah, one of the Cities of the Plain. He believed God's wrath caused the Dead Sea to rise and cover the lost cities.

"Unfortunately, Baney's ideas were disproved about twenty years later when the water level of the Dead Sea dropped and exposed the site Baney had explored. Other archeologists from your country concluded that the plain had been uninhabited since at least 3,000 B.C—one thousand years before the destruction of Sodom and Gomorrah.

"However, those very same archeologists did uncover five sites near the south end of the Dead Sea. The sites match the location and age of the Cities of the Plain, and at least one of the ruined cities appears to have been destroyed by fire," Joseph concluded.

"Ah, you can see the Dead Sea now," Joseph said as we dropped even further into the valley. "And look straight ahead, across the sea. To your right is Jerusalem, and to your left is Bethlehem."

I stared and saw clusters of lights on a desert ridge on the other side of the Dead Sea as I marveled at the thought of just how deep into "The Holy Land" I was.

"Everything is just so close together," I said, thinking that the Dead Sea seemed very small and more like a dead lake than the sea I had envisioned.

"We are a tightly knit part of the world," Joseph countered. "That small area, the state of Israel, just across the Dead Sea is sandwiched between Egypt and the Gaza Strip to the west, Lebanon to the north, and the West Bank, Syria and Jordan to the east," Joseph explained.

"You know the city of Jerusalem is very small, less than one square kilometer, only about a third of a square mile. It is one of the oldest cities in the world, over four-thousand years old. It is the holiest city in Judaism and the spiritual center of the Jewish people. It contains many Christian holy sites and is considered the third holiest city in Islam. How is that for being closely knitted?" Joseph asked.

"It is all just so amazing and eye opening. I thank you for such an enjoyable and educational ride," I said.

"Well, our time is almost at an end. But I do have time to tell you one more story. You know of the Ark of the Covenant of course?"

"Of course, another Indiana Jones reference," I answered.

"The Ark was the symbol of the ancient Israelites. God instructed Moses how to construct the Ark. It was a chest about four feet long, two feet wide and two feet tall made of wood but covered in gold plate. It was carried on two gold plated poles inserted through four gold rings attached to its feet.

"The Ark held the Ten Commandments and has been lost to time. Many feel that finding the Ark of the Covenant would prove all the religious skeptics wrong. Think what it's discovery could mean. An American claimed to have found the Ark here in Jordan," Joseph explained.

"Really? I never heard anything about it," I said thinking that perhaps there was some vast conspiracy to cover it up orchestrated by the Catholic Church—it was a Dan Brown, *Da Vinci Code* moment.

"Yes, a man by the name of Croster said he found the Ark during a secret dig here in Jordan. He claimed to have photographic evidence but would only show the proof to David Rothschild, the famous international banker.

"Rothschild refused to see him; so Croster agreed to show the photos to a biblical archaeologist, Siegfried Horn. There were a dozen photos in all. Horn claimed that ten of the photos were completely blank while two did show images of a gold plated box, but the photos showed nail heads on the surface indicating it was a box of recent design.

"My government was furious with the unauthorized excavation and the bad publicity it received; so they denied a legitimate excavation the following year, which is unfortunate because I believe the Ark of the Covenant is in Jordan, just waiting to be discovered," Joseph concluded.

"So this Croster was a con artist," I stated.

"He was a fraud. The year was 1981 when the first Indiana Jones film came out. Perhaps he was trying to attract publicity for himself. I think he might have been a bit insane as he also claimed to have found Noah's Ark, the Tower of Babel, the City of Adam and even the stone used by Cain to kill Abel!

"Here we are, at the lowest spot on earth," Joseph said as we pulled up to a guarded gate at the entrance to the Kempinski Ishtar Resort.

Our car was searched again, and then we were allowed to pass as the giant gates swung open permitting us to enter the resort property. My luggage was taken away to be x-rayed, and I walked through a metal detector in order to enter the lobby of the hotel. Check-in in the Middle East is a very different experience from checking into a hotel in the States.

I waved goodbye to Joseph as my new contact, Hassan, greeted me in the lobby. Hassan was educated in the United States and actually had seen my show while he was in college in Cincinnati at Xavier University. An eighteen-year-old Muslim man from Kuwait attends a Catholic university in Ohio, sees my show at his orientation and six years later we're meeting again halfway around the world at the Dead Sea. It is a small world!

After our initial greeting, I proclaimed to Hassan, "What a beautiful hotel."

"It is indeed. It's designed after the legendary Hanging Gardens of Babylon. Take a stroll in the morning. You'll find stunning views of the Dead

America's Dairyland to the Lowest Spot on Earth
to the Conch Republic

Sea as well as gardens, lagoons, waterfalls, ancient olive trees, bamboo palms and numerous pools."

"What about the pools? Can I go swimming?"

"Oh yes, there is the main pool and also some lap pools located throughout the property," Hassan replied.

"Do I have to stay covered up to and from the pool?" I asked, remembering how strict the rules were when I was in Saudi Arabia.

"No, no, no. Jordan is very progressive. Men and women can even share the same pool. You may even see a bikini or two. In fact, would you like a glass of wine in the lobby lounge?" Hassan asked as I began to realize that Jordan was nothing like Saudi Arabia when it came to strict Muslim law.

We enjoyed a glass of wine, and then I was off to bed but not before standing on my balcony taking in the sight of the Dead Sea, a full moon and swaying palm trees.

The next morning I did get to enjoy the property. I swam some laps, floated in the Dead Sea and even saw a bikini!

The performance was scheduled for that evening after dinner. I did my sound check in the late afternoon and returned to my room to change. I was in the room for less than five minutes when there was a knock on my door. I opened it to find a uniformed attendant who smiled and offered me a sealed envelope. I opened the envelope to read a note informing me that my flight to New York the following morning had been cancelled, but I had been re-booked on another flight. The only problem was that the other flight left a day later and would get me back to the States a day after my next scheduled presentation. I ran off to find Hassan!

"Do not worry Craig, we will take care of it. You see, our company also owns a travel agency," Hassan tried to reassure me.

"Just get me back to the States. For example, is there anything direct to Washington, D.C.? D.C. is not far from where I live. Or, try to route me to Miami. That's where my next performance is." I was trying to give Hassan as many options as possible.

"But you were going to Pittsburgh, would that destination suffice?"

"Sure, as long as I can get there in time to catch my flight to Miami," I answered.

"You focus on your show, we'll work on getting you back in time," Hassan said.

I met Hassan for dinner with the group and he handed me my new travel itinerary. I would leave on a night flight that very evening to Frankfurt. After a seven hour layover in Frankfurt, I would go on to

Washington Dulles where I had less than forty-five minutes to clear customs and catch a connecting flight to Pittsburgh. Not *ideal,* but at least I would be back in time to catch my flight the following day to Miami. I relaxed and enjoyed my meal.

It was a fascinating group of people from many different countries. All of them did business with the company Hassan worked for. I met Hassan's employer, a dark skinned, dark eyed, handsome man dressed in an expensive Italian business suit. Even though he was dressed in Armani, I could easily picture him sitting on horseback in full Arab dress, a falcon perched on his arm. His father actually had started the company. He had become wealthy during the rebuilding of Kuwait after the Iraqi invasion and what has become known in the United States as the "First Iraq War" in 1990 and 1991. When the company expanded to include private equity, a beautiful, brainy, U.S. educated, blonde Russian woman was chosen to head up that division. This was a very progressive Middle Eastern business concern.

The show was very well received. Everyone spoke or at least understood English, and while the humor didn't translate as well as it usually does, I was greeted very warmly.

My bags were packed and sitting in the back of the banquet room. I collected them after the performance and joined my hosts in the lobby bar for a nightcap before meeting my driver and heading off to the airport.

This new driver wasn't nearly as chatty as Joseph, and that was just as well as my nerves were a bit on edge. You have to remember that I flew overnight from San Francisco to London and then on to Jordan. I did have a decent night's rest on my arrival in Jordan, and I did get to briefly enjoy the Kempinski Ishtar Resort's amenities before doing a sound check followed by a performance and a "meet and greet." Then it was off to the airport for another overnight flight to Germany followed by a seven-hour layover and then a flight back to the United States if all went well.

As we arrived at the Queen Alia International Airport (named after Queen Alia Al Hussein who ironically died in a helicopter crash in 1977), an energetic Jordanian youth grabbed my bags and shouted, "Follow me!" and we headed toward the terminal.

He hustled me (in more ways than one!) to the check-in counter. There seemed to be a problem with my D.C. to Pittsburgh flight; so the bags were just checked to Dulles. I figured I could reclaim them, which I had to do anyway before clearing customs and then check them to Pittsburgh. The entire process was a bit of a blur, but my smiling new friend helped me

America's Dairyland to the Lowest Spot on Earth
to the Conch Republic

through the entire procedure. I handed him 20 U.S. dollars and he was back out the door, and before I knew it, I was on my way to Frankfurt.

The long layover in Germany was uneventful as was the flight to Dulles. However, upon arrival in D.C., customs was a madhouse. By the time I cleared customs, my Pittsburgh flight was already in the air. The next flight to Pittsburgh was four hours later at 11:00 p.m. It was the last flight to Pittsburgh that day and was already overbooked. At this point, I wasn't sure how long it had been since I had slept in an actual bed, and I was exhausted but I really wanted to get home; so I rented a car and drove the four-and-a-half hours to West Virginia.

Charlotte greeted me with a hug and a kiss. Our dogs, Dolittle and Connor P. McNasty, gave me a lick or two and the four of us headed to bed. The next morning we drove from our house to the Pittsburgh International Airport, Charlotte in our personal vehicle (which we would leave parked at the airport) and me in my D.C. rental car that I had arranged to drop off in Pittsburgh. We left Connor and Dolittle behind in the kitchen, their heads tilted to one side probably wondering, "Where is he off to now? He just got home." I think that's one of the reasons Charlotte and I have never had children.

"Don't worry boys, we'll be right back, and Laura will be here soon," I said as I closed the kitchen door. Laura was their favorite dog sitter.

We made it to Miami without a mishap. After my morning presentation and my final performance for 2007 at the Ritz-Carlton Key Biscayne, Charlotte and I jumped into our rented convertible and drove to Key West. The plan was to spend a few days in the Conch Republic to unwind and celebrate the end of 2007 as we planned for 2008. We were also celebrating my 50th birthday that had occurred without ceremony a couple of weeks before.

It's about 150 miles from Miami to Key West, and the trip takes about three-and-a-half hours. What a spectacular drive! You travel on U.S. 1, known as the "Overseas Highway" in the Keys. What is collectively known as the Florida Keys is essentially island after island connected by this one and only roadway. During the drive, you cross many, many bridges the most famous of which is Seven Mile Bridge. The bridge is, you guessed it, seven miles long (actually just under seven miles but 6.79 Mile Bridge doesn't have the same ring to it!). This particular bridge is an engineering marvel. The bridge arches high into the air to allow tall ships to pass beneath it. You are surrounded by gorgeous blue water that ranges from light to dark in color. The sun sparkles off the water and the site is truly something to behold.

The current bridge was completed in 1982 and replaced two other bridges. The first was a railway bridge built by the wealthy and eccentric transportation mogul, Henry Flagler. This bridge served as part of the Florida East Coast Railway's Key West extension and was completed in 1912. At that time, it was considered by many to be one of the wonders of the world. The bridge was badly damaged during a hurricane in 1935, was refurbished by the United States government and reopened as an automobile highway and extension of U.S. 1. Much of the old bridge is still intact, and it parallels the new bridge. You see people fishing off it as you drive by. It's kind of bizarre and beautiful—just like the Florida Keys!

We arrived in Key West, checked into our hotel, headed out to the pool and ordered some tropical drinks. That night, we caught some street performers and watched the sunset at Mallory Square before heading to Blue Heaven for a wonderful dinner of sautéed yellowtail snapper with citrus beurre blanc sauce and, of course, a slice of Key lime pie.

Blue Heaven is a wonderful restaurant located in a shuttered, blue painted building. The restaurant has a history of entertaining going back over one hundred years. During its history, the property has hosted cock fighting, gambling, Friday night boxing matches hosted by Ernest Hemingway and more recently, impromptu concerts by Jimmy Buffett. The outdoor courtyard where Charlotte and I enjoyed our dinner is paved with slate pool table tops left over from when the lower level of the building was a pool hall and ice cream parlor. Roosters still roam the courtyard, but no *fighting* is allowed!

The second floor has served as a dance hall, a playhouse and even a bordello. Currently, the upstairs is dedicated to the Bordello Gallery and exhibits colorful local artwork. There are still a number of small rooms in the upstairs gallery and "peep-holes" in the doors to those rooms which were used to spy on the working girls. You can still look through them, but you won't see any action! Well, it is Key West—you just might!

The current owners, Suanne Kitchar and Richard Hatch started serving black beans, rice and fish to lunch customers in 1992. They would motor over from their houseboat home on Christmas Tree Island each and every day, provided the weather cooperated. After a year-and-a-half of building their lunch business, Richard's brother Dan, a formally educated chef, was brought in to develop a dinner menu and the rest is history. You can't get a better meal in Key West.

As we roamed the streets of Key West after dinner, we saw a shirtless man in boxer shorts, boots and a Santa Claus hat riding his bike down the street. As he peddled, he would point at various women and say

America's Dairyland to the Lowest Spot on Earth
to the Conch Republic

"Ho, Ho, Ho!" I had to laugh thinking back over the last five days. Coast-to-coast appearances in the U.S., a trip to the Holy Land and the lowest spot on earth, and now I was standing at the southernmost point in the continental United States as a perverted Santa Claus in his underwear pedaled by. I looked at Charlotte and thought it would be nice to take her to Jordan and spend some time there. We could visit Petra, see the biblical sites, climb Mount Sinai and maybe even make that side trip to Syria! But at the moment, Key West was exactly where I needed to be.

CHAPTER TWENTY–FOUR

The Father of Modern Magic

There are people who come into your life who you know will always be a part of you, true friends. Charlotte and I didn't have many friends. We don't have any children; so there isn't the socializing with other kids' parents, and neither of us has ever had a nine-to-five job; so we don't meet anyone at work. Charlotte, who is much more outgoing than I am, does stay in touch with a group of four women: Tanya, Tandy, Tammy and Lou Anne, all of whom she has been friends with since grade school. It's an amazing relationship. None of them lives in our town and she only sees them three or four times a year. As a couple, we have "performer friends" who are scattered about the country. There's Tom, the hypnotist, and his wife Sara in Orlando; Kevin and Cindy, the illusionists, in Lynchburg, Virginia; and Pat and Barry who perform a multimedia presentation on the history of rock and roll and live part of the year in Boca Raton, Florida, and part of the year in the Catskill Mountains in New York. These couples are special. We've become friends because we each tour the college market in the U.S. We see each other at trade show conferences throughout the year and occasionally visit each other's homes or catch up on the road. We have so much in common, (my father used to refer to us as circus people), that we just click and can talk about things that other people simply wouldn't understand unless you've spent your life barnstorming the country trying to entertain the masses.

The Father of Modern Magic

A while back, Charlotte met a local couple at a wine tasting—Joel and Cynthia. I met them a bit later, and eventually we became very good friends. Cynthia and Joel are two of the most interesting people I've ever met. They truly know how to live life to the fullest. They also came equipped with a large circle of friends; so we went from hardly knowing anyone locally to having more friends than we could keep up with. Our life hasn't been the same since.

Joel and Cynthia live in our town, Wheeling, West Virginia, most of the year. However, for three to four months each year, in month-long increments, they take up residence in Paris, France, at an apartment they own on Ile Saint Louis. They invited us to visit them one summer, and it became a summer tradition for us for three years, from 2006 through 2008.

Cynthia and Joel make a striking couple. She is of Caucasian-Asian descent with porcelain skin and dark black hair cut in the style of a China doll. In fact, she looks like a walking, talking China doll. While Cynthia is short, Joel is tall and lanky. He sports a little "soul patch" beneath his lower lip, and his head is attached to a jungle of wild, curly, dark hair. He usually wears a pair of funky eyeglasses, as well. And then there's Toulouse. Toulouse is the pair's Brussels Griffon, a breed of dog you're probably familiar with if you've ever seen the film *As Good as it Gets* with Jack Nicholson, Helen Hunt and Greg Kinnear. He is the most unusual looking canine. He's small but sturdy with a butterscotch blonde coat, a little black button nose and a near human expression. He has large, black almost bulging eyes and short, pointed ears. He looks like a cross between Gizmo from the film *Gremlins* and Chewbacca the Wookie from *Star Wars*! Toulouse goes everywhere with Cynthia and Joel—even to Paris. He is welcomed in the finest restaurants and hotels. Once, while dining at the five star Hotel le Meurice, Toulouse was given his own pillow to sit on and a sterling water bowl to drink from. The real irony is that while Toulouse can go almost anywhere in Paris, dogs are barred from most city parks!

The five of us have had some wonderful times in France. The first year, I would only commit to four days. People think I'm crazy traveling to Europe for just four days, but with the amount of time I spend away from home that's all I really want to be gone. Plus, I have a theory: four days and no budget! I mean how much trouble can you get into in just four days? In Paris, plenty! Our 2007 trip was expanded to five days and 2008, to six. If we keep this up, perhaps one day we'll visit for a month!

Paris is a beautiful city and contrary to popular belief, I have found the people very friendly. It may have something to do with the fact that both

Joel and Cynthia speak fluent French, she with a Parisian accent. If you were to compare the hospitality of the Parisians with a similar city in the U.S. (think New York) I believe you would find that Paris would win out when it came to friendliness and courtesy.

Our first Parisian adventure was a whirlwind of activity. We taxied in from the airport to our hotel in the Marais section of Paris. It was a very cool boutique hotel called Hotel Bourg-Tibourg. The room was tiny, but we weren't going to spend much time in the room. We walked over to Joel and Cynthia's apartment on the island. As we crossed the Seine on Pont Marie, one of the oldest bridges in Paris, I was struck by the fact that it was almost as if we were leaving the city of Paris behind and entering a small village. The noise level dropped, the streets narrowed, and it all seemed so magical.

While the island is village-like, there is much to do. You can go boutique shopping for everything from clothing to antiques. There is even a store devoted exclusively to puppets! There are many wonderful restaurants as well as bakeries, foie gras shops, fromageries and the most magical chocolate shop. Then there is the ice cream! Berthillon ice cream is famous, known for its rich colors and intense flavors, and you can only find it on Ile Saint Louis. Ile Saint Louis is connected by Pont Saint Louis to Ile de la Cité, its sister island and home to Notre Dame Cathedral. Pont Saint Louis is a pedestrian bridge, and you can frequently enjoy colorful street performers as you walk across the bridge. And, of course, since you are on an island, the beautiful Seine always surrounds you.

Joel and Cynthia's apartment is a charming place in a building dating to 1635. You press the security code, walk through the gates and enter a flagstone courtyard leading right up to their front door. The apartment is small by U.S. standards, more like a nice hotel suite with an attached kitchenette, but it is beautifully decorated. They re-tiled the floor with ancient, reclaimed chateau tile. French antiques are all around. Exposed brick and stone walls and a beamed ceiling complete the picture. It is just beautiful and so well done.

That first visit has become a blur. We did a speed tour of the Louvre. You cannot understand how large that museum is unless you visit it. It goes on and on. My best memories of the Louvre are of watching a mob of Japanese tourists surrounding the Mona Lisa (it's very small) and seeing Napoleon's furniture in a special display. Quite honestly, your head literally spins as you try to take in as much as you can, knowing that you could spend a year in the building and not fully appreciate everything.

The Father of Modern Magic

We ended our first day in Paris with a champagne toast at night as we watched thousands of sparkling lights adorning the Eifel Tower dance in a special show.

Charlotte fell in love with Le Marché aux Puces, the Paris antique market. It is stall after stall of the most wonderful European antiques. Prices aren't cheap, but you will see things there that you will never see anywhere else. Have you ever walked into an antique store and seen something so unusual and beautiful that it took your breath away? If so, you probably thought, "Where did they find such a thing?" The answer could well be the Marché aux Puces!

Charlotte's first Marché aux Puces souvenir was a glazed terracotta decorative roof tile in the shape of a lamb. The lamb is life size and has glass eyes. The piece is from Normandy and dates to the mid 1800s. Those glass eyes now watch over us as we prepare meals in our kitchen as the little lamb has found a home there. During our second visit, a French church processional figure from the late 1700s came home with us. He now resides in our living room.

We visited the Baccarat Museum in the beautiful former home of famed patron of the arts Marie-Laure, Viscountess de Noailles; the Paris Opera House; Notre Dame Cathedral; the white-domed Basilica of the Sacré Coeur in the Montmartre district; and the Tuileries Gardens. We also browsed the antique book and paper dealers who line the Seine looking for treasures.

This first visit coincided with Bastille Day, the French Fourth of July. We watched the most spectacular fireworks show I have ever seen at the Eiffel Tower as we enjoyed a picnic dinner. It is a sight I will never forget and one of my favorite memories of Paris.

We also had some of the best meals I've ever had. My favorite was lunch at Le Grand Véfour. This was the first of the grand restaurants in Paris and dates to 1784. You sit in early 19th century neoclassical elegance amid gilded mirrors as tuxedoed waiters hover around you attending to your every need while delivering the most scrumptious four-course meal. Well, technically it's a four-course meal, but when you factor in the house confections, the signature angel food cake and the cheese cart (a highlight of any French meal), it's more like seven courses. Over the years, all of the Parisian "movers and shakers" have dined there and brass plaques on various seats indicate whose posterior predated yours: Victor Hugo, Jean-Paul Sartre, Napoleon Bonaparte and Josephine, for example. Lunch lasted four hours!

Eating and drinking are two highlights of any of our trips to France. On this first trip, I became addicted to Hôtel de Crillon, one of the oldest luxury hotels in the world located right at the foot of the Champs-Elysees. The front of the hotel is a car lover's dream. You'll see Bentleys, Ferraris, Maseratis and a Rolls Royce or two. With rooms starting at about $1,000 per night, we've never stayed there, but we have had dinner, and we made a friend of Kevin, a bartender. We make it a tradition to stop in for the Crillon version of Pimm's Cup.

The Pimm's Cup cocktail was created in England in the mid 1800s and is a refreshing afternoon drink after a day of walking around Paris. The usual Pimm's Cup is made with Pimm's #1, a gin-based beverage the color of dark tea with subtle tastes of spice and citrus fruit. Pimm's claims the beverage is still made according to James Pimm's original recipe, a closely guarded secret known only to six people. To the Pimm's #1, you add some fruit, ginger ale and garnish with cucumber. The Crillon version of this concoction is made with champagne instead of ginger ale and is served in a Baccarat crystal pitcher. It's very decadent. One year, Kevin gave Charlotte and Cynthia two Crillon champagne glasses engraved with a scripted "C." "C" for Charlotte, "C" for Cynthia, "C" for Crillon!

Another favorite "watering hole" is the Hemingway Bar at the back of the Ritz Hotel. It's an intimate space decorated with Hemingway memorabilia where the drinks are very expensive but very good, and you never know who you might see.

On our second trip to Paris, we added a day and drove to the country to spend some time in the Champagne region. Joel and Cynthia met us at the airport where we rented a car, and with Joel behind the wheel, we headed to Champagne.

We stayed for two nights at Château Les Crayères in Reims, the heart of Champagne country. The chateau is stunningly beautiful and sits amid a 17 acre park. As you enter the chateau, you are surrounded by 18th century opulence. The chateau was the home of Madame Louise Pommery. She took over her husband's winemaking business when he passed away in 1858. The widow Pommery was thirty-nine years old at the time. During the following thirty years, she built a small winemaking business (which specialized in red wines) into one of the most successful champagne houses in the world. Pommery currently produces seven million bottles of bubbly each year.

Our dinner the first evening was at Château Les Crayères and what a dinner it was. We enjoyed a seven-course meal with each course being accompanied by a different champagne. I think this meal and my first meal at Le Grand Véfour are the two best dining experiences I've ever had.

The Father of Modern Magic

While in Reims, we toured several champagne houses. At Lanson, Joel and I stood transfixed as we watched a professional bottle wrapper ply her trade. She was a pretty blonde, wearing red lipstick, a white lab coat, black-framed glasses and red high heels. There was something quite arousing about the entire process! At Taittinger, Toulouse began to get into the act and by the time we finished up at Pommery, the Brussels Griffon was a bit tipsy!

The Pommery tour was the most interesting. The main buildings above ground were primarily built in the 1870s in the neo-Elizabethan style popular in England at the time. This was intentional, as Pommery was trying to publicly acknowledge the strong ties the champagne house had to the English market.

Below ground is where it really gets interesting. The buildings sit over two-thousand-year-old chalk caves, and these caves store 20 million bottles of champagne. There was a temporary modern art installation throughout the caves when we visited. These modern works of art competed for your attention with permanent artworks on the cave walls done by workers over the last one-hundred-thirty years.

We went further out into the country for dinner at another chateau our second night in Champagne. It was very good, but couldn't compare to the meal at Les Crayères. Before we knew it, it was time to return to Paris.

We checked into a different hotel from the year before. Hotel Jeu de Paume is right on the island and just around the corner from Joel and Cynthia's. The hotel got its name from a French sport very much like American handball and a precursor to modern day tennis. Jeu de Paume literally means "game of palm." The hotel was originally a royal, 17th century Jeu de Paume court used by the court of Louis XIII. In 1987, an architect discovered the site and decided to convert it into a luxury hotel while preserving its history. Consequently you have a high ceilinged common area (complete with a glass elevator), and three-hundred-year-old timbers surround you. The common areas are unique and inviting, the rooms, not so much. But it is a very unique place which blends the past with the present, and I get a special feeling every time I walk through the large wooden carriage doors and step into the beautiful lobby.

We now come to our most recent French excursion in 2008. This time we decided to go to the chateau country of the Loire Valley in addition to spending quality time in Paris, but first, Marché aux Puces! Joel met us at the airport and we taxied to the market. Joel and Charlotte left to go antiquing, and I went with the luggage to Joel and Cynthia's apartment. We were only going to spend the night in their apartment, as we were to leave for the Loire

Valley in the morning. Cynthia, Toulouse and I met Joel and Charlotte at the antique market, and this year Charlotte couldn't find anything despite being there from opening to closing. The dollar to euro ratio was particularly tough during this trip, and I think that had a lot to do with it. However, Charlotte did come home with a treasure when she purchased a late 19th century Guignol puppet show theatre, complete with puppets, from Joel and Cynthia's bedroom wall. Guignol is like the Southern French version of Punch & Judy. Our friends were going to start to rent their apartment when they weren't in residence and didn't want to leave the theatre on the wall for fear something would happen to it. It now resides on our home office wall, and the puppets are actually just over my shoulder watching me type this!

The following day, we picked up a rental car and headed to the Loire Valley. Cynthia, Joel, Charlotte, Toulouse and I took up residence in yet another wonderful chateau, Château de Noizay. The plan was to tour some of the amazing castles up and down the Loire River, the longest river in France. While castle hopping we would also visit a troglodyte or two. Troglodytes are cave dwellings hollowed out of the chalk cliffs and are common in this area of France. Some are still occupied as primary residences, some are used as storage facilities and some have been converted into restaurants or bars. On our final night in the Loire Valley, we had dinner at Les Hautes Roches, a hotel where the rooms are actually cut into the hillside. As we were motoring up and down the Loire Valley, we would stop at a roadside troglodyte, have a glass of Vouvray wine, chat a bit with the person working there and then be on our way. The hillsides are littered with troglodytes but you have to look closely as they blend in so well.

As for the chateaus, we left everything up to our two Francophiles. They chose one chateau for the best garden (Château de Villandry); another spanning a river for its stunning location (Château de Chenonceau); another smaller chateau for its jewel box-like beauty (Château Azay-le-Rideau); and yet another for its unique architecture (Château Royal de Blois).

As we headed toward Château Royal de Blois, I saw a road sign and a tingle ran down my spine.

"Did that sign just read 'Bloyz?'" I asked.

"No, I don't believe so," Cynthia replied.

"I'm certain it did. Maybe I'm not saying it right. The town was spelled B-l-o-i-s," I spelled it out.

"Oh yes, that's where we're going—*Bluwaa*," Cynthia answered in beautifully accented French.

The Father of Modern Magic

"OK Contessa Tini," I said, "Je ne parle francais." (We call Cynthia "Contessa Tini" because of her royal bearing, her passing resemblance to Ina Garten, the Barefoot Contessa, and the fact that she makes one mean martini!).

Joel and Cynthia speak wonderful French, and when I heard them mention the Château Royal de Blois, I heard Château Royal de Bluwaa never connecting the sound Bluwaa to the city Blois. It's fun to watch and listen to them work on their conversational French. The year before when we were headed to Reims there was much good natured arguing back and forth on how to properly pronounce Reims with a lot of throat gurgling and strange sounds coming from both of them.

The reason I was excited was due to the fact that Blois was the home of Jean Eugene Robert-Houdin, a performer known as the Father of Modern Magic. Born on December 7th, 1805, Robert-Houdin is credited by many magic historians as the performer who took magic out of the fairgrounds and marketplaces and into the legitimate theatre. I had heard about a wonderful museum in Blois dedicated to this master magician and I had always wanted to visit it.

"I think that's the town the Robert-Houdin magic museum is in. Do you know anything about it?" I asked Cynthia and Joel.

"No, but we'll ask around once we get there," Joel replied.

We didn't need to ask around. As soon as we got into town, we saw signs for Maison de la Magie everywhere. Apparently, it was as big a draw as the chateau.

The museum is housed in a three-story mansion and is just across from the chateau. On the hour, a half dozen automaton dragons poke their heads and tails out of the windows and roar. It's quite a site. The dragons are actually supposed to be salamanders, the symbol of Francois I, who was known as the Salamander King. He brought the renaissance to France building many of the chateaus in the Loire Valley in order to entertain his court. Outside the museum sits a life size marble statue of Robert-Houdin. After taking in the dragon/salamander show, I couldn't wait to get inside.

There are actually four levels to the museum. You enter into the lowest level called the Rotunda. Displays around the Rotunda trace the history of magic over the ages, from the ancient Greeks to the 19th century. From this brief history lesson, you travel through a hall of optical illusions and then into a display area of posters, props and stage illusions used by magicians throughout the world. There is a 400-seat theatre on site and a daily magic show. In the foyer of the theatre there are many other wonders to behold: more colorful magic posters, a mummy's sarcophagus and a sword box illusion, to name a few.

We sat in on the magic show and it was well done. It was a three person show performed in pantomime, with a very European feel. While I thoroughly enjoyed the performance, I couldn't wait to get to the heart of the museum and get to know Robert-Houdin.

Before reaching Robert-Houdin Hall, we passed through the Harry Houdini Passageway. If you think the names sound similar, you're correct. If you think that it's a coincidence, you're wrong! Harry Houdini, arguably the most famous magician of all time, was born Erich Weiss in Budapest, Hungary, in 1874. Young Erich moved with the rest of his family to Appleton, Wisconsin, in 1878 to join his father, Rabbi Mayer Samuel Weiss. Erich fell in love with magic at an early age. In 1891, he read the American English translation of Jean Eugene Robert-Houdin's autobiography, *The Life of Robert-Houdin, The King of Conjurors,* and became enchanted by the French performer. Erich Weiss changed his name to Houdini thinking adding the letter "i" would indicate he was like Houdin and also believing that his idol's name was Robert Houdin. The Harry came about because it sounded like an American version of Erich.

Harry Houdini went on to fame and fortune. He also became a student of the history of magic. He would visit magicians' graves and oftentimes pay for the upkeep on them in order to keep the performers' names alive. In the early 1900s, Houdini was touring France. He desperately wanted to meet with the descendants of his idol, Robert-Houdin. When he contacted the remaining family, they refused to meet with him. They were actually unfamiliar with Houdini and thought that the American was cheaply exploiting their ancestor's reputation.

Houdini was deeply hurt and insulted by this reaction. He went on to use his extensive collection of magic memorabilia in an attempt to discredit his former idol. In 1908 he published his controversial book, *The Unmasking of Robert-Houdin,* claiming that performers before Robert-Houdin actually invented many of the illusions credited to the Frenchman. While there was some merit to Houdini's work, most magic scholars agree that, for many reasons, Jean Eugene Robert-Houdin truly deserves his title, the "Father of Modern Magic."

After looking at some interesting Houdini artifacts, it was on to meet Robert-Houdin! As I walked into the hall, my eyes darted around trying to take in all the wonders before me. At this point, it was just Charlotte and I.

Cynthia had stayed outside with Toulouse, and Joel had bailed after the magic show. Magic doesn't cast a spell on everyone!

There, his top hat and wand! A note inscribed by Robert-Houdin himself was on the wand. Translated, it read, "This wand has served me in all the performances I have given during my entire artistic career." If your image of a magician is a man in a tuxedo, you have Robert-Houdin to thank. Before Robert-Houdin, most magical performers would wear some type of costume, a conical hat and wizard robes for example. However, Robert-Houdin chose to dress in formal wear, in accordance with what his audience would be wearing in the 1800s when they attended his performances in Paris. His dress, which wasn't a costume at all, became the standard dress for magicians for more than one hundred years.

"I can't believe all this stuff survived, and I'm looking at it as if I were in Robert-Houdin's theatre," I exclaimed as I stared at what appeared to be a large leather portfolio with the words "Carton Fantastique de Robert-Houdin" on the front.

"That's Robert-Houdin's 'Fantastic Portfolio,'" I explained to Charlotte.

"He would enter the stage with this thin portfolio under his arm. He would rest the portfolio across two sawhorses and then open it. From it, he would produce paintings, women's hats, four doves, three copper pots (one filled with beans, one with water and one with fire) more birds, this time in a cage, and finally, his young son, Eugene!"

"Wow!" Charlotte said, "He really was a wizard!"

"The king of conjurors," I agreed.

"Look at this," I said, pointing to one of Robert-Houdin's "Mysterious Clocks." "Before he was a magician, he was a clockmaker. He was actually so much more than a magician. He was an inventor, a scientist, a true Renaissance man." I was trying to keep Charlotte hooked so I wouldn't lose her like I'd lost Joel. But that didn't seem to be a problem given her knowledge of magic and her love of antiques. She seemed almost as interested in the exhibits as I was.

We looked at a beautiful 19th century clock with a glass face and a single hour hand. The hand would move correctly around the dial without any apparent connection. These creations of Robert-Houdin won many prizes and awards and sell for tens-of-thousands of dollars today.

"That's not something he would use on stage, right?" asked Charlotte.

"No, but *that* is," I said as I pointed to the "Aerial Clock." A large, transparent clock dial suspended in mid-air by two thin cords. Beneath the dial there was a crystal bell.

"Anyone from the audience would call out an hour and the clock hand would move to that number as the bell rang out the correct hour. Both the clock and the bell were passed out to the audience for examination prior to and at the completion of the routine.

"Robert-Houdin used many marvelous mechanical devices onstage. They were called automatons. There's one over there, the 'Pastry Cook of Palais-Royal,'" I explained.

We looked upon a miniature pastry shop complete with a tiny pastry cook. "The audience would request various items like hot buns, cakes, ice cream, even liqueurs, and the little mechanical man would dart into the shop and return with the requested item," I tried to explain the routine to Charlotte.

"As a finale, a borrowed ring would vanish from a box while the owner held it. The pastry cook would come out of the shop carrying a small cake. Inside the cake would be the ring!

"And look over there," I continued, "that's one of his most beautiful creations, the 'Marvelous Orange Tree!' The magician would borrow a handkerchief and vanish it. Next, Robert-Houdin would vanish several oranges. A vial of elixir would be ignited and its vapors would swirl around a small orange tree. Orange blossoms bloomed and then oranges appeared. One of the oranges broke into quarters and inside was the borrowed handkerchief! Two butterflies attached themselves to the corners of the handkerchief and spread the fabric for all to see."

I stared at the display shaking my head and marveling at the genius of the man and then a small stool caught my attention.

"What are you looking at now?" Charlotte asked.

"That stool."

"What does it do?"

"I think Robert-Houdin's teenage son, Emile, used to sit on it! Doesn't sound very interesting, does it?" I knew better as we walked over to the display and verified that this was indeed the stool young Emile sat upon as he performed "Second Sight."

"Emile would be blindfolded and his father would walk through the audience asking the sightless Emile to identify various objects offered to the conjuror by his spectators. The master developed this routine further so that he would not speak a word but only ring a handheld bell when Emile was to give his impression.

The Father of Modern Magic

"This same stool was one of three used in one of Robert-Houdin's most famous illusions, one that is still in the repertoire of many magicians performing today. It was called the 'Ethereal Suspension' and capitalized on the fact that in 1847 ether and it's possible uses provided a popular topic of conversation. The conjuror claimed (for theatrical purposes only) that if a human breathed in the proper amount of ether, it would cause that person's body to momentarily become as light as a balloon. Robert-Houdin proceeded to demonstrate using his little son Eugene as the subject. The three stools would be placed across a bench. Eugene stood on the center stool and two canes were placed upright on the stools to each side of the boy. Eugene would rest his arms on the canes. At this point he would supposedly breathe in the ether. His eyes would close and his head would slump to his chest. Robert-Houdin would remove the stool Eugene was standing on, leaving him supported by the two canes alone. Then, remarkably, he would remove one of the canes along with the stool, leaving Eugene suspended by only one cane. To take it further, Robert-Houdin raised his son with one finger to a horizontal position, suspended by only one cane beneath one arm. It was an impossible looking sight," I concluded.

"That's like the illusion Kevin and Cindy used to do in their show with the brooms," Charlotte said referring to our illusionist friends the Spencers.

"One and the same and it's been around since 1847."

I was in heaven strolling through this temple of magic. Everywhere I looked, I saw treasures reminding me of the fantastic life that Robert-Houdin lived. He actually started his public performing career rather late in life (at the age of 39) when he opened his Theatre Robert-Houdin in Paris on July 3rd, 1845. The theatre was elegant but small, seating about 200 people. It was designed to resemble a drawing room of the Louis XV period painted in white and gold with fine draperies, candelabra and period furniture. The show was called *Soirées Fantastiques* and it was two hours of the most amazing magic anyone had ever seen. Robert-Houdin attracted all manner of people to his theatre and became the talk of Paris.

After a year of wonderworking in his theatre, the magician received a special request. King Louis-Philippe summoned Robert-Houdin to the St. Cloud palace for a performance. The "King of Conjurors" prepared a special, one-time-only presentation for the King of France. The illusionist borrowed and vanished six handkerchiefs. He then asked the King to choose any location and the magician boldly stated that he would cause the handkerchiefs to reappear in that very spot. The King considered a number of possibilities before declaring that the handkerchiefs should reappear in an orange tree planter on the palace grounds. A servant was dispatched to search the planter. As he dug into the planter, he unearthed an antique strong box that looked as if it could have been buried for a century. The servant immediately brought the box to the king. When the box was opened, the handkerchiefs were found inside! In addition to the squares of fabric, there was also a note from the famed 18th century mystic Cagliostro, who died in 1795. The note read: "This day, the 6th of June, 1786, this iron box, containing six handkerchiefs, was placed around the roots of an orange tree by me, Balsamo, Count of Cagliostro, to serve in performing an act of magic which will be executed on the same day sixty years hence before Louis-Philippe of Orleans and his family." The aged parchment containing the mystic's message also held the authentic seal of Cagliostro!

News of this incredible performance spread and Theatre Robert-Houdin began to draw the very highest levels of society. He had received the royal stamp of approval.

Robert-Houdin's performing career was relatively short, just eleven years. During that time, he traveled to Belgium, Germany and the British Isles (most notably England) where he gave two royal command performances for Her Majesty Queen Victoria.

The magician retired in 1851 to his home, The Priory, in Saint-Gervais near Blois. Robert-Houdin was anything but idle after leaving the stage. He authored several books (including his famous memoirs which inspired Erich Weiss) and worked on numerous inventions including an electric light he created years before Thomas Edison produced a commercial light bulb.

The Priory itself was a magical place. When you approached the front gates, you were instructed to push a button that was actually an electric doorbell. A sign reading "Robert-Houdin" changed to read, "Enter" as a servant in the main house opened the gates remotely. When the mail was delivered, another electrical signal was sent to the house that not only indicated that the mail had arrived but how much mail there was. There was an automatic feeder for the horses' stable on property and at the shooting range, if you hit a bulls-eye, a crown of flowers suspended from the ceiling would appear over your head.

Perhaps the most interesting story about Robert-Houdin occurred after his official retirement. In 1856, there was turmoil in French Colonial Algeria. Marabouts (tribal shaman, religious fanatics and wonderworkers), were encouraging the various Arab tribes to revolt against French rule. The

The Father of Modern Magic

French government called upon the "King of Conjurors" to travel to North Africa and demonstrate that his powers were greater than those of the Marabouts, thus implying, don't mess with France!

A performance was arranged expressly for the chieftains of the various Arab tribes and Robert-Houdin was in fine form. In addition to his classic effects, he invited a giant of a man on stage and told him he would take his strength away. The magician asked the man to lift a box from the stage and the Arab did so easily. The magician then claimed to have taken the man's strength away and the giant could not budge the box. A child was invited onstage and asked to lift the box and the child did it effortlessly. The giant was asked to try to lift the box again. Once again he failed, and this time he yelled out in pain (courtesy of an electric shock he received). This was Robert-Houdin's famous "Light and Heavy Chest" which used the very advanced (in 1856) principle of electromagnetism.

In another feat, Robert-Houdin invited a young Moor to stand atop a table. The boy was covered with a cone. When the cone was removed, the boy had vanished. Some of the magician's audience vanished, as well, running from the theatre in fright!

Robert-Houdin also performed his version of "The Bullet Catching Trick" during this theatre show. This infamous illusion has claimed the lives of 12 different magicians over the years. There are different versions of it, but essentially a bullet is fired at the performer and the magician catches it on a plate, in his hand or in his teeth. Penn and Teller perform a modern version of the illusion in their Las Vegas show with the magicians firing guns at each other and each catching a marked bullet in his teeth.

After his successful theatre show, Robert-Houdin was sent out on a desert road show to bring his magic directly to various tribes. News of his theatre performances reached the tribal communities, and at one stop a Marabout challenged him to perform the gun trick. The magician was not prepared and said so. The Marabout laughed and called him a fraud. Robert-Houdin promised that if he was given time for prayer and meditation, he would be able to perform the feat the following morning.

In the morning, a crowd had gathered to watch this battle of magic. Two pistols were produced. The pistols were loaded under the watchful eye of the Arab holy man. Robert-Houdin walked 15 paces and turned to face the Marabout. The Arab took a pistol and aimed at the Frenchman. He fired! Robert-Houdin immediately opened his mouth revealing that he had caught the bullet between his teeth! The Marabout was furious and attempted to grab the second pistol in order to try once again to shoot the magician. Robert-

Houdin beat him to it. He grabbed the pistol and aimed it toward a freshly painted white wall. He proclaimed that his aim was much more dangerous than the Marabout's. He fired at the wall and a spot of red appeared. As the spot of red began to spread and cover the wall, the Marabout ran up to the wall and trailed his finger through the stain, smelling and then tasting it, verifying it was indeed what it appeared to be—blood! The crowd was awestruck. Robert-Houdin and his entourage mounted their horses and rode off into the desert.

Before Robert-Houdin left Algeria, he was summoned to the governor's palace. There he was greeted by the Arab chieftains, all wearing red robes as a symbol of their loyalty to France. The tribe leaders presented the magician with a scroll testifying to his unmatched magical powers. This has always been one of my favorite Robert-Houdin tales. And as I stood in the Maison de la Magie, I could feel my jaw drop as I peered into a display case and saw that very same Algerian scroll with the wax seals of all the Arab tribal leaders still intact one-hundred-fifty-two years later.

After his Algerian adventure, the magician returned to The Priory and continued to write and invent. The Franco-Prussian war ended the magician's peaceful retirement. The war claimed the life of his son, Eugene. The little boy who used to mysteriously appear out of a thin portfolio and defy gravity by floating in mid-air grew up to become a soldier and died in battle. On December 10th, 1870, the Prussian army came to Blois and Saint-Gervais and took control of The Priory. Robert-Houdin, his wife and family lived like prisoners in their own home until early March 1871 when the Prussians left the area. Things were never the same after that. Robert-Houdin tried to get back to a normal life, but he kept falling ill, finally succumbing to pneumonia on June 13th, 1871.

After taking our walk through magic history, Charlotte and I headed up to the fourth level of the museum to experience l'Hallucinoscope. This was an interactive visual illusion. We each donned special eye wear, blocking our forward vision. We walked along a trail guided by a handrail. As we walked, images of sea life from the ceiling were reflected around us and it was as if we were walking through the ocean. It was very odd and unique but couldn't compare to the *Soirées Fantastiques!*

After our Loire Valley tour, the five of us returned to Paris for fine dining and high-end bar hopping. We returned to Le Grand Véfour and one of the three best meals I've ever had. This time we were greeted by Michelin starred head chef, Guy Martin as we entered the restaurant. As we were enjoying the four-hour lunch, it dawned on me that we were actually in the

Palais Royal, the former home of Robert-Houdin's theatre, and I thought the trip had come full circle. I also thought that the décor of this famed restaurant had probably not changed much since Robert-Houdin's day. I could imagine him enjoying a fine late night meal here after a successful performance of *Soirées Fantastiques.* I looked in vain for a brass plaque with the magician's name on it. While there is no brass plaque in Le Grand Véfour honoring the "King of Conjurors," I was comforted knowing that streets were named after Jean Eugene Robert-Houdin in both Paris and Blois.

On our final night in Paris, the five of us toasted another extraordinary trip with a bottle of Ruinart champagne on a stone bench next to the Seine. It was the perfect ending to a wonderful holiday.

Au revoir Paris, until next time.

Bon Voyage

I hope you enjoyed the journey! It has been said that you can't travel and return home the same person and I can attest to that. After thirty years of roaming the world, I have found that the extraordinary is everywhere and you can find it if you only learn to open your eyes, your ears, and your mind—to be aware. I hope this book brought back fond memories of a place you've been or has inspired you to visit one of the places I have described within these pages. It is my wish that the stories in this book motivate you to seek out the extraordinary, be it on the far side of the world or in your own backyard.

Wishing you extraordinary travels....

"It is not down on any map; true places never are." —Herman Melville